Rescuing Spelling

Melvyn Ramsden

First published 1993 by Southgate Publishers Ltd
Reprinted 1999

Southgate Publishers Ltd
15 Barnfield Avenue, Exmouth, Devon EX8 2QE

Printed and bound in Great Britain

British Library Cataloguing in Publication Data
A CIP catalogue record for this book is available from the British Library.

ISBN 1-85741-090-4

Acknowledgements

I am grateful to Margaret Aze, Elly Babbedge and Jayne Morgan at Pinhoe School for their professional enthusiasm and personal support; their gently positive nagging made sure that I wrote this book in the first place. Nick Hockings in Bordeaux descended on the draft text with a thoroughness which was both pernickety and provocative; several important modifications resulted from his self-imposed labour.

Contents

PART THREE: SELECTED ACTIVITIES AND THEMES

Signs and Conventions Used in This Book

☞ This pointing hand indicates a practical suggestion for teaching which arises from the text in which it occurs. In this way the teaching point is embedded within the part of the book which explains and justifies it.

✎ This icon indicates an item from a running glossary which gives a definition of a term in the accompanying text.

❒ One of the very few absolute rules of English spelling is indicated by this icon. I call these real rules *laws* and they apply without exception.

✠ This icon indicates a structural principle of English spelling

✿ This icon indicates a pattern of English spelling.

(The terms *law, principle* and *pattern* are explained in Part Two, Chapter 6.)

¯ (Macron) Written over a vowel the macron indicates that the vowel is 'long', i.e. it represents the sound of its name. Thus /ā/ is the vowel in *fame* and /ō/ is the first vowel in *only*.

˘ (Breve) Written over a vowel the breve indicates that the vowel is 'short'. Thus /ă/ is the vowel in *fat* and /ŏ/ is the vowel in *hot*.

> < (Guillemets) These are used to indicate the actual written letter of the alphabet enclosed between them. Thus >h< represents the written letter aitch, however it is pronounced in a word.

< > Used this way round guillemets indicate established letter-strings which are the elements of words. For instance, *unkindness* is <un> + <kind> + <ness>.

// (Slash Brackets) Letters and symbols enclosed in slash brackets are to be taken purely as indications of sound. E.g. *echo* could be represented as /ĕkō/, both *know* and *no* would be /nō/, and *right, write* and *rite* can be represented by /rīt/

*** (Asterisk)** An initial asterisk is used to mark an unacceptable form of a word, e.g. **thay*.

Conventions of Matrices

The matrices introduced in this book are a powerful teaching and learning tool because they are an embodiment of the order and regularity of the English writing system and the way its orthography represents the meaning of words. Because teachers who use this book must become thoroughly familiar with the conventions of these word matrices, here is a summary of the conventions of their use, together with annotated examples.

- Elements which are only *phonetic* building blocks are printed in an italic (chancery script) type face *which looks like this*.
- Base words/elements are printed in bold roman type **which looks like this**. Affixes are printed in ordinary roman, often in a smaller size and look like this.
- Only single, complete words are formed from a matrix.
- Only one element per column per word may be used.
- It is not necessary to take an element from every column of a matrix, but columns may not be 'leapfrogged'.
- Shaded areas cover elements which will go together around the base element.
- Spelling patterns and conventions must be operated when words are built from the elements in the matrix. Reminders of these are rarely given with the matrix; the word builder must be on the lookout for them – indeed, opportunity to apply spelling conventions is one of the functions of matrices.

Italic type indicates that this matrix consists of *phonetic* elements

b	
cr	*awl*
dr	

Roman type indicates that this matrix consists of morphological elements, which are —

prefix	base words	suffix 1st set	suffixes 2nd set
	play		ly
un	**help**	ful	ness
	hope		
	care		

shading shows that the prefix is only used with base word **help**

Examples of non-permissible words:

***hopely** – this leapfrogs the second column; no column can be omitted between the first and last element of a word made from a matrix

***carefulnessly** – this takes two elements from the same column; only one element per column should be used to build a word.

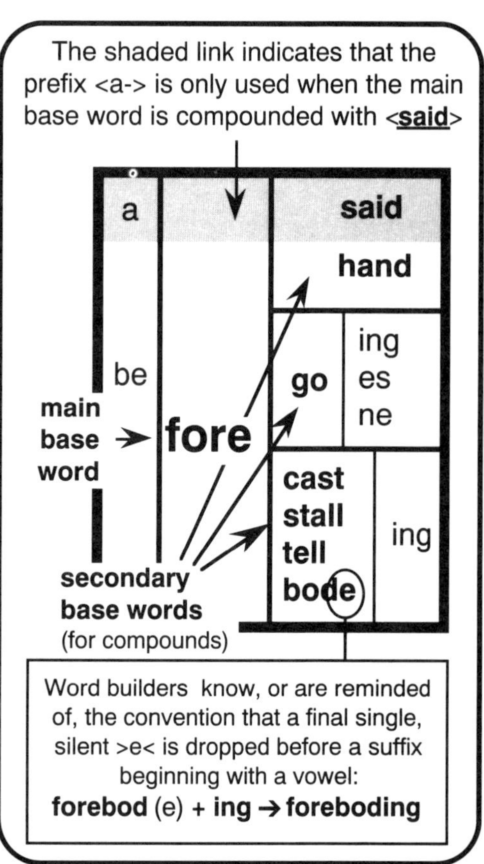

INTRODUCTION

Spelling needs to be rescued!

Spelling, with its general image of tedium and pedantry, is probably the prime candidate for the title of least loved element of the curriculum.

During the first few years of my time in primary schools my teaching of spelling was frankly incompetent and misleading. I was enthusiastic enough; in fact I was quite good at turning much of the drudgery of spelling into a series of games. But that was all skirting round the issue of what spelling really is. I was still labouring under the grand misapprehension that English spelling is supposed to be mainly a representation of the *sound* of words, and that when it wasn't doing that it was just an inconsistent and unreasonable fact of life that we all have to put up with.

In those early years as a primary teacher I needed rescuing from my ignorance about what English spelling actually is, and the children in my classes needed rescuing from my own incompetence. How I regret that I did not know then what I know now:

- **The English spelling system is logical and almost entirely self-consistent.**
- **'Exceptions', far from being widespread, are extremely rare.**
- **There is a reason for every English spelling.**
- **When I found myself saying that English spelling is awkward and contradictory I should not have been blaming the system – I had my basic 'rules' wrong!**
- **Attention to spelling is not a hindrance to writing; being able to spell increases, rather than hinders, breadth of expression and creative flow.**
- **English spelling is primarily the representation of MEANING.**

Surprising claims? I'll be justifying them in this book because spelling needs to be rescued from its own image of being inconsistent and riddled with exceptions.

Sadly, the same misconceptions and plain misinformation that clouded the issue of spelling in my teacher training, and subsequently characterized my attitude to it in the classroom, are still around. This book is what I would like to have encountered in my training and at the beginning of my teaching career; if I had then I might have avoided the problems which I both met in my teaching and caused to the children in my care. It gives an account of the real structures of English spelling (something that not many people seem to know about), and offers ways in which this theoretical knowledge can be transformed into effective practice.

Spelling needs to be taught

I am convinced of the importance of spelling and its crucial role in empowering children to organize their thinking effectively in the context of language.

Students taking examinations can now lose up to 5% of their score for inefficient spelling. In the sense that this stricture gives a strong signal that ability to spell is now considered to be important then it just may have some point. But we cannot avoid addressing the question of why takers of GCSE examinations may be bad spellers, whether it is really their own fault if they are, and what we can do to ensure that they reach that stage as good spellers.

> The onus has been thrown entirely on the pupil to *learn* to spell, in that most schools rely on the children being able to absorb a knowledge of spelling from their general reading, aided by nothing more than a few – generally bogus – so-called spelling "rules", together with a vague strategy of giving children lists of spelling to learn by heart. In no way can such practice equate with that proper guidance of children in *how* to learn to spell.
>
> (Jean Augur, Educational Officer to the British Dyslexia Association, TES 1.2.91)

It can be something of a problem for those to whom accurate spelling comes intuitively and easily to understand that it involves the acquisition of a number of specific skills, each of which may need to be actively taught. Most teachers now in schools were not themselves taught to spell when they were at school. Their subsequent training courses, confirmed by many who give advice to teachers on matters of language, may have marginalized understanding both the nature and importance of spelling and created a climate in which some teachers still assume it to be unnecessary for children to know about the structure of their own language.

If we wish to raise the general level of spelling ability in our schools in a way that does not penalise sixteen-year-olds for something which is not really their fault, we should be looking at the *teaching* of spelling. We need to realize that **the structures of spelling have never really been taught in English schools; spelling has only been corrected and tested**. There is an overriding need for a programme of training for teachers so that understanding of the structures of our language can become more widespread. Only in this way can the standards of spelling be improved.

The National Curriculum has made spelling the legal entitlement of all children as English Attainment Target 4. Sadly, the Programmes of Study only give a sketchy outline of how that entitlement might be realized. It is a very inadequate document, but it is a start. The book you are now reading responds to the requirements of the National Curriculum, but it gives structure to its vague and imprecise elements, and offers a conceptual framework which embraces it but is almost entirely absent from the document itself.

Spelling is rooted in thinking

Ability to spell is not a merely a cosmetic or superficial addition to written language. It is an aspect of knowledge about language which can empower writers to organize and reorganize their verbal thinking, and in the process sharpen and strengthen that thinking. We fail our children if we marginalize spelling by characterizing it as an encumbrance or of little importance.

PART ONE

FINDING THE RIGHT PRINCIPLES

It is only when we have achieved ... spelling that is automatic, predictable, and infallible that we are really free to write with confidence, with no backward glances to see if a word 'looks right', and with no offering of a less precise synonym or phrase because the right one is difficult to spell.

(Peters, page 5)

CHAPTER 1: PUTTING SPELLING IN ITS PLACE

> The arguments about spelling go back a long way. Almost a century ago to this very year there was openly expressed anxiety about standards; and certainly around the turn of the century the debate was in progress as to whether spelling should be directly taught or could be breathed in naturally if the air was right.
>
> (Bullock Report, 11.44)

The Broader Picture of Language

To teach any aspect of language and make sound judgements about its appropriateness you need to have a view of language as a whole, so that is where we start.

One of the best and most accessible brief statements of the nature of language is the four-page Chapter 4 of the Bullock Report of 1975. Reading and re-reading it from time to time will provide a stimulating focus for thinking about language and learning. The simple diagram at the bottom of this page will help to remind us of language activity as a whole.

When we use language in any form we are organizing and reorganizing what we make of the world within and around us. Writing is part of language so we can say that

> **When we write we are constructing sense. We think through what we write, and since spelling is part of that then spelling also plays its part in imposing order on our world and the way we respond to it.**

Let's look more closely at this idea that our thinking organizes itself while we are actually writing or speaking.

We do not know *exactly* what we are going to say before we start speaking. We sort that out as we go along. As teachers we know this process; we constantly reorganize our knowledge by the need to make sense of it for our children; we do

A diagrammatic model of language which shows the four modes referred to in Bullock and their role in the representation of meaning through language

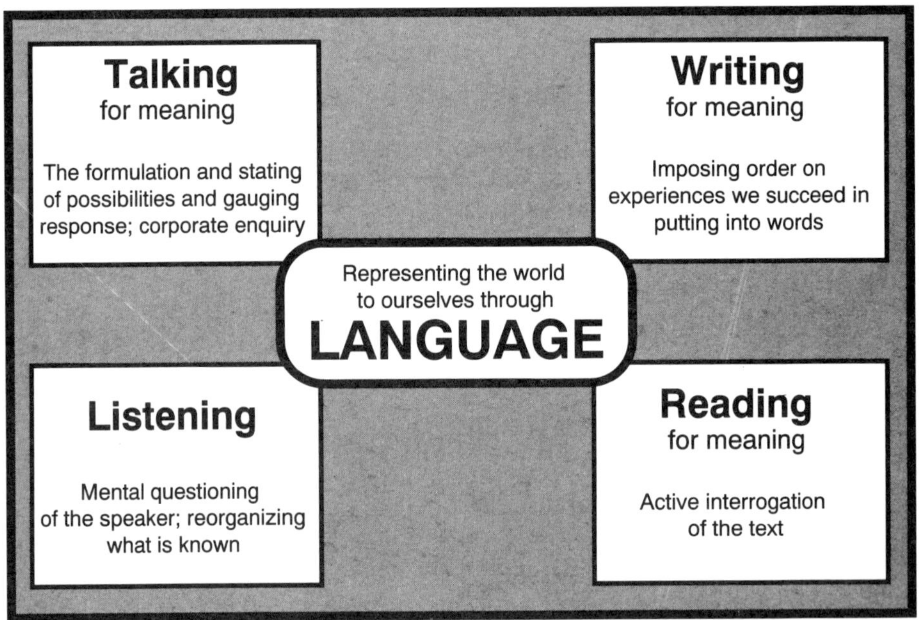

it principally by talking to them and *the act of talking constantly refines the way we understand it ourselves.*

The same happens with writing. As we begin we may have a general idea of the context of what we intend to write; we may even have some sort of sequential structure in mind. But it is only in the act of writing that we sort out the details and reorganize our thinking. In writing such a paragraph as this I had a good idea of what I wanted to say, but I am having to bring it to order as I go along through the act of writing.

Speaking and writing are media through which we operate and bring order to our thinking.

The element of writing which we call spelling is specific to words, the building blocks of written texts.

Spelling brings order to our thinking because it is a way of representing the meaning of words.

Spelling and the Senses

Traditionally most teaching of spelling has concentrated almost entirely on only two of our senses: sight and hearing.

Spelling by Sight

The heavy reliance on the sense of sight for spelling is apparent in a notion that words are perceived as a whole; the conclusion is drawn that words are remembered as a whole too. (We shall see later that words are rarely 'wholes'.)

Over-reliance on the sense of sight gives rise to the common advice that all you have to do to check a spelling is to write it down and if it *looks* right then it is right. Yet most people I talk to have experienced the situation in which the more they look at a word they have written the more unsure they become of it, *even* when it is correctly spelled. Try this for yourself: which of the following alternatives is correct?

withold / withhold
consensus / concensus
supercede / supersede
mispelling / misspelling
milennium / millennium / millenium

benefitted / benefited
ecstacy / ecstasy
apartment / appartment
playwright / playwrite
analyze / analyse

☞ **It is not necessarily helpful to emphasize the look of a word as an indication of its correct spelling.**

When you have done this little exercise (and checked whether you were right!) ask yourself what your strategies actually were in coming to your decision; were they really *confined* to the sense of sight? It is more likely that you used other strategies which were to do with thinking about the words' structures, or even about patterns and conventions of spelling which you may have come across before. Certainly the sense of sight is prominent but it is often unreliable.

The assumption that we learn spelling by sight is sometimes linked with an idea that the spelling of words is 'picked up' through reading.

Good Readers and Spelling

The assumption that children who are efficient and fluent readers must be able to spell the words they are reading ignores the simple fact that it is usually easier to recognize something than to reproduce it.

Being able to read, however fluently, will not necessarily bring efficient spelling. Many children (and adults) are efficient readers but inefficient spellers. The received wisdom of many teachers and parents is that there must be an automatic carry-over from reading to learning spelling; this has resulted in a tendency to characterize children as 'careless' when their writing has not matched the competence of their reading.

Why spelling is not necessarily consequent upon reading will become more clear if you consider the nature of reading. Reading operates on only partial clues from inside the word; the major clues come from the *broader context* in which the word is situated *at the time of reading*. It is a process of constructing sense. Indeed, a mature reader does not actively engage with every letter of each word, or even necessarily with every whole word in a given passage. If you read,

'Once upon ◊ ◊◊◊◊, ◊◊◊◊◊ ◊◊◊ ◊ ...,'

you know what words are represented by the diamonds.

> We do not have the time to pay attention to letters. Reading at the relatively modest rate of 200 words a minute would entail recognizing more than three individual words a second, an average of 15 letters or more a second, with the added complication of trying to discover the appropriate sound for every letter and to blend these sounds together to try to make a recognizable word. The human brain works fast, but not as fast as that.
>
> (Smith, page 145)

You can test this process out for yourself by photocopying a short passage of text, and blotting out parts of several words (or even the whole of one or two words); replace the eliminated parts with some sort of mark and give the passage to a friend to read. Here is an example for you to try for yourself; it is from E.M. Forster's *A Passage to India*.

> The news hurt Ronnie very m◊◊h. He had heard Aziz ann◊◊◊ce that she w◊◊◊d not return to the country, but h◊d paid no att◊◊◊◊on to the rem◊rk, for he nev◊◊ dreamt th◊◊ an Indian c◊◊◊d be the ch◊nnel of commu◊◊◊◊tion betw◊◊n two Eng◊◊◊h people. He contr◊lled h◊◊self and s◊◊d gently, 'You nev◊◊ said we sh◊◊◊◊ marry, my dear girl; you ne◊◊r bound either your◊◊◊f or me – don't let this ups◊t you.

Only partial clues, then, are needed for the reading process to be successful. The word is principally constructed from its relationship with the other words among which it finds itself in that particular passage at that particular time. Reading might, then, be said to depend crucially on the *contextual*, rather than the internal, dimension. In reading you are *constructing* sense from clues and expectations outside the word.

Spelling a target word is different. The individual word is known before you start; the task is not to *detect* or *construct* its meaning and sound, but to *represent* them. In order to spell the word – to represent its meaning in writing – you need to have at your disposal full clues about every part of the word you want to write. This necessitates an ability to examine the target word outside the ordinary context of reading. What you do is to think of how the word is embedded in a set of words of similar formation and meaning. This demands word-attack skills which recognize each *meaning segment* of the word. You certainly need to know of possible letter-to-sound matches, the phonic dimension. But above all, you need an internalized vocabulary of *letter-to-**meaning*** matches.

The work of Utah Frith (1980) will be of interest to those who wish to pursue this matter of the uneven relationship between reading and spelling. She investigated those children who are rapid and fluent readers but are incompetent when it comes to writing. Frith calls reading (and listening to speech) an *input* process; writing, on the other hand, is an *output* process. The conceptual processes for 'input' and 'output' are, she argues, not only independent but also at times incompatible; we can conclude that the processes of the one are not necessarily relevant to the other.

☞ **Do not assume that good readers should automatically be good spellers.**

With such different processes and skills involved it becomes clear why children can often read words that they cannot spell, and why profoundly deaf writers, for whom the phonic dimension does not even exist, are still capable of spelling words correctly. Although, then, it may seem to go against common sense, reading competence need not have much effect on ability to spell.

Spelling by Hearing

The sense of hearing is also heavily relied on, a result of the misconception that English spelling is primarily about the sound of words.

Beware of Phonics!

Let's suppose that English spelling is phonetic (it isn't, but we'll assume for the moment that it is). We immediately encounter some fundamental problems.

First problem: There are more sounds in English than there are letters in the alphabet.

Depending on who is speaking and where English is being spoken, there are between 40 and 50 basic sounds in English and about as many more complex ones. It is immediately clear that a one-to-one correspondence between letters and sounds is impossible. Two solutions to this problem might be suggested.

The first solution would be to increase the size of the alphabet so that the number of letters would match the number of sounds in the language. To some extent this has already been done in the evolution of English spelling. The alphabet we inherited is Roman; it was developed to write Latin, which had a different phonetic make-up from English. The original Roman alphabet did not contain the letters J, W, Y or Z (K was hardly ever used, but it was there and available). There wasn't a separate form for the letter U either; the letter V served to represent that vowel.

So we have extended the alphabet a little, but if we took the idea of inventing letters to its logical conclusion we should end up with an English alphabet of about 50 letters, nearly double the size of the one we in fact use. Not surprisingly, that solution has not been adopted.

A second possible solution is to use letter-combinations to represent basic sounds. This solution has been adopted in some cases. For instance, the sounds of /θ/ and /ð/ which do not occur in Latin are both represented by the letter combination <th>; the sound /ʃ/ is sometimes represented by <sh>; the sound /ɔɪ/ is represented by <oi> and <oy>.

Children need to know that they have to use and look for *combinations* of letters.

This is a rather better solution since it does not involve a drastic increase in the number of letter symbols we need. It does mean, however, that young learners must know from the very beginning that ***letters do not operate in isolation***.

Second problem: The sound of English varies from speaker to speaker.

If we are to tie spelling to the sound of the language, whose English are we to use as the model? The south-east? 'Standard' English? Scottish? American? The pronunciation of fifty or a hundred years ago? One of the many advantages of the current spelling system is that it can be understood throughout the United Kingdom and all over the world where forms of English are spoken with varying phonetic systems; we can also maintain intimate contact with the English of our forebears over the last four or five hundred years even though the sound of the language has changed, in some cases quite radically, in recent centuries.

Spelling is not tied to the sound of any particular form of spoken English, not even 'Standard British English'.

Communication with our contemporaries and with our past would be difficult and sometimes impossible if we tied the writing system exclusively to sound.

Third problem: The sound of English words is variable from one context to another.

Sometimes when a word is inflected the sound changes quite markedly. The following examples will illustrate this.

- The word ***say*** will rhyme with *hay* when it occurs simply; yet when it acquires an >s< (as in *he says*) it will rhyme with *fez*.
- The word ***do*** will rhyme with *coo* when it occurs simply; when it acquires the suffixes <-es> or <-ne> (as in *does* or *done*) the results rhyme with *fuzz* and *bun*.
- In the word ***house*** the final /s/ sound becomes /z/ when the word is plural – *houses* sounds like /howziz/.
- The words ***mean*** and ***deal*** (which rhyme with *been* and *meal*) change their sound when they acquire the suffix <**-t**> for the past tense forming ***meant*** (rhyming with *sent*) and ***dealt*** (rhyming with *belt*). A similar thing happens to the word ***clean*** when it acquires the two suffixes <**-li-**> + <**-ness**> to form ***clean**liness*.

In the course of fluent and connected speech the same individual words become phonetically elastic as they form the semantic music of whole sentences. This is not a failing of English; the expressive potential of the language is richly enhanced by this phonetic elasticity. Words in spoken English change their sound depending on how they are being used in a sentence. The simple word ***are*** rhymes with *car* if you say it in isolation, but in such a spoken sentence as *The men are here* it is more likely to sound like /er/ (in this sentence the words *The men are* rhyme with *the tenor*).

If spelling slavishly followed sound rather than represented meaning we would end up with an impossibly complicated and inconsistent writing system!

If we made phonetic considerations paramount then the spelling system would become *more* complicated, not less. We would have the absurd situation of a single word needing to be spelled in several different ways depending on the grammatical and expressive context in which it was spoken, as well as on who was speaking and when it was spoken. **Above all spelling would lose much of its relationship with the meanings of the words it was supposed to be representing.**

Problems with 'Sounding Out'

Another example of over-reliance on the sense of hearing is the misleading and ultimately confusing advice to 'sound out' a target word in either reading or in writing. 'Sounding out' means reading out the spelling of a word using not the alphabetical names but the so-called phonetic names. The classic example of 'sounding out' is representing the word ***cat*** as "kuh, a, tuh." Try 'sounding out' the following words, all of which I have found in books for early learners, and compare the sounded out version with the sound of the real word.

someone love buy television school
neighbours eight suddenly each two

It is a fallacy to think of spelling as primarily a phonic system; don't present it as such to children.

There is a further problem with concentrating attention on sound: what words actually sound like is not necessarily what we *think* they sound like! As Frank Smith puts it, 'even when [the conventions of spelling] are related to the sounds of speech, they in fact represent *conventions* of what the sounds of speech are thought to be, rather than what the sounds actually are.'

Hearing what we *think* we should be hearing is like what happens when we read. When we read text we only take in as much as we need in order to make sense of what we are reading – a mature reader does not actively take note of every letter or even every word; we respond to what is necessary to make sense of what we are reading. A similar thing happens when we listen to speech: we only take notice of what we need in order to make sense of what we hear. Let me give an example.

In a class of mainly six-year-olds one young writer had written:

I **sutis** go fishing with my dad.

He was representing the mystery word 'sutis' phonetically – exactly as he said it in connected fast speech. And what is more *you* probably say the word ***sometimes*** (for that is what he was intending to write) something like /su'ties/ when it is embedded in a quickly spoken sentence. But you probably don't *think* you do because as soon as we know how to spell words we convince ourselves that we can hear the spelling of the words we speak.

Another example is *didn't*; you almost certainly pronounce that word as /dint/ when you use it in connected speech. Similarly most early learners, brought up to trust only in sounding out, will write 'going to' as *gonna* or *gunner* or the like.

In the same piece of writing my six-year-old also wrote:

The **furs** time I went ...

This is a further clear illustration of how the writer was representing only the exact **sound** of the way he spoke – and you, too, almost certainly do not sound both the final >t< of ***first*** as well as the initial >t< of ***time*** in connected speech. You only think you do because you know how to spell.

Here are some further examples of sounds that we think we hear in words, but often don't actually pronounce in connected speech:

/t/ in: soften chestnut Christmas often
/d/ in: handsome handkerchief grandmother
/p/ in: consumption temptation empty
/i/ in: family

One of the results of this unawareness of what is actually happening when we hear words is that we often distort the normal way of saying a word in order to prove to children that spelling does represent sound! I well remember trying to convince a child that the word *prints* is pronounced with a definite /t/ as distinct from the pronunciation of the word *prince*; the child was unimpressed and rightly put me in my place by telling me that nobody pronounced ***prints*** like that and that it sounded exactly like ***prince***.

A final example can be seen in H.E. Bates' *The Darling Buds of May,* a book popularized more recently by the television adaptation. This is the splendid word '**perfick**'. You may *think* you pronounce the word ***perfectly*** just as it is written, with a short >e< and a distinct >t< , and you may just do that if you are saying the word on its own. But in your quickly spoken ordinary speech you almost certainly pronounce it as /perfikly/. If you remove the common suffix <-**ly**> from that pronunciation you are left with the Larkins' word 'perfick'. What is wrong about that spelling is not that it is unconventional but that a word such as 'perfick' has lost its connection with such close meaning relatives as *perfected* and *perfection*. It is precisely this incongruity that makes the word 'perfick' so amusing.

I am not saying that sight and hearing are of no importance in the representation of words in writing. Of course they are. What I am suggesting is that exclusive emphasis on them is not always helpful and can occasionally be misleading. Other senses are important too.

Perceiving through 'Tasting'

The 'sounding out' of words is inappropriate when it is the sole strategy in achieving a target word because it takes no account of the sense and little of the structure of a target word.

A form of sounding out *is* constructive when a word is spoken or chanted in order to segment it and identify its component parts – what are often referred to as syllables, though I shall argue later against using this term.

Ask learners to concentrate more on what the word *feels* like in the mouth than what it sounds like when they hear it.

Instead of directing exclusive attention to listening and the sense of hearing when we are 'sounding out', we should ask learners to concentrate more on what the word feels like in the mouth. In that way they are combining two of their senses in their perception of the word. Involving the feel of the word as it is generated through the throat and the mouth can engage children in a more realistic approach to the phonic dimension of being able to spell. What we do is tell our learners to speak the word out loud and to feel the result, and I often refer to this process as 'tasting the word in your mouth'.

Language is Sequential

Language is by nature sequential; it *sequences* elements of meaning. The order of sounds in a word and of words in a sentence are crucial in the construction of sense. The sentence *The cat attacked the mouse* completely changes its meaning if it becomes *The mouse attacked the cat*. Similarly, *God is love* is not the same as saying *Dog is love.*

Awareness of this sequential element of language gives us a further reason why over-reliance on sight and hearing is not entirely appropriate in learning to write. The sense of sight perceives a complete picture as a whole or, at any rate, in no *necessary* sequence. Of course it is possible to 'read' pictures, but there is no universal or even conventional way of doing so, unless it be by analogy with the directionality of text – and that depends on the writing system used by the viewer.

☞ **Of all the senses involved with language sight is least reliant on and appropriate to sequential perception.**

Sequential perception may be of greater prominence in hearing but our short term auditory memory may be subject to some confusion; we may remember the elements of what we heard, but we will not necessarily recall them in the order in which we heard them.

I have short-term auditory memory problems. I was lucky enough as a child to meet a teacher who told me that if I needed to remember something like a telephone number for short-term recall I should repeat it out loud as soon as I was told it. 'Your voice has a better memory than your ears,' she told me, and she was right.

Lack of appreciation of the sequential nature of language has lead to misconceptions about writing too. It has been common to assume that handwriting and drawing strategies are interrelated. We all know of children whose art and drawing are executed with excellent fine motor control and attention to detail, yet they are incompetent in handwriting. The commonly given advice that bad writers should practise drawing skills in order to help their handwriting is both misconceived and of no practical help. Drawing strategies are not of necessity sequential; a completed picture of a cat is still a cat whether the drawing was started with the tail or the whiskers, or whether the cat faces to the right, left, front or rear. With writing it does matter where you start and the order in which you write is crucial.

Learning through the Sequential Senses

The sense of touch as expressed in the integrated patterns of writing, and what I call the sense of taste when applied to the production of the spoken word are more efficiently sequential than sight and hearing. When we write words it involves integrated movement patterns and the manipulation of pen or keyboard – the senses of touch and movement are also present in the generation of words.

A Multisensory View

We must understand that our engagement with language is *multi*sensory. Those of us who also work with children with specific learning difficulties in language tend to be more aware of this fact. Such children may well have had their difficulties exacerbated by early teaching which concentrated on only auditory and visual sequencing, the sound and sight of words. The feel and taste of words are of equal, if not greater, importance to learning how they are represented in writing or print.

Because spelling is an *intersensory* activity it draws on all our experiences of words, whether through 'taste', through our vocal memory of the sequence of letters as we spell them out loud, through hearing, and through the tactile and visual encounters with the integrated movement patterns which produce written words.

Spelling as a Convention

Writing, as part of language as a whole, exercises and develops our thinking processes. Being able to spell is important because the more fluent our writing, the more powerful and efficient its ability to explore and organize thought. Efficiency and ease in spelling adds to fluency in writing.

There is an influential body of opinion which regards attention to spelling as the very opposite of fluency. When I was a student teacher my training college lecturers told me that spelling is of low priority and doesn't really matter. Attention to spelling has sometimes been regarded as the province of pedants and of little relevance to the great issues of language.

Justification for this view of the unimportance of spelling sounds very plausible. We must, then, spend a little time rescuing spelling from this beguiling dismissal of its integral part in the generation of written thinking.

Spelling and Fluency

It is said that undue concern with spelling can inhibit both writing and learning to write. True, as far as it goes – but how far *does* that argument go?

True – insistence that early learners spell correctly every time they write will overload them and confine writing to trivia.

True – expectation of flawless spelling in early drafts of writing will restrict writers to what is safe; risk-taking will play no part in the writing process.

True – marking of work irrespective of its purpose and stage of drafting will deflect attention and care from overall structures and genres. If we are looking at early drafts of writing whose purpose is the exploration of imagery or experimentation with overall form then that is what we should first respond to.

These are examples of *undue* concern with spelling. Spelling is not there to be punitive and restricting.

Due concern with spelling, however, grows from an understanding that spelling is actually an **enabling** element of writing.

Words have to be written somehow, so what tools are given to our young learners? Much is made of what some call 'invented spellings'. Such spellings are what early writers produce as they move towards a discovery of the conventional way of writing words. The trouble is that denigration of spelling conventions abandons children to the reinvention of the spelling wheel by giving them little to go on and making every word a fresh codification problem. The only clue that children are usually given is that spelling is somehow tied to the representation of sound. And if there is one stratagem which *guarantees* failure in writing most English words it is phonics!

☞ **Confidence in spelling frees the child to write and fulfil his purpose.** (Bullock, 11.43)

Children who are not at ease with spelling still have to take each individual word one at a time in order to work out a way of codifying it. As Frank Smith has put it, **it makes writing much easier to know there is an agreed spelling for every word than to try to think of a spelling that a reader might be able to understand.**

A further argument is brought forward to justify the view that time spent on spelling is unnecessary. It is said that in a technological age the business of identifying and correcting spelling mistakes can be left to the software on the word processor. But there are still problems once you run a text through the spell-check. For one thing it will not identify a wrong word when it is spelled correctly (*sale* for *sail*, for instance). Chapter 9 deals in detail with the limitations of spell-checks. Over-reliance on these is reminiscent of traditional attitudes to dictionaries. Children who want to know how to spell a word have often been told to 'look it up in the dictionary'; the problem is that you have to be able to spell the word before you can find it in dictionaries; they are about meanings and only incidentally about spellings.

The Standardization of Spelling

> It is sometimes suggested that spelling is a convention and if it is of any consequence at all this is slight compared with so many other considerations in the teaching of English. There is no question of its being a convention, but in our view it is a convention that matters. It is of little relevance for today to argue that in "Faerie Queene" Spenser spelt 'hot' in at least six different ways; or that the Oxford Dictionary lists 30 versions of 'little' by the 16th and 17th century writers.
>
> (Bullock, 11.42)

The last few decades have seen a fashionable assertion that spelling and creativity are mutually incompatible. In support of this recent orthodoxy I have heard quite eminent educationalists support that argument by referring to Shakespeare's inconsistent spellings. 'There you are,' they say, 'Shakespeare couldn't spell but he wrote some pretty good stuff.' This attitude takes no account of the state of the language in Shakespeare's time. The point is not that Shakespeare was a bad speller; he was spelling according to current conventions. The English language was still consolidating its form and its pronunciation was still fluid. The printing presses were beginning to make the spread of the written word more possible. There were no important or comprehensive works of reference in English (it was only in 1604 that the first English dictionary made its appearance). Latin was still the medium of learning, thought and science.

Come the seventeenth century, however, the country was growing smaller in terms of travel and communication, literacy was becoming more widespread and, with the continuing growth of English nationalism, the English language was increasingly the medium of study and learning. Scientific thought was progressing apace; *there was now a need for increasing precision in language.*

Phonics and Consistency

A need for **consistency** in the written word was developing, and consistency could not be achieved by tying the writing system entirely to the fluid, varying and changing *sounds* of the English language.

> It is a commonplace that English spelling is quite seriously unrelated to pronunciation. The reasons are well-known to linguistic scholars, but hardly at all to laymen. In general terms, written English has remained relatively static since the invention of printing about the middle of the fifteenth century, but spoken English, in its received form, has changed repeatedly since then.
>
> (Burchfield, page 144)

The freeing of the written language from phonic fetters has been of lasting benefit.

> The main reason that English spelling so poorly represents the sounds of English is because representing the sounds of speech is a relatively low priority for spelling in any case; there are two overriding considerations, consistency and meaning. Despite the many apparent anomalies of English spelling for one historical reason or another, a basic principle that always has priority is that **words and parts of words with similar meanings should be spelled alike**. This is one facet of spelling that makes life easier for both reader and writer... For the reader, words that look alike have a similar meaning; for the writer, words that have similar meanings tend to be spelled alike.
>
> (Smith, page 149)

The patterns and principles of English spelling have evolved (and continue to do so) along with the consolidation and development of the language as a whole. The result is a better and more natural match than would be achieved if we were to try to impose a complete system from scratch.

Landmarks in English Spelling

This is not the place to give a detailed account of the development of English spelling, but it will be useful to mention some of the important landmarks. Before the advent of printing at the end of the fifteenth century the writing of English was rare and when it was written it was usually scribes trained in Latin and in latinate conventions who did so, using adaptations of the writing conventions of Norman French and Latin. They brought order to the chaotic spelling of English words.

The invention of printing was the innovation which did more than anything else to encourage the use of writing and to create the climate in which more people wanted to read. The printer Caxton and his successors at the presses created a need for a consistent writing system which could easily be understood over the wider areas of the country to which the more readily available printed books would be distributed. The pronunciation of English was still in a state of flux at the time and there were wide variations in the sound of words from region to region; overreliance on the pronunciation of any one typesetter could produce such idiosyncratic spellings as to be confusing to other readers.

The surge in the publication of printed matter in the sixteenth century meant that the need to standardize the spelling of words towards relationships of meaning was becoming increasingly obvious to scholars. The first book on English spelling was published in 1568, but it was written in Latin and raised the question without providing any real solution. I have already referred to the appearance of the first English dictionary in 1604. This date marks the beginning of what some have called the age of lexicographers, during which the classification and listing of the words in the language achieved increasing sophistication and consistency. It was a time when knowledge was growing apace and works of reference of all sorts were increasingly needed. For these works of reference to be of any practical use the principle of alphabetical order needed to operate and words had to be written with established and regular sequences of letters. The age of lexicographers culminated in England with the publication of Dr Johnson's famous dictionary in 1755. The principle of English spelling as reflecting relationships of meaning was now thoroughly established and accepted as being entirely appropriate to the nature of the English language. Dr Johnson's world of the eighteenth century was a time of wider education and the intensification of trade and travel. Competition and the broadening of people's outlook made it evident that discipline and consistency in spelling was not a luxury but essential. The need for precision in writing meant that doubt about meaning could only be eliminated by developing and observing conventions. Practicality, not pedantry, made spelling conventions necessary.

We are now in a further phase of the development of consistency in our spelling system with the advent of the word processor. Spell-check systems are standardizing our spelling to an even greater extent than before.

Conventions of Spelling

It is worth summarizing the resulting conventions of the English spelling system.

1. Spelling's overriding concern is the representation of meaning.

— Words or parts of words which have similar meanings are written similarly.

— Shared origins indicate shared meanings; spelling will indicate the origin of words, often by using aspects of the spelling system of the source language.

2. Letters are used to indicate sound only for the clarification of meaning.

Letters (usually in combinations and strings rather than individually) often represent elements of sound in words. Different combinations of letters can represent the same sound. The reason for our ability to represent the same sound in different ways is crucial: *where two words sound the same but have different meanings then if you can spell them differently you are likely to do so.*

Letters sometimes indicate no sound at all. This can be either (i) because they are indicating something about a word's origin, or (ii) because a letter unpronounced in one word may indicate a sound that is pronounced in another related word.

This whole book is about how our spelling system represents relationships of meaning, but it will be useful at this point to give some examples of the principle in operation. You will see that, of course, an *element* of phonics is present, but however prominent it may appear it is always subordinate to the needs of indicating relationships of meaning. Take the following words:

damn — The letter >n< is written in this word because of its relation with ***damnation***. The spelling ***dam*** gives a word which *sounds* the same, but since it is spelled differently will have a different *meaning*. (You now know why there is an >n< on the end of ***autumn*** and ***hymn*** – they are related to the words ***autumnal*** and ***hymnal***.)

real — There are two possible ways of spelling the words which sound like /ri:l/ – ***real*** and ***reel***. But which is which? The word ***reality*** offers the clue to the meaning in this case, as would the related word ***realize***.

muscle — What is the letter >c< doing in this word? Think of the word ***muscular***, and you will know. The word *mussel* sounds the same but the different spelling shows that it means something different and unrelated to ***muscularity***.

accident — Or is it *accidant*? The word *accidental* supplies the answer.

author — Or is it *auther*? The combinations <or> and <er> would sound the same when spoken. The word ***authority*** supplies the answer in this case, and we also know from this which of the spellings *authorize* or *autherize* is correct.

grammar — Or is it *grammer*? Both would sound the same when spoken. Your answer is in the related word *grammatical*.

Other cases might include such words as ***government*** where the >n< (usually unpronounced) is needed to relate it to ***govern***; the >t< is needed in ***Christmas*** because of ***Christ*** and the >g< in ***length*** to relate it to ***long***.

3. Certain letter combinations are preferred to others for reasons of visual clarity in type and ease of reading.

These are sometimes referred to as 'orthographical rules'; they have developed as aids to reading and therefore indirectly to helping the meaning to be clear. Examples include:

— The combination <ii> never occurs in an English word (when written it looks like ü): use <yi> instead.

— No complete English word ends with the letter >i<: you usually use >y<.

— There is no such spelling as <uv>: use <ov> instead.

— No complete English word ends with >v<: use <ve>.

The National Curriculum of 1990

Children in schools now have a statutory entitlement to know how to spell. The English National Curriculum has five Attainment Targets; one of them is entirely devoted to Spelling. After Level 4 (roughly the end of primary education) Spelling coalesces with Handwriting under the joint title of Presentation; this merging is not altogether arbitrary since, as we shall see later, the way we learn to write has a significant influence on our ability to spell.

There are no Levels 8-10 and Programmes of Study which refer to spelling are almost entirely confined to Key Stages 1 and 2. We might infer, then, that the National Curriculum assumes that the bulk of the work of learning to spell should be more or less complete for most children by the end of the primary phase. The National Curriculum is, perhaps necessarily, rather skimpy. It does, however, seem to be based on conceptually sound assumptions:

- It avoids explicit mention of the phonic fallacy (the assertion that spelling is principally the representation of how words sound).
- While it never manages a clear definition of spelling it nevertheless appears to know that English spelling is predominantly the **representation of** [relationships of] **meaning**.
- It does not talk of spelling rules (which always have exceptions) but of **patterns** and **conventions** (which don't have exceptions).

The document uses a number of technical terms and phrases which it expects us to understand. They include:

complex regularity	consonant	spelling conventions
grammatical feature	inflectional suffix	letter string
lexical features	long vowel	monosyllabic
polysyllable	prefix	roots
short vowel	stress	sound-symbol relationship
word families	suffix	

As you read this book you will encounter explanations of these terms together with other terminology which is essential to the understanding of English spelling.

CHAPTER 2: ELEMENTS OF ENGLISH SPELLING

Knowing How to Spell

Having a grasp of spelling means more than just being able to produce on demand the correct form of an isolated word; it means *understanding the principles on which the writing system is based.* It means knowing when English spelling represents sound, but also knowing when it is not representing sound because it is doing the far more important (and consistent) job of representing meaning. Only then will you have the ability to put into practice the written representation of any target word, even one that you may never have written or even read before. You will also have analytical skills at your disposal by which you can check the spellings of words.

☞ **Emphasis is placed on the relationship between spellings and meanings and not just spellings and sounds.**

(Bullock, 6.24)

As teachers we ourselves must have this knowledge in order to help our children take control of their own writing.

The Use of Proper Terminology

We all need a grasp of the theoretical dimension of spelling. It is an early priority to recognize the need for some precision in the language we use to discuss orthography. Avoiding precise terms perpetuates vagueness. As teachers we need to have the correct terminology in order efficiently to evaluate teaching methods. Children also need correct terminology in order not to cloud their thinking. Romantic and patronizing attitudes to children have tended to deny them proper terminology; they are often confined to short or chatty words (like the unhelpful practice of referring to upper and lower case letters as 'big' or 'little').

☞ **Giving children correct terminology empowers them consciously to own the execution of their work.**

> Knowledge about language, including the use of terminology, is an important part of children's work in English... The main function of such terminology is to consolidate what is already known intuitively. What is already known can be made more explicit or conscious by terminology.
>
> (Cox, 5.3)

The word *spelling* itself is both ambiguous and emotive and is probably best avoided in the classroom, except in very specific senses. It can have a verbal sense, referring to *what a writer can do.* Thus you might say, 'Soon I will be spelling most of my words correctly on the first draft.' In this sense, spelling means the *ability to write words* correctly according to the conventions. Secondly it has a nominal sense as in, 'Many people do not seem to know the proper spelling of *accommodation.*' In this sense the word means *the accepted principles and structures* of the writing system.

You need to have a *knowledge* of spelling before you will be *able* to spell correctly.

Another problem with the word *spelling* is its emotiveness. To children the very mention of the word brings memories of the tedium of the weekly spelling test and so-called rules which seem to have more exceptions than cases which conform. Teachers often groan at the thought of hours of corrections and queues of children wanting spellings.

✎ **Orthography**: The proper term for *spelling*, which in English is the representation in letters first of meaning and only secondarily of some aspects of sound when meaning is affected by such sounds.

When I want to refer to spelling as the process of constructing words in writing I often use the term **word building**, useful because 'construction' and 'building' are near synonyms. There is a technical word which refers specifically to conventional principles of word structure and has none of the negative connotations of the word *spelling*. I suggest that we use it whenever possible. That word is **orthography**. It is the structure of *orthography* that I discuss and try to define in this chapter.

Written Symbols

✎ **Grapheme**: The letter or letter combination used to represent a unit of sound or of meaning.

In order to be capable of written representation a language needs a repertoire of signs which correspond to units of the language they represent. Such orthographic symbols are called **graphemes**. The basic building blocks of English graphemes are the twenty-six signs which we know as the alphabet. Our graphemes are formed from single letters or combinations of letters.

Not all writing systems are alphabetic. Some, like Chinese, are *logographic*; a single sign represents a whole word or idea. Logographic systems have little relationship to the sound of words. This is not necessarily a disadvantage since people who might not understand what is being *said* in another region could still understand what is *written*. The grapheme is fulfilling the function of making *meaning* clear.

Some systems have *pictographic* elements, that is to say signs which resemble what they represent in some way; many road signs are pictographic and, therefore, international. Egyptian hieroglyphic writing was an interesting combination of alphabetic and pictographic elements.

Some writing systems are *syllabic*; single signs represent combinations of sound which commonly occur in the language they are representing. There is a strong syllabic element in the system of graphemes used in Japanese.

The Alphabet

We must have some detailed knowledge of just how our alphabet copes with the representation of meaning, and how this interrelates with its secondary function of indicating some aspects of the sounds of words.

In common with many other languages of the Western World English has inherited the Roman alphabet, a series of signs developed to write Latin. English, however, is not Latin, so the Roman alphabet has had to adapt to the needs of representing English. We saw in the last chapter that some of these adaptations include new letters and signs. The letters themselves have developed different functions which suit the needs of English rather than those of Latin. Other languages which have inherited the Roman alphabet make their own adaptations and adjustments.

Because other languages make use of an alphabet which is very similar to ours it is easy to fall into the trap of making assumptions about the English system by (false) comparison with those languages. For instance, it is fashionable to complain about the English spelling system by contrasting it, say, with Italian where there is a near complete correspondence between its sounds and the way they are written. 'Why can't English be as straightforward and consistent as that?' people ask. The answer is quite simple: English is not Italian! English has an elastic sound-system while that of Italian is very rigid. What the alphabet has to do for Italian and other languages is necessarily different from what it has to do for English.

It is not always understood that not only is **the English spelling system not primarily one of representing sounds,** but also **it is not even *possible* accurately and consistently to represent the sound of English in writing!**

Of course the letters of the alphabet do have some relevance to sound, but it is crucial to understand that such a connection is by no means straightforward, nor is it the overriding function of letters to represent sound.

Mastering the Signs

Basic to all word building is the writing and recognizing of all twenty-six letters. As soon as possible children need to know:

The alphabet and its order must be one of the first learning experiences of young learners.

- **The names of the letters**. This means the real names, not the so-called 'phonetic' names. More will be said about these below.
- **The conventional order of the letters**. Knowing alphabetical order is a fundamental of the skill of referencing. The Alphabet Song will help early learners to consolidate alphabetical order (the music is in Part Three, p.103).
- **The sounds that each letter can sometimes represent**. Many letters of the alphabet can represent several sounds depending on the letter-string in which they occur.
- **The fact that letters sometimes do not themselves represent sounds at all**: they are giving important clues about what the word means.

Upper and Lower Case

Early learners should learn to write only the lower case until their basic word building is established.

Early learners should deal only with the lower case at first; twenty-six signs are quite enough to consolidate in one go. Learning the upper case letters at the same time would increase the number of letter patterns to be remembered to fifty-two, and will generate confusion. The upper case should be introduced to children once their basic word building is established.

Calling letters 'big' or 'little' (like 'big A', 'little a') is as inappropriate as it is misleading (see my *Putting Pen to Paper*, pages 29-30, for a full discussion of this point). Use the proper terms from the beginning: **Upper case** (or **Capital**) and **Lower case** letters. Both >T< and >t< are the letter *Tee*: the former is upper case while the latter is lower case. The decision as to whether to use upper or lower case depends on aspects of the meaning of what is being written and is nothing to do with sound.

The 'Phonetic' Names of the Letters

Phonetic: Any analysis or representation of words which only takes account of the *sound* of a word is phonetic. A phonetic representation of a word is conventionally indicated by enclosure in slash brackets; for instance, the phonetic representation of the word *heads* is /hedz/.

Splutterings such as 'kuh', 'tuh' and 'guh' for the letters >c<, >t< and >g< are examples of a way of learning the alphabet which claims to call the letters by phonetic values. This sort of practice results in such nonsenses as 'a, nuh, yuh,' when spelling out the word ***any*** and 'eh, ih, guh, huh, tuh' for ***eight***.

Knowing >t< and >h< as 'tuh' and 'huh' is unhelpful when children encounter the grapheme **<th>** which is needed to represent the two phonemes [θ] (as in ***thin***) and [ð] (as in ***that***); similarly, [ʃ] is represented by **<sh>** – ess aitch, not 'suh-huh' – (as in ***shut***). Two of the possible sounds of >s< are not 'suh' and 'zuh'; the word ***yes*** is not 'yesuh', and the word ***these*** is not 'theezuh'! The two phonemes referred to are more like 'sss' and 'zzz'.

When you are associating sounds with the letters, be very careful not to use the 'phonetic' alphabet.

The letter >c< is often called 'kuh' by proponents of these so-called phonetic names. But >c< can represent the phoneme [s] as well as [k] (and follows a completely consistent pattern when it does). In combination with >h< it forms the grapheme **<ch>** which can represent three further, different, sounds (e.g. ***chemist, chin, machine***). Children who have been given the early impression that >c< is 'kuh' are guaranteed confusion in their subsequent word building.

Don't mislead and confuse early learners by using the so-called 'phonetic' names of letters; use the conventional names (>d< as 'dee', >m< as 'em', >k< as 'kay', >r< as 'ar', >h< as 'aitch', >w< as 'double-U', >z< as 'zed' etc.)

Not long ago I was working with a young dyslexic who had only recently been referred to me. He had written <f-i-t> and I was asking him to read the word that he had written. 'Fuh, ih, tuh,' he said. I covered up the >f< and asked him to read the remaining letters as a word, and he had no trouble in recognizing *it*. I then asked him to put the sound of the letter >f< before it and tell me what the new word was. He became increasingly uncomfortable and refused even to have a go. I did my best to encourage him, assuring him that I wasn't worried if he didn't get it right but still he refused, beginning to get quite upset. I asked him to tell me what was worrying him and he told me that he thought I was asking him to swear. Then it dawned on me – he could only read it as 'Fuh it'! I quickly shared with him the knowledge that >f< represents the sound 'fff' here, not 'fuh'. He read the word *fit* straight off and the relief was writ large all over his face!

> I am not saying that the letters of the alphabet are not related to the sounds of speech, or even that knowledge of these correspondences is not helpful in reading. But this knowledge, even if a beginning reader could painfully acquire it all, will rarely permit the sounding out of visually unfamiliar words with sufficient precision to make them recognizable as known words in English speech. For a start, there are too many possibilities. There is not a single letter in English writing that does not correspond to more than one sound (or to silence) in speech. In a relatively small sample of 20,000 common words there are over 300 of these correspondences; over 300 different ways in which our 26 individual letters of the alphabet are collectively related to the sounds of English speech. It is scarcely possible to exaggerate how difficult it is for a child to identify an unfamiliar word in written English without any other kind of clue.
>
> (Smith, page 146)

It should be understood by all that single letters can rarely indicate and represent a sound in isolation. Letters work in *combination* with others, and it is those combinations which follow consistent patterns.

A Model of Orthography

It is fundamental to a proper understanding of the conventions of the English writing system to realize that the prime concern of letters is **the representation of meaning**. This is why it is fundamentally wrong to give the impression that letters are tied to sound. **Orthography is the representation of meaning in writing.**

Children should be told from the beginning that spelling is our way of showing what words *mean*.

English orthography is made up of three interrelating elements: the way a word is written depends on all three. To build up our model we now consider each of those three elements in turn, beginning with the least important.

Phonology

Phonology is a study of the sound system of languages. The building blocks of sound are called **phonemes**. Representation of phonemes is the lowest level of writing and for many people this is the only aspect of language that is consciously known. Since almost all current and traditional teaching of spelling, and reading for that matter, seems to be based on the "sound it out" approach it will be useful to look at phonology in a little more detail. Some examples will illustrate what phonemes are.

In the word ***bat*** we recognize three constituent sounds: /b/, /ă/and /t/; we use three letters when we write that word. In the word ***right*** we recognize the three phonemes /r/, /ī/and /t/, but in this case we use five letters to represent it.

✎ **Phoneme**: The smallest unit of sound of a language that can affect meaning.Standard English has 44 such phonemes. The signs that represent phonemes are often indicated by square brackets; for instance, in the word *practice* the last phoneme [s] is represented by the grapheme <ce>.

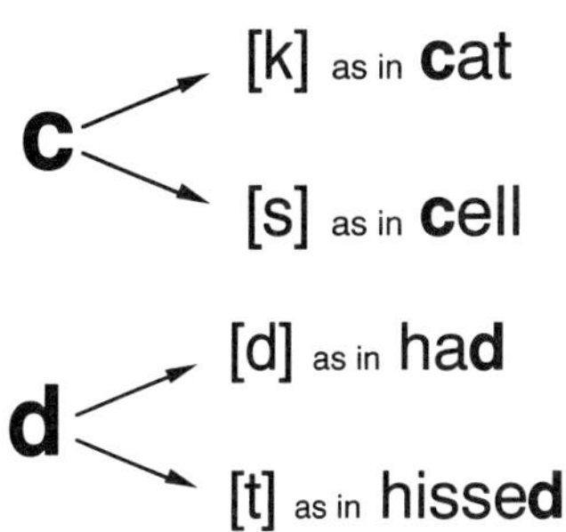

There is an indefinitely large range of sounds heard in languages, and no two languages have the same set of phonemes. Each language operates with a relatively small range of phonemes – I am told that Hawaiian has only thirteen while others use as many as eighty. Analysis has suggested that Standard English has forty-four basic phonemes – twenty-four consonants and twenty vowels and vowel-combinations. With only twenty-six letters at our disposal it is immediately clear that we do not have a one-to-one relationship between twenty-six single letters and forty-four constituent phonemes of English.

One way in which this mismatch is solved is to make some letters have dual function (in fact most letters of the alphabet can represent more than one sound as well as no sound at all). For instance, the letters >c< and >d< can each represent at least two different sounds, as is illustrated in the diagram.

Another way to represent a phoneme is to use linked pairs of letters (known as **digraphs**). Thus the single phoneme which distinguishes ***ship*** from ***tip*** is represented by the digraph >**sh**<. Other digraphs which are used to represent single phonemes include: >**ch**< as in *chin*; >**th**< as in ***thing*** (but note that the phoneme in ***then*** is different from that in ***thing*** even though it is written the same, so digraphs as well as single letters can do double duty!).

More precisely a phoneme is **the smallest segment of sound which can distinguish words**. So ***bad*** and ***mad*** are only distinguishable by the initial sounds of /b/ and /m/. Similarly, ***bad*** and ***bid*** are distinguishable by the vowels /ă/ and /ĭ/.

The interesting thing to note here is that even though we have been concentrating on aspects of *sounds* of the language, we still only classify those sounds when they can signal distinctions of *meaning* between words.

Phonology is only one of the three interrelating aspects of orthography. The first stage of our diagrammatic model is shown below.

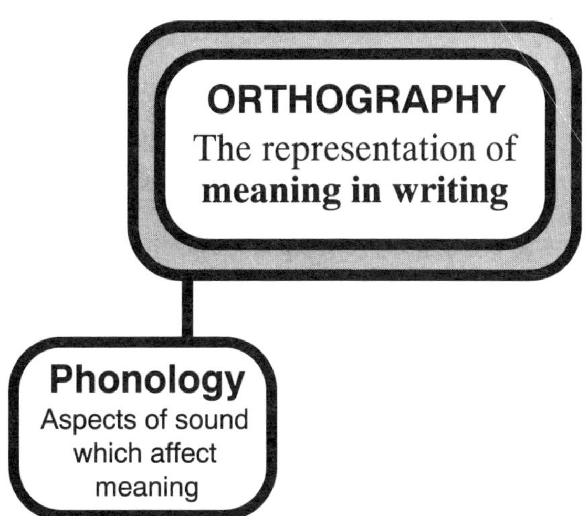

The representation of the sound of words is often the only aspect of English spelling that many are aware of. But phonology is only one aspect of our writing system, and a lower-level one at that. To confine children's perception of spelling to simple phonics is to deny them the proper tools of the job.

Explicit teaching of the phonemes of English is often confined to individual letters and a very few digraphs such as <**th**>, <**ch**>, <**sh**>, and perhaps <**ng**>. But the real sound-units of English are rarely represented by just one letter in isolation. Even what may seem to be a simple one-letter correspondence between sound and symbol is not actually that simple; for instance, it is an old cliché that 'A is for Apple'. This is most unhelpful, since it is also for **A**re, **A**im, **A**ny, **A**way, and **A**ll! It also stands for other sounds in words such as b**A**n**A**n**A**, wom**A**n, w**A**s, and me**A**n.

Letters are rarely specific in what they represent when written singly: the essence of writing is the *combining* of letters. Handwriting then is an important element of word building. This is why any system of handwriting which hinders children from writing letter combinations from the very start is at best unnecessary and at worst a severe drag on fluency in the representation of meaning. A fundamental property of any handwriting system must be the facility of generating strings of letters which are unities in terms of movement. There must be a means of obviously grouping letters into words apart from simple juxtaposition. It is interesting that the opposite of *orthography* – the wonderful word *cacography* – not only means bad spelling but also bad handwriting. (See *Putting Pen to Paper* for more on this point.)

Written letter-strings also have an even more important function to perform than approximation to sound. That is concerned with the next element of orthography.

Morphology

✎ **Morpheme**: An element having a meaning or grammatical function that cannot be subdivided into further such elements.

The most important element is morphology, the actual structure of meaning within words. It introduces us to the unit of meaning which makes up words called a **morpheme**.

The word ***unknowingly*** has four sequenced elements of meaning: <un-> + <**know**> + <-ing> + <-ly>. Each one of those morphemes could be a 'building block' of meaning in all sorts of other words

*The constituent morphemes of the word **unknowingly** can each be elements of other words. It could be a useful project for a small group of children to generate as many words as they can from each morpheme; the possibilities are almost limitless!*

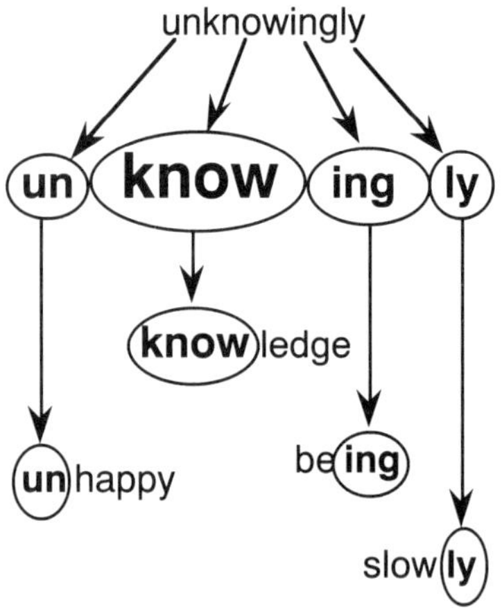

unknowingly
un know ing ly
knowledge
unhappy
being
slowly

A further example will help. Each of the words ***kids*** and ***kits*** has two morphemes, <**kid**> + <-s> and <**kit**> + <-s>. Again, each of those morphemes could be a building block in other words:

<**kid**> as in ***kidnap***; <**kit**> as in ***kitbag*** and ***identikit***; <-s> as in ***books*** and ***pens***.

Interesting points arise from these examples which clearly illustrate how morphemes and meaning are more important than phonemes and simplistic phonics. Look again at the word ***unknowingly***. There are two kinds of morpheme in it. At its core is the morpheme <**know**>; this morpheme can occur by itself as a complete word – it is what is called the **base word** of *unknowingly*.

✎ **Affix**: A bound morpheme which must be fixed to a base element; when appearing before the base element it is called a *prefix*, after the base element it is called a *suffix*.

The other morphemes in the word – <un->, <-ing> and <-ly> – cannot occur as a complete word on their own and are technically known as *bound* morphemes, which is why I write them with a connecting hyphen to show that they have to be attached to something else. Bound morphemes – those which need to be *fixed* on to others in full words – fall into two categories: those which need to appear in *front* of the base element are called **prefixes**, and those which appear *after* the base element are called **suffixes**. Collectively, prefixes and suffixes are called '**affixes**'.

The centre of meaning of a word (usually, but not always, a free morpheme) is called the word's **base element**. We have already recognized that the words ***unknowingly*** and ***knowledge*** have the same base element – the free morpheme <**know**>. When the base element can be a free-standing word (and most base elements are) then it could also be called a **base word**. Bound morphemes which are attached to the base element are **prefixes** and **suffixes**. This basic structure of the English word can be simply represented like this:

Notice that the base word **<know>** might change its sound in different combinations. Thus in *unknowingly* the base word is pronounced to rhyme with 'flow', the >o< is 'long' – /ō/. But in *knowledge* the same base word is pronounced differently, the >o< is 'short' – /ŏ/. **But even though the sound alters, the spelling does not change because the *meaning* of the morpheme has not altered.**

The arrowed line which connects morphology and phonology in the diagram is a reminder that the two elements interact in our spelling system. Wherever possible, however, ***it is the representation of morphemes that takes precedence over the relatively fluid representation of phonemes.***

A similar thing happens with the plural morpheme <-s>. In ***kits*** the <-s> is pronounced /s/ while in ***kids*** it is pronounced /z/. Again, though the *sound* of this plural morpheme changes from word to word, its spelling does not because **the English system of spelling principally represents *meaning*.**

This means that spelling will only be affected if there is a change of meaning. It also means that where there is a strong relation of meaning between two words, then that closeness will be reflected in the spelling. For example ***heard*** is written like that because it relates to ***hear***; and because the word ***herd*** means something completely different then it is spelled differently. Another simple example can be provided by the base word **<can>**. On its own it is pronounced /kăn/ and it would sound like that in such a sentence as, 'Can you cook?' In a spoken phrase such as, 'I can swim well,' the vowel collapses and the word sounds something like /kŭn/; in the common form of its negative, ***can't***, the base word itself sounds like /karn/. If spelling were completely tied to sound then the same base word would have to be spelled in three different ways. But since the meaning does not change, *then the spelling does not change either.*

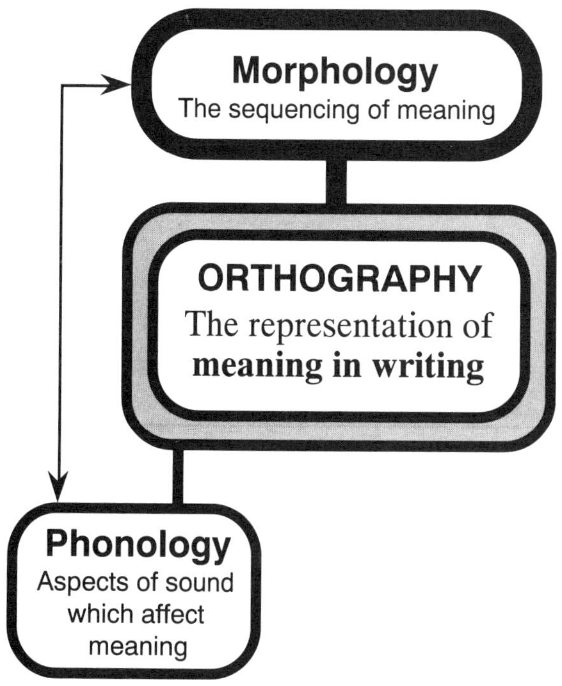

We can now extend our diagrammatic model of English orthography. The elements of morphology and phonology interact in English spelling, but the representation of the morphemes takes priority over the representation of sounds.

From the earliest stages of their school life children must engage with the organic connection between handwriting and spelling. A sound teacher of the written aspects of language links handwriting with this crucial element in the sense-making that written language explores. How this can be done is discussed in Part Two (page 45 ff.) when details will be given of how knowledge of morphemes is translated into practical teaching.

It is important to link morphemes with the way they are written. Since hardly any morphemes are represented by only one letter even the youngest learners should be writing *strings* of letters so that they can link their handwriting with morphemes.

Etymology

Etymology is the remaining element of orthography. It also concerns the representation of meaning, but in a different way; it points to a word's *relationship with other words* of associated meaning. It shows the *interconnections* between words. To adapt John Donne we might say, 'No word is an island, entire and of itself.'

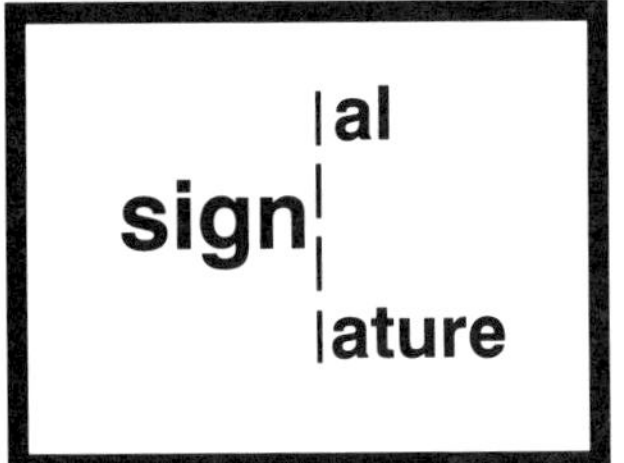

An example will illustrate this; take the word ***sign.*** What is >g< doing in it? Ask most people and they will probably say that it is a 'silent g'. True, but why should it be a >g<? Why not a 'silent x', or a 'silent k', or any other letter for that matter?

The answer is simply that >g< is there for etymological reasons: it indicates a connection of meaning with closely related words. When you ***sign*** a document it is your ***signature*** that you write. A sign that is given or made is a ***signal***. Here, then, an interaction between phonology and meaning is at work. The >g< is pronounced in the two words ***signature*** and ***signal***. Its presence is needed in ***sign*** to represent the connection of meaning even though it is not actually pronounced in that word.

✎ **Homophone**: A word which sounds exactly the same as another word which has an unrelated meaning.

At this point it is interesting to contrast ***sign*** with ***sine***, a word which sounds exactly the same; the words are *homophones*. Because of the etymological dimension of orthography, the difference of meaning between ***sign*** and ***sine*** can be related to a difference of spelling. You will have heard of a 'sine curve'; ***sine*** is related to the word ***sinuous***. A >g< would be as inappropriate in ***sine*** as it is important in ***sign***. **English spelling is also the representation of *relationship* of meaning.**

The base word ***sign*** can be the central point of an interesting word web. The one given here was generated by a group of Year 4 children. Word webs are powerful illustrations of the way the interrelationship of meaning between words is reflected in their orthography. The production of such webs should be a regular feature of children's orthographical activities.

This example shows the powerfulness of word webs in reinforcing an understanding of the morphological nature of English spelling.

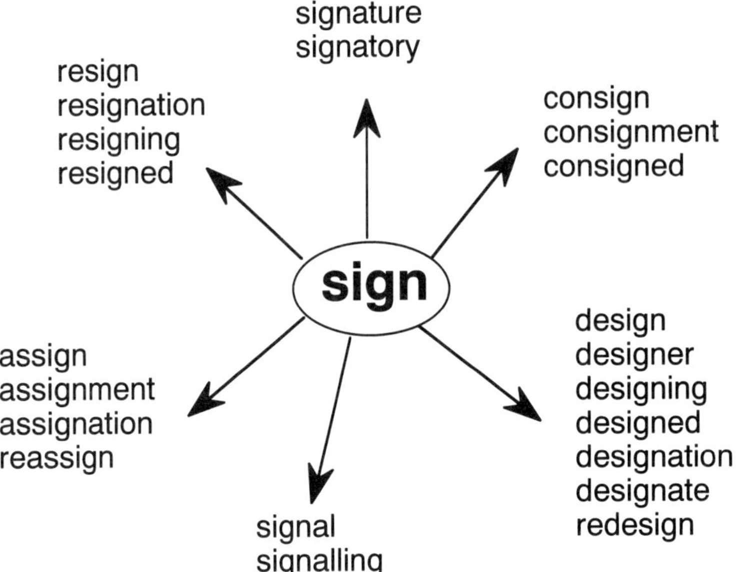

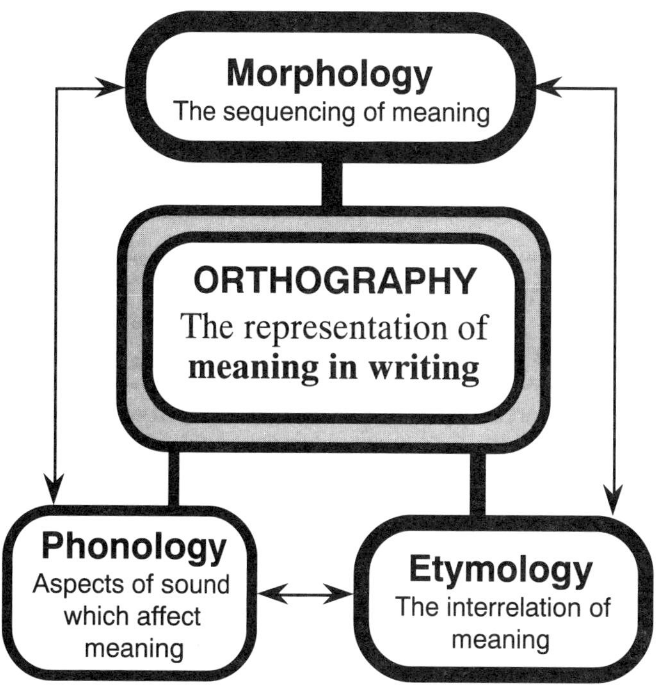

I have been using the term *etymology* to describe this element of orthography. The term is, however, commonly understood to have a more restricted meaning, referring only to the study of the history and origins of words. The Collins English Dictionary, for instance, defines etymology as **the study of the sources and development of words and morphemes**. Consequently it is often assumed that a knowledge of ancient languages is essential to be able to operate on an etymological level. But we have already seen with the word ***sign*** that we have operated etymologically without a knowledge of Latin. It is a matter of interest that the common ancestry of ***sign*** and ***signal*** is the Latin word *signum* but it isn't necessary to know that; we knew about the need for the silent >g< from its related words.

I will, therefore, need to redefine the term *etymology* as **that element of orthography which indicates how words relate in meaning to each other as a result of common histories and origins**.

We can now complete our model of the component elements of the English spelling system. Etymology takes its place as the element of orthography by which we signal the interrelationship of words.

Working with Basic Word Structure

In recent years such terms as 'whole word' approaches have been used to describe methods of teaching reading and writing. Such notions grow from an understandable reaction against the barrenness of the simplistic phonics. We know that the phonic element of writing is unstable and can even be confusing or misleading if it is taken in isolation; we have seen how phonology is the lowest level of orthography. Learners certainly need rescuing from methods which are limited to phonics. 'Whole words' sounds like a good idea.

Unfortunately the 'whole word' reaction is not necessarily helpful either. It rests on an assumption that words are 'wholes' and unfortunately for the theory, and therefore for the resulting practice, they often are not. An understanding of morphology reveals that words are rarely seamless wholes. The ability to recognize or to spell the however many tens of thousands of individual words there are in the English language does not depend on having a memory of each isolated word as a whole; it depends on recognizing the elements of meaning of which each word is constructed. The next chapter will show that **the mind does not store whole words: it stores morphemes.**

We saw above that there are two broad categories of morpheme: bound and free. Bound morphemes are those (like <-ing>, <-ly> and <-ness>) which cannot stand on their own as words; free morphemes are those like <**know**> and <**whole**> which can stand on their own.

There is a relatively small number of prefixes and suffixes in the language, and children can quickly build up a repertoire of known affixes. An interesting consequence of this is that the longer a word is the more likely it is to consist of familiar parts. To many it is a strange paradox that **longer words are almost always easier to spell than shorter ones**!

The diagram given on page 23 shows the structure of most English words. There is also another class of word which consists of *two* base elements joined together to make a new word. These are called **compound** words.

✎ **Compound Word**: A word which consists of two base words combined into one new one. Each element is spelled as it would be as an independent word; no modifications are made when they are joined as a compound.

prefixes and suffixes can then be added to the compound

Here are some examples:

playtime postbox somebody takeaway headache slowworm

More will be said later about compound words, but it is worth mentioning a property they have which affects the way they are spelled. *The spelling of each base element in a compound word is the same as the base word on its own.* Two of the words above illustrate this clearly.

You probably know that the single silent >e< at the end of ***take*** would be dropped in front of a suffix which begins with a vowel:

take + ing → taking.

But ***away*** is not a suffix, it is another base word so no change is made with the resulting compound:

take + away → takeaway

Some dictionaries follow increasingly modern practice by spelling the name of the legless lizard ***slowworm***, without a hyphen. The structural principle of compounding words leaves no problem with the >w< written twice; the form ***slowworm*** is constructed on the same pattern as its alternative name ***blindworm*** (never ***blind-worm***).

slow + worm → slowworm.

*This matrix makes clear why <h> needs to appear twice in the compound word **withhold**.*

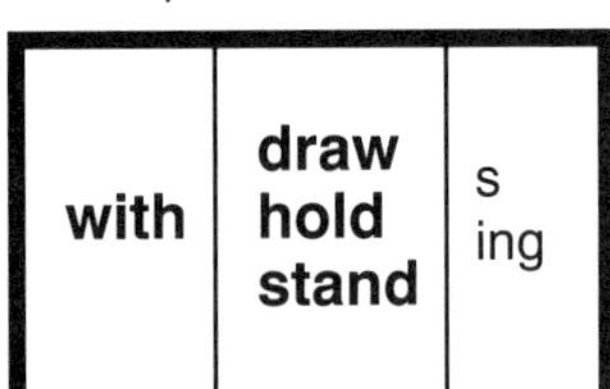

People often have a similar difficulty with ***withhold*** – or is it ***withold***? It's no use just gazing at the two suggested spellings to see which *looks* right; only one of them can *be* right. Think morphologically rather than on a simplistic phonic level and you will know which has to be right. I might offer the matrix in this margin to a class who needed to consolidate this principle for themselves.

Illustrations

The etymological dimension of spelling is present very widely and can often provide insights into spelling which are accessible even to quite young children. The following two illustrations occurred recently when I was working with a class of Year 4 children.

Someone in the class asked me why the word ***yolk*** (of an egg) was spelled with >l<. He had spelled the word as ***yoke*** in a piece of work and the teacher had corrected it. 'Why *not* spell it Y-O-K-E?' he asked.

We first established that there are two homophones which sound /yōk/ and that one of them means an implement which is placed over the neck for carrying or pulling; the other one is the part of the egg. The group knew the important principle that when two words sound the same but have different meanings then they will also be spelled differently if that is possible. They now knew why there were two different spellings for the same-sounding words.

The discussion then moved on to questioning the presence of >l< in ***yolk***. It was quickly established that an egg contains 'white' and the *yellow* part. Several voices quickly piped up with no prompting from me that ***yellow*** and ***yolk*** might be connected. This was confirmed by reference to the dictionary in the class's scriptorium (the area set aside for writing activities and reference materials).

This basic word chain was produced by children to illustrate that the 'silent' >w< in ***two*** *signals a connection in meaning with other words which include the idea of the number 2 where the <w>* ***is*** *sounded.*

Someone then offered the hypothesis that ***folk*** and ***fellow*** might be connected in a similar way.

The same group continued an investigation on what they had learned to call the 'silent' letter. The question arose as to where >w< in ***two*** comes from. Telling them that it is a 'silent w' doesn't really answer the question since that doesn't indicate why the silent letter is >w< in particular. What they produced to summarize their own explanations is in the margin and should account for the >w< in ***two***.

With these words ***yolk*** and ***two*** we see how the 'silent' letters >l< and >w< are there for etymological reasons; they are indicators of a connection with words of related meaning in which those letters *do* form part of the phonology. Each of these base words could, of course, acquire affixes: examples include ***yolkless*** and ***twosome***.

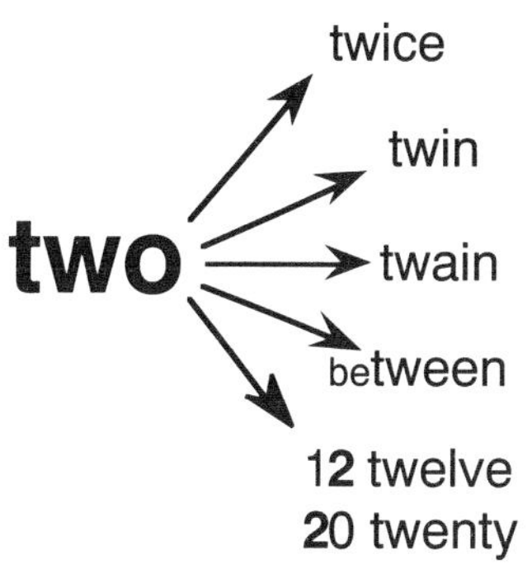

In a further example of words which have been investigated by various groups of primary children, here is a word web which grows from the starter word ***unhelpfulness*** which is clearly not a seamless 'whole'. Each of the morphemes of that central word in turn is made the basis of its own word list.

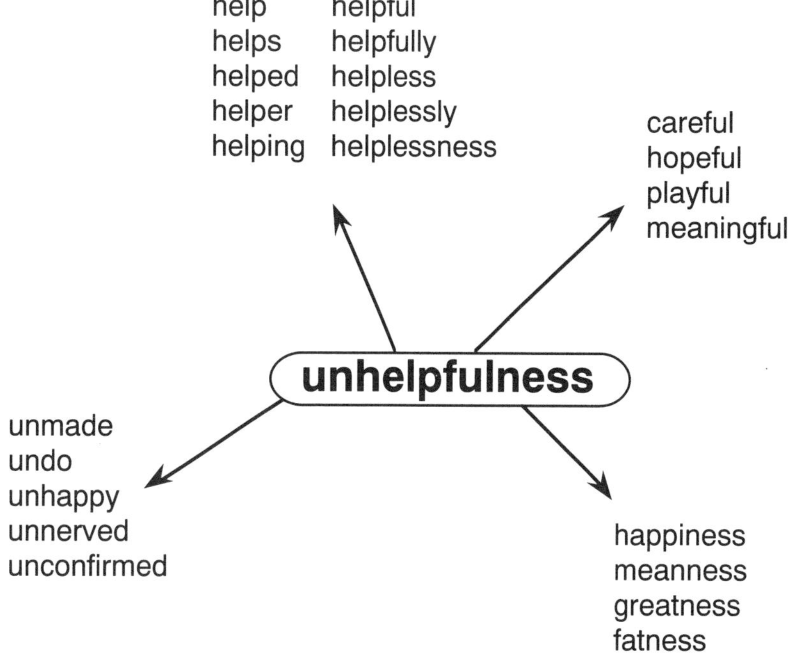

people

p o pula	te
p o pula	tion
p o pula	r

A word web can also be useful for illustrating other etymological characteristics of the spelling of some words. Here are two examples.

The spelling of **people** shows an interesting combination of phonology and etymology. It came into English in the thirteenth century as the Old French *pople* (itself from the Latin *populus*). Over the years it has changed the sound of its vowel in the spoken language, but the original vowel is retained in the written language so that the word's semantic connections are not lost. The silent presence of >o< in the word recalls its sounded presence in words to which it might be related. Incidentally, the reason why *popular* has to be spelled like that with <ar>, and not as **populer* with <er>, can readily be seen when we look at the related word *popularity*.

A large number of the university undergraduates I taught regularly misspelled the starter word of the following web as **definate*. From a simplistically phonic point of view there seems no reason why it should not be spelled like that – after all it sort of rhymes with such words as *fortunate* which do end with the suffix <-ate>.

*This word web shows clearly why the suffix in **definite** has to be written as <**-ite**>; the related words are, after all, not ***defination** or ***finate**!*

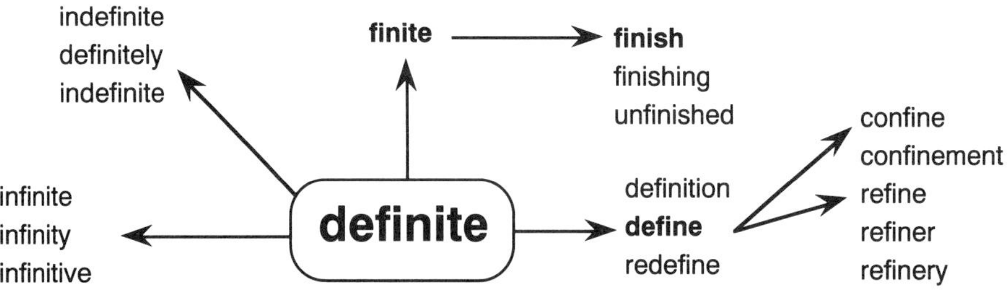

Sometimes building word webs will result in unexpected insights about words. Here is an example which comes from a Year 6 group spelling project.

*This web led its makers to an etymological discovery. I clearly remember the glee with which, as a result of making this word web, a small group of children realized how **disaster** came to mean what it does. The link they discovered with the base element <**aster**> suggests that at some time in the past people tended to attribute misfortune to the malign influences of the stars and planets. As the Collins English Dictionary puts it:* C16 originally in the sense: malevolent astral influence.

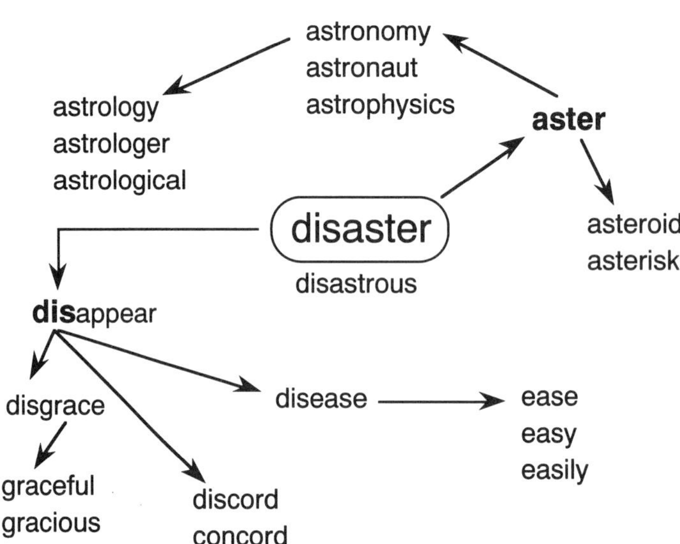

More will be said later in the book about how word webs such as these can be actively incorporated into teaching and learning strategies.

CHAPTER 3: HOW THE WRITER'S MIND ENGAGES WITH SPELLING

Knowing what the structures of orthography actually are allows us to give conceptual coherence to our presentation of spelling. We must ensure the appropriateness of our teaching by considering how the mind engages with these structures.

The Lexicon

The word ***lexicon*** has an interesting history. Until this century *lexicon* and *dictionary* were virtual synonyms; the difference was merely one of etymology – *lexicon* derives from Greek while *dictionary* is from Latin. This synonymity is assumed in Dr Johnson's famous definition – **LEXICOGRAPHER**: A writer of **dictionaries**, a harmless drudge. If there was any divergence of meaning it was that *dictionary* tended to be used for alphabetical lists of English words and their meanings, while *lexicon* was often used of ancient languages such as Greek and Hebrew, and therefore less common than *dictionary*.

✎ **Lexicon**: the set of all the morphemes of a language.

The growth of the academic study of linguistics has created a need for precise and specific terminology. As a result *lexicon* has acquired a specialized meaning relevant to our consideration of the nature and processes of orthography.

While a dictionary consists of lists of entire words, the lexicon is thought of as composed of the small units of meaning which are the *components* of words.

> The lexicon should contain all the information that is idiosyncratic to a particular lexical item. This also includes ... semantic and phonological features. In fact, rather than thinking of items in the lexicon as words, a more accurate conception would be that each lexical item is a bundle of features. These would include ... everything about a word that is relevant to its use in the language.
>
> The basic notion is that the lexicon provides a pool of lexical information about words which can be channelled appropriately into every part of the [language] system.
>
> (Greene, pages 62-3)

The term lexicon in this sense is now also used by psychologists of language; the **personal lexicon** is that part of our memory which stores what we know of the building blocks of language. It contains our vocabulary of base words, affixes and all the elements of complete words that we know. In our personal lexicon we store:

- Our collection of the units of language; from these units we know how to build up complete words.
- Our ability to match some sort of meaning to those units of language.
- Our orthographical knowledge: that is, our ability to represent the meaning of these units in writing.

The Basic Lexical Process

A closer look at this somewhat technical subject will help us to understand more clearly the process by which children (and we) reach the point when we can make a written representation of the meaning of any target word.

In an admittedly simplistic way we could describe the process like this. We 'feed' that target word into our lexicon and match it to what we know of the 'building'

blocks from which words are formed. We identify the building blocks from which the target word is built and use our knowledge of how those blocks are written to compile the whole of our target word.

This process is rather like making a lego model. We start with an idea of the sort of model we want to make; then we go to our collection of lego blocks and components and sort out what we need; finally we fit them together in order to produce the finished model. For mature writers and spellers the process is so practised that it has become internalized and happens almost unconsciously. The overall process by which a mature writer spells a target word may be simply represented by the accompanying diagram.

Base and Combining Elements

Words are built up from morphemes; many complete words contain more than one morpheme.

We do not necessarily hold complete words in the lexicon; we hold the *elements* of words. The contents of the lexicon which relate to spelling have been met in the last chapter; they can best be understood as:

1. **Base Elements**, often able to stand as whole words, but not necessarily so.
2. **Combining Elements** such as prefixes, suffixes and the inflectional endings of nouns and verbs.

Here are a few examples to illustrate what is meant.

The Base Element RUPT

The base element <**rupt**> usually suggests that a word which is built around it may have a meaning which is something to do with ***breaking***.

This morphological diagram illustrates how this base element can combine with various affixes to produce a large number of different but interrelated words.

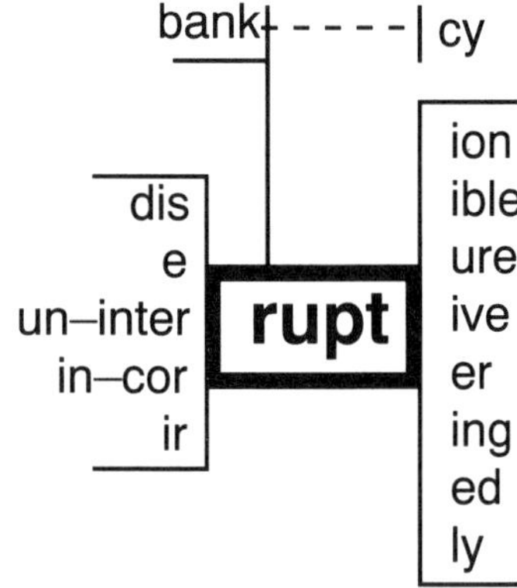

The web is also a representation of the information stored in our lexicon from which we can assemble such words as the following:

disrupt	disruption	disruptive	disruptively	erupt
eruption	erupted	erupting	interrupt	interruption
interrupted	interrupting	rupture	ruptured	rupturing
corrupt	corruption	corrupted	corruptible	incorruptible
irruption	bankrupt	bankruptcy	corruptly	uninterrupted

Our model makes it clear why in words such as ***interrupt*** and ***corrupt*** we need to write the >r< twice; one belongs to the prefixes <inter-> and <cor-> while the other is needed for the base element <**rupt**>.

The Base Element SCI

The base element <**sci**-> usually suggests that a word built around it has something to do with ***knowing*** and the acquiring of knowledge. For instance, when you are *conscious* you ***know*** what is going on around you (and when ***unconscious*** you don't know!); by your *conscience* you ***know*** what is right; a *scientist* is one who investigates and classifies ***knowledge*** of the physical world.

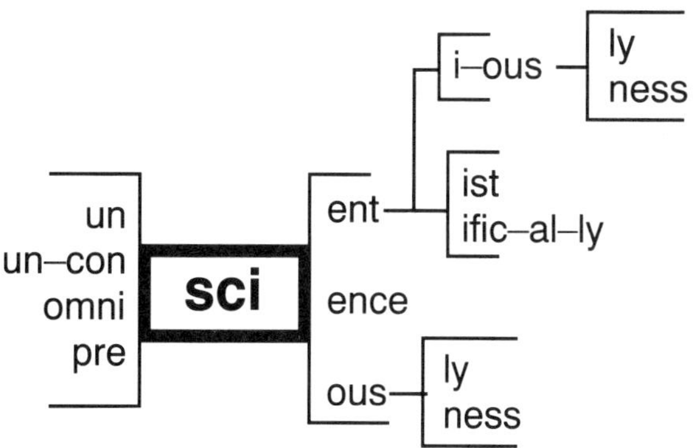

This cluster of morphemes contains the elements of such words as:

scientist	scientific	unscientifically	science
conscience	conscious	consciously	unconsciousness
prescience	omniscience	omnisciently	conscientiously

This base element is interesting from a phonic point of view since the sound represented by <sci-> is variable. The phonic value depends on the combination of elements. In *scientist* it is /sī /; in *conscience* and *conscious* it is [ʃ]; in *conscientious* it is /ʃĭ/; in *omniscient* it is /sĭ/. But the spelling remains the same because the semantic base (the fundamental meaning) does not change. Morphology and etymology take precedence, as they always do, over phonology. The presence of <sci-> in all these words is also an etymological signal of a common relationship of meaning and history of the words. (It is interesting, but not necessary, to know that all these words trace back to the Latin verb *scire*, which means *to **know**.*)

Why Isn't *they* Spelled **thay*?

A recurring, and for some irritating, problem of basic orthography is the spelling of the two related words ***they*** and ***their***. Why isn't ***they*** spelled *****thay*** and ***their*** spelled *****thair***, or even ***there***?

We know enough about orthographical structures to hypothesize that since ***they*** and ***their*** are closely related in meaning then they will be spelled as similarly as possible. You may also know that >i< and >y< are sometimes interchangeable (e.g. duty→ dutiful). A combination of these two principles will explain the transformation **they → thei → their**.

The question still remains as to why ***they*** is spelled with an >e< in the first place. An answer may be found by relating them to the third word in this trio of meaning – ***them***. The interrelationship of the words ***them, they,*** and ***their***, and therefore of their orthography will be registered in the lexicon. The following diagram can indicate the way the lexicon may represent this information to itself.

This diagram shows clearly how the spelling of *their* can be approached and justified. In the case of its homophone *there*, link it with the word *here* to which it is related in meaning and therefore in spelling. In turn, *here* itself has a homophone – *hear*. Link this last word with the word *ear*; *hear* is what you do with your *ear*.

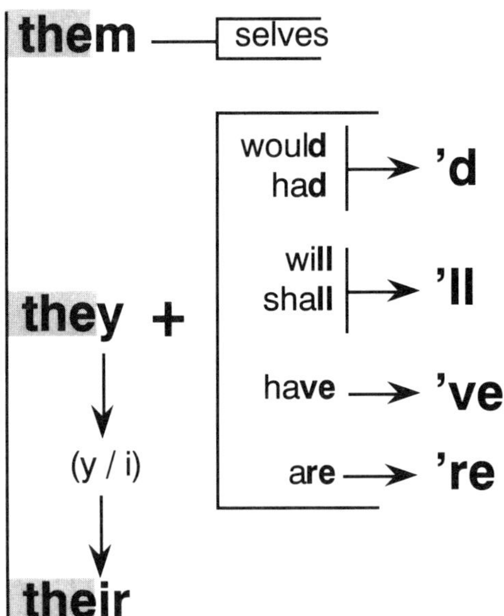

This provides the means of building such words as the following:

them themselves they they'd they'll they've they're their

Segmentation

The lexicon is the mental data bank from which we construct words. It also gives us the means of *analysing* words – recognizing their constituent parts. This is how we make sense of a previously unfamiliar word when the written or spoken context is of little help. Look at this process of analysis with the following complete words separated into their component parts.

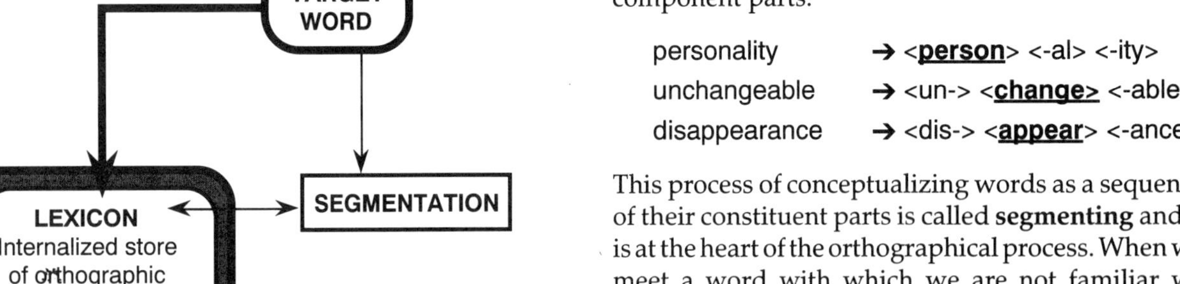

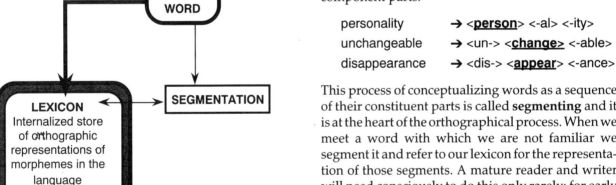

personality	➔ <**person**> <-al> <-ity>
unchangeable	➔ <un-> <**change**> <-able>
disappearance	➔ <dis-> <**appear**> <-ance>

This process of conceptualizing words as a sequence of their constituent parts is called **segmenting** and it is at the heart of the orthographical process. When we meet a word with which we are not familiar we segment it and refer to our lexicon for the representation of those segments. A mature reader and writer will need consciously to do this only rarely; for early learners this is their commonest conscious strategy.

This is the process with which we should deliberately and consciously engage young learners as they come to grips with orthography. It is an early priority that they should learn the habit of segmenting their target word and checking whether they recognize any of the resulting segments.

Most of the examples given so far are *morphemic* segments; the words are divided into their units of meaning. But we do know that phonology is also an element of orthography, though it is the lowest-level element. Segmenting on a phonetic basis can also take place. Phonetic matches are the lowest and most primitive level of orthographical strategies. Thus a very early learner, when faced with a target word which has not yet been learnt as a sequential whole, may engage in a process rather like this further extension of our model. (*Graphemes*, you will remember, are the written alphabetic representations of phonemes and morphemes.)

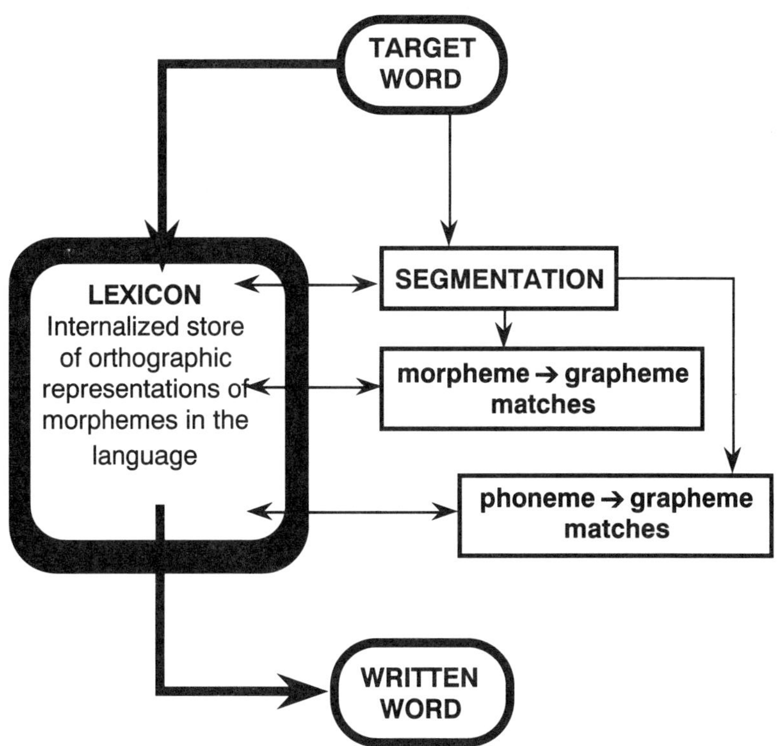

This complete model of the personal lexicon helps us to understand the way in which we process the need to represent a target word in writing. Knowledge of this process can suggest an explicit strategy for word-attack skills.

Here is a framework for the process of word attack which I share with even the youngest of the learners with whom I work.

1. Segment your target word.
2. Do you recognize any of the segments?
3. Do you know how to write these segments?
4. Write down the segments you know in the right order.
5. Leave a blank for those segments you don't know and ask someone you trust to help you with those segments.

PART TWO

FROM PRINCIPLE TO PRACTICE

The system we have is good for the reader, especially the fluent reader. The way words are spelled makes it easy to see the meanings quickly. It's not so good for a beginning reader who's trying to work out a lot of new words. It's particularly bad for spellers. But it's worst of all for spellers who try to work out spellings from the sounds of words only. That's not how the system is designed to work. It's not designed to show you how the language sounds like.

Our spelling system is designed for people who speak the language and who know about how words are linked together and built up. It shows you what words mean and where words come from. It will teach you about the English language – how words are related; which languages words come from. It will tell you something about our history – who conquered us, where we built an empire, where we traded, who came to settle in this country. If you want to be a good speller you have to take an interest in all this.

(Pratley, page 116)

CHAPTER 4: HAND, VOICE AND EYE

Two assumptions underpin the traditional teaching of spelling: they are that the basis of spelling is phonic (but with exceptions) and that memory for spellings is visual. Teaching methodology has relied on a combination of two elements:

- Giving lists of words to learn, usually with some variation of the test in view;
- An expectation that providing spellings when they are requested and correcting misspellings when they appear will lead to 'picking up' correct forms.

From the account of the real nature of English spelling provided in Part One we can conclude that traditional approaches consisting of testing, correction and visualization rely on a partial and truncated appreciation of orthography.

This chapter deals with how the intersensory nature of the process of spelling must lead us to engage more than just the visual processes in the organizing of children's acquisition of spelling. Later chapters will deal with constructive alternatives to correction and testing.

Handwriting

Handwriting is an important part of language activity and is embedded within the broader processes of language. It is also integrally bound with the way we learn to spell. The research of Margaret Peters, among others, has clearly established that fluent handwriting is an aid to good spelling while poor and inefficient handwriting is a positive hindrance.

☞ **Teaching children print script, or allowing them to write in capitals, will hinder their orthographical development.**

The reason why handwriting affects our ability to spell is because we have a tactile movement memory by which we learn word formation and the reproduction of words in writing. Try closing your eyes and writing your name; even though you do not see what you are writing such familiar words are easy to write.

Since handwriting is principally concerned with the representation and organization of meaning there is more to it than just style and appearance. The connection with spelling suggests that real handwriting should be characterized by fluency and continuity of the movement of the pen-in-hand. Such practices as print script in lower case or writing in block capitals will hinder continuity of movement and inevitably hinder the implementation of the action of the motor memory.

☞ **Tell children that handwriting is a dance of the pen – the dance turns into writing because the pen leaves a trail of where it has been.**

In a quite literal way writing *moves* into spelling. Bradley (1980) is a strong supporter of what she calls a 'running hand' and states that 'failure to establish motor patterns ... could hamper the normal development of spelling'.

> Integrated movement patterns are the basis of fluent writing... Handwriting would not be possible – not if we were trying to compose words at the same time – if we had to labor along one letter after another... Very rapid and precise combinations of plans for movements have been what psychologists call "overlearned", which means that they are so highly practiced that they demand little or no conscious attention.
>
> (Smith, page 142)

Smith's use of phrases like *integrated movement patterns* and *precise combinations* helps us to understand that the construction of words is not simply a question of writing rows of individual letters. Sequences of letters called **letter-strings** have a predictability which is based on patterns of meaning and some approximate representation of sound. A good handwriting system will give the facility for generating **strings of letters which are unities in terms of movement too.**

Real Handwriting and Spelling

I discuss the nature and teaching of handwriting fully in my book *Putting Pen to Paper*. You will need to consult it for a justification of the following statements.

Handwriting works very closely with spelling so the teaching of the one is best combined with the other.

- Spelling and handwriting are not fully effectively taught in isolation from each other. Fluency in handwriting depends in part on knowing how to spell, and learning how to spell is mainly learned from writing.
- Printing is not only inefficient, but it also fragments the writing of words. Print script concentrates attention only on the finished shape of a letter which is all that is checked. It is little surprise that frequently the route taken by the writing instrument in the formation of printed letters is perverse, reverse, and counter-productive to fluency. Such teaching of writing which concentrates on 'round' forms and circular movements is unhelpful because they do not conform to the natural movement of the pen-in-hand. Indeed, merely copying the traditional round forms of the sans serif print can only reinforce some letter confusions. In the traditional rounded infant print script >b< and >d< are mirror images of each other; it is inevitable that such reversals should occur quite widely. (The plain sans serif type so often used in early readers is no help either; in that simplistic and tiring type face >b< and >d<, again, are mirror images. In mature and regular type face they are not.)
- Machines print; people, however, **write**! Children should not print but learn to write a fluent style from the start of their schooling. When letters are learned as a process of motor formation rather than merely copying shapes then such confusions as the lower case >b< and >d< almost never arise; the two letters are formed completely differently, they 'feel' different as they are being written, and they do not even look similar when they are written down.
- If real writing is taught from the beginning of learning then there is not a great Rubicon to cross when 'joined-up writing' is announced. An ergonomically sound and consistent script will contain within itself the structures of its own ligatures as well as the roots of its own speed.

Ligature: A stroke which is added to a letter or is a continuation of a stroke of the letter by which a join is effected to the following letter.

Ability to form and therefore to identify letters in connected strings is crucial to the orthographical process. Children's handwriting should be capable of generating connected strings of letters from their earliest learning.

Written Letter-strings and Spelling

In those groupings of signs which we call words, component letters need to *feel* as if they belong together as we generate them in writing. Our primary aim should be to help children to write sequenced letter-strings which flow naturally from the pen in as continuous a 'dancing' sequence as can appropriately be achieved.

This written morpheme has the advantages of being mainly composed of falling verticals, and of having both an ascender and a descender which give it an obvious visual wholeness.

Giving practical experience of the power of the motor memory in generating and recalling strings which correspond to meaning can take place at any stage of learning. Ideally, of course, it should happen from the earliest writing, but it is impressive whenever it happens. In order to do this the common bound morpheme <-ly> is a useful one to start with. It is most appropriately written as a unit – the pen need not leave the paper. Writers should be encouraged to make sure that the descending 'tail' of the >y< swings below the >l< as well in order to emphasize the unity of the morpheme.

When children are well into the rhythm of writing this morpheme (probably only a minute or two) ask them to try writing it with their eyes shut, and prepare yourself for squeals of delight when they open their eyes and see how well they have done. Tell them that they have now discovered one of the great secrets of writing; it is that **the hand has a sort of memory of its own**, and that they don't have to look at each letter of a part of a word they are writing. You can usually trust your hand to get it right! In the words of an American writer, the form is 'grooved' in the writers' tactile memory and it will not be long before they can make the metaphorical statement of 'doing something with one's eyes shut' a personal reality! Indeed, **we can often spell words when we *write* them even if we were not able to reconstruct them accurately from visual memory alone**.

☞ **Encourage writing for spelling recall rather than just mental visualization.**

mad	ly
love	
proper	
nice	
sad	
real	
most	
glad	

When we put pen to paper we often just set the writing in motion and the hand's movement memory will do the rest. It is not unusual for us to be able to recall the spelling of a word or morpheme through writing when we were not sure of it by mental visualization. Children whose first encounters with the morpheme <-ly> are by writing it as an integrated movement pattern will never write it as <*le>, <*lee>, <*ley>, or the like.

After some oral work in which children practise telling you what various base words will become when <-ly> is suffixed to them let them enjoy writing the results. The matrix given here will provide you with examples both for preliminary oral work and also for subsequent written work. A copy could be given to each child as the beginning of a spelling resource collection.

Introduce the equally common bound morpheme <-ful> quite quickly after <-ly>. Young word builders will need to use their knowledge of ligaturing from the crossbar of the >f<, completing the morpheme without lifting the pen. Remind them to bounce up high towards the >l< as it is a tall letter. As with the <-ly> they can try writing it with their eyes closed to confirm that the hand can be trusted to 'remember' how to write it. They will soon be ready to try another word matrix, not just with <-ful>, but with <-ly> as well.

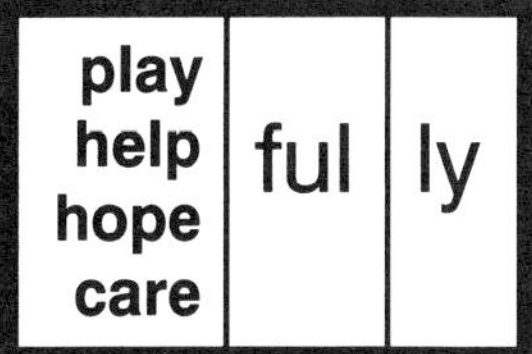

play	ful	ly
help		
hope		
care		

An incidental point worth making at this stage is that the suffix <-ful> is spelled differently from the base word ***full***. Sharing this knowledge with children will be a useful opportunity for further confirmation of the principle that differences of meaning and function are, wherever possible, reflected in spellings of words.

Write Words a Morpheme at a Time

Clearly it is a powerful teaching stratagem to base the process of word building on the conceptual structure of the words, that is the sequencing of the morphemes from which they are constructed. In this way learners are helped to conceptualize words not as seamless wholes but as sequences of elements of meaning.

> At the heart of the [spelling] process is the concentration of attention on the internal structure of words, and this is something that rarely takes place when the conventional mark/correct procedure operates.
>
> (Bullock, 11.12)

☞ **Children should not be handicapped by the obstacle of print script or its relatives if they are to represent the relationship of letters in morphemes in a completely tangible way.**

This approach to building words is appropriate for writing. Each morpheme in a word is *written* as a unit rather than attacking the word as a whole. For instance, the word ***uninterruptedly*** consists of two prefixes, a base element, and two suffixes – five sequenced morphemes; ***orthographically*** consists of a base element and four suffixes. They would be written in this way:

☞ **Encourage children to check each morpheme of a target word as they write it.**

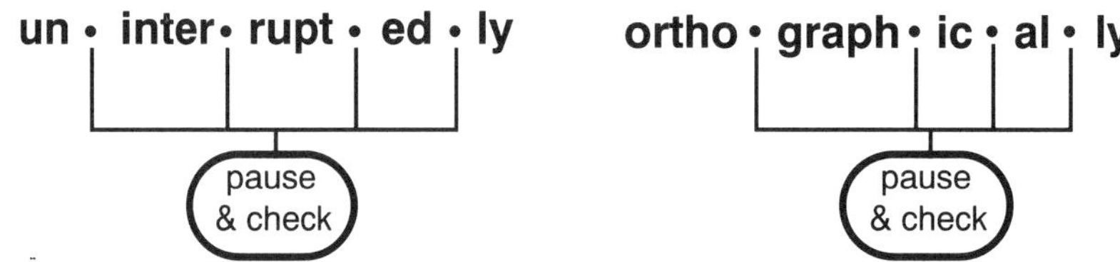

br cl fl k r s sl st str w wr	ing

Apart from reinforcing the conceptual structure of the word this approach also enables the checking of the spelling of words 'on the hoof' as each *morpheme* is quickly checked before moving on to the next. This is more efficient than checking whole words or even whole sentences.

j m s t	ing	le

Another important morphemic letter-string is the common suffix <-ing>. Its unity is emphasized by connecting the written forms of its component letters as a continuous movement without pen-lift, only dotting the >i< when the string is finished. When early learners are first working with the string <-ing> I tell them to say 'ing!' out loud as they complete it with the dot.

This string is also a stable phonetic unit so can also be used for word building of an entirely phonetic nature.

Writing it in this way will also help to establish a habit of only dotting an >i< when any string in which it is present is completed; it is a further encouragement not to think of words letter by letter.

A powerful letter string which can be introduced to quite young children is the four-letter sequence **<-tion>**. This string is easy and satisfying to write. Like **<-ing>** the >i< is dotted only when the constituent letters have been completed; as that dot is written I ask the children to say a triumphant 'shun!' since the string is phonetically stable and represents that sound (represented as /ʃun/).

Children will know that whenever they see the string **<-tion>** it will always represent the sound /ʃun/; this is one of many ways in which writing feeds the learning of reading. They will also know that if they are writing a word which has a segment identified as /ʃun/ it is likely to be represented by **<-tion>**.

ac na op ra lo po sta suc sec igni peti devo no	**tion**

com e loco	**mo**	**tion**
at con	**trac**	
in im | per	**fec**	
re con ex	**cep**	

di e cor	**rec**	**tion**
in de con ob	**struc**	
de sub in con pre	**scrip**	

It is a useful project for a few days to make a class collection of words which end with **<-tion>**. Prepare to be surprised by words that quite young children will contribute. The matrix here can be given as a useful resource for generating a starter collection of such words.

The project can be extended to classifying these words according to whether they end with

I have seen <-tion> referred to as a suffix in some spelling books; that is not correct as strictly speaking the suffix element is only the <-ion>. The following matrix illustrates this.

act	ion
opt	
intent	
direct	
elect	
perfect	
inspect	

-ation, **-etion**, **-ition**, **-otion**, and **-ution**, or end with **-action**, **-ection**, **-iction**, **-oction**, and **-uction**. The results will provide rich material for vocabulary extension, wordbuilding consolidation, and the development of fluency in the handwriting of the letter-strings concerned.

A Further Note on Infant Print Script

Print script, invented in the first two decades of the twentieth century, is a system of writing in which the letters are twenty-six separate shapes with no rhythm of writing common to all of them; attention is inevitably focused on the separate formation of individual letters. That is a sure way of preventing the conception of wholeness and continuity within words. This fragmentary system of much infant printing allows no means of obviously grouping letters into words apart from juxtaposition, and almost all writing of it allows the winds of heaven to blow between the letters. Print script is a motor and conceptual obstacle race.

If you wish to facilitate your children's ability to spell you need to give them a style and form of handwriting that is ergonomically and conceptually sound. Print script will not provide this.

The main conclusion of this section about the role of handwriting in orthography is that quite often we find that we can spell a word once we start **writing** it *even if we were not sure of the spelling in our head only*. The hand goes on to a sort of autopilot!

The Voice and Spelling

Teaching of spelling, then, should involve integrated movement patterns of letter-strings that are part of handwriting. **The hand has a sort of memory of its own.**

And so does the voice.

'Spelling Out'

From the earliest learning ensure that children spell out using letter *names*, not the so-called phonetic names; thus *care* is 'cee, ay, ar, ee', not 'kuh, a, ruh, eh'.

'Spelling out' describes words by naming their component letters in the right order.

Using the proper *names* of the letters of the alphabet gives a powerful structure for the learning of spelling. Any one of the hundreds of thousands of words in the language can be definitively described by using just twenty-six symbols, each of which can be referred to by a single *name*.

'Spelling out' also means that the letters are spoken in the right *groupings* which correspond wherever possible with units of sense – the morphemes of the word. Pauses should be made between the various parts of the word which will coincide with the connections between the constituent morphemes. Thus the word ***described*** is spelled out as D-E (pause) S-C-R-I-B (pause) E-D. Further illustrations will establish this process.

The word ***playfully*** will be spelled out as P-L-A-Y pause F-U-L pause L-Y. Clearly, even at an early stage of learning, it is important to ensure that the word is not conceived as '... F-U-Double-L-Y'. There is no phonetic reason for the *double* >l<; but there is every reason for writing >l< twice from a morphemic point of view: one >l< belongs to the morpheme <-ful>, and the other to the separate morpheme <-ly>. Here are further examples.

sadly → S-A-D (pause) L-Y

unkindness → U-N (pause) K-I-N-D (pause) N-E- double-S

carefully → C-A-R-E (pause) F-U-L (pause) L-Y

really → R-E-A-L (pause) L-Y (**NOT:** R-E-A - double L - Y)

meanness → M-E-A-N (pause) N-E- double S (**NOT:** M-E-A- double N...)

In this last case this ***is*** 'double S' because >s< invariably appears twice inside this particular morphemic unit.

☞ Children should spell words out loud using the proper letter names, grouping them according to the word's constituent morphemes.

Most of us who teach in primary schools have been imbued with ideologies which react against parrot-fashion learning; we feel uneasy about 'spelling out' if it seems to be a case of chanting as learning. But the real objection to parrot-fashion repetitions is that they are devoid of meaning. (It is, for instance, not much use being able to chant the nine times table if we cannot then sort out what *thirteen* nines are.) Similarly it is not much use being able to chant N-A-T-I-O-N as the spelling of ***nation*** if we cannot then spell ***international.***

Spelling out a word may sound like chanting, and indeed will be if the way it is spoken out does not correspond to the structure of meaning in the word.

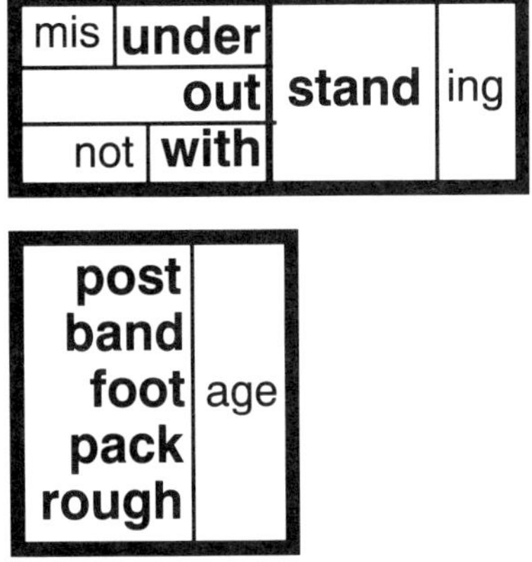

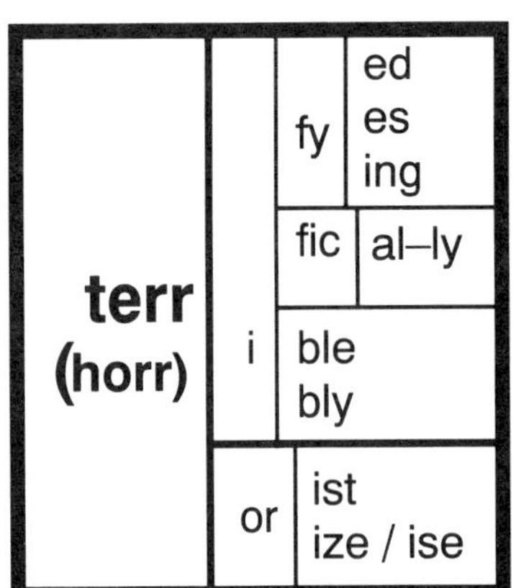

When spelling out a word is linked with its writing and follows its correct segmentation, then not only the sequence of the segments but also the sequence of the letters in each segment will be established in the memory both of the voice and the hand, and each will reinforce the other. Try out this process for yourself by using these matrices. As you write the words spell them out, making sure that you *pause between the morphemes.*

☞ Children should know that they are much more likely to be able to spell a word by speaking and writing than by trying to work it out all in advance by inner visualization.

Spell-checking by Spelling Out

Just as children should be encouraged to spell words out loud as they write them so, more importantly, they should also do so when they are checking the spelling of a word when it has been written. I have frequently seen children detect their own spelling miscues by reading spellings out loud when they did not detect them merely by looking. As they read out the spelling the voice often falters if it reaches a part of the word where the letters are not in the expected order or where there is an unexpected letter. The reason for this has been alluded to earlier in the book: the voice and the organs of speech operate with a more powerful sequential element than does the sense of vision, and their sequential memory is stronger.

Voice and the Phonological Dimension

When phonic aspects of spelling are being dealt with it seems like common sense to concentrate attention on hearing. But this is to forget that the sound of words also *starts* somewhere – it is produced by the mouth and the vocal organs.

☞ When tracking phonic elements of words direct children's attention more to the 'feel' of the sounds in the mouth than to reception of the sound by the ear.

Phonology is as much to do with representing the *production* of sound as with the perception of it.

Clearly, then, it will always be helpful to direct a learner's attention to the *production* of a target segment or word; what the throat and mouth are doing as they form the constituent sounds of words is more accessible to the learner than hearing the result of someone else forming words.

There is a further reason for teaching awareness of the production of sound in dealing with phonics; the obviously physical process of speech relies more heavily on a powerful sense of sequencing than does hearing. Just as the voice's 'memory' is often more reliable than visual memory, so the use of the voice can also be superior to the sense of hearing – *even* when only the phonics of a word are being attended to. Sequencing is not a powerful element of the sense of hearing; you hear the component sounds of a word, but you may not necessarily be able to reconstruct that sequence afterwards by using your 'inner' ear. By *speaking* the word again you can reconstruct a sequence of sounds more effectively.

☞ Make the experience of phonics more holistic for learners by encouraging them to concentrate on what the target word or segment *feels* like in the mouth as it is being produced; tell them to 'taste' the word. In that way the component parts of the word can be identified and their proper sequence established.

Like anything being tasted you can draw out the 'savouring' of the target word so that you can really identify its constituent phonemes. It is particularly effective for establishing the proper order of phonemes. For example young writers sometimes confuse the spelling of the prefixes <per-> and <pre->. Try saying out loud each of the two words ***perfect*** and ***prefect*** very slowly, but instead of *listening* to what they sound like concentrate on *what they feel like in the mouth* as you say them.

The 'phonetic' alphabet has many drawbacks, several of which have already been mentioned. A further problem with its use arises from the fact that the staccato nature of the values given to the letters fragments the production of sound to a series of hiccoughs. Thus a young child weaned on this system, trying to write the word ***play*** eventually wrote it as ****pula*** – the inevitable result of trying to phoneticize it as 'puh-luh-ay'. (A similar problem is caused by this phonetic alphabet to reading; I saw a child who had been limited to a phonic strategy read ***centre*** by first speaking it out as 'kuh-eh-nuh-tuhruh-ee' and saying 'country'.) This 'hiccoughing' fragmentation of words can be prevented both by avoiding the phonetic alphabet in the first place, and mainly by training learners to sound out target segments and words as a *continuous* sound in which the phonemes slide into each other. I told one child to stretch out the word he was saying as if it were a piece of bubble gum; he took to the idea instantly.

Keep Phonics in Its Place

Phonics is important. There is no question that one of the pillars of the orthographical system is an approximate representation of *some* aspects of sound.

☞ In the word attack process phonics comes into action only after segmenting has taken place.

The proper place of phonics is to associate letters with sounds but *only when that serves the purposes of representing meaning.* As such phonics serves morphology and etymology. For this reason phonics is sometimes referred to as a 'low-level' orthographical activity; this is not because simple and common words are principally phonic – most are not – but because phonics will always be overridden by the needs of the other pillars of orthography.

Avoid Mispronouncing Words on Purpose

'The phonetic fallacy' generates apparently helpful approaches which are actually conceptually wrong and therefore counterproductive. An example of this re-inforcement of the phonetic fallacy is the deliberate mispronouncing of words in order to 'help' a child with spelling.

For instance, you might pronounce **says** as if it rhymes with ***ways***. However, the child brought up to understand that spelling represents relationships of meaning before sound will have no difficulty with **<say> + <-s> → *says***, whatever the shift of pronunciation in the base word.

In the case of the word **stationary** you might pronounce the suffix <-ary> to rhyme with ***fairy*** in order to distinguish the word from its homophone ***stationery.*** The conceptually sound approach is much simpler and not misleading: call attention to the fact that *stationery* is what a *stationer* sells.

Confronting Children's Accent

The phonetic fallacy underlay my strategy of teaching spelling by deliberate mispronunciation. The same fallacy underlies the statement that I hear from time to time to the effect that if children spoke properly they would spell correctly. A consequence of this (untrue) notion that correct spelling reflects Received Pronunciation (RP) gives rise to an attitude which attempts to teach spelling by confronting local accent. The entirely understandable cause of helping spelling generates the questionable practice of denigrating a child's speech. The irony of this is that *even RP is not faithfully represented in spelling.*

I was put in my place on this matter in the early months of my first teaching job in London. That old chestnut pronounced by the children as /sumfink/ had arisen and I began the standard strategy of getting them to pronounce it according to RP. 'If you said it right you would spell it right,' I castigated them, and demonstrated the 'proper' pronunciation of ***something***, clanging the final <g> to ram home my point. A child in the class then observed that if ***thing*** had to be written down as I said it then he would write the first part of the word as S-U-M which was also exactly as I was saying it. When another child suggested that ***nothing*** should be spelled N-U-... I could only reply that the right spelling just was the right spelling; I had probably set back the class's route to orthographic maturity by implying that spelling *should* be about correct sounds but much of the time *actually* wasn't.

Look-Cover-Write-Check; Current Orthodoxy

The conclusions of Margaret Peters have influenced much current teaching of spelling. Her work has been particularly informative and of value in clarifying the nature of the spelling process and its structures. She points out, for instance, that good spellers recognize word *forms*, often see what she calls 'words within words', and perceive letter *sequences* and patterns. She also notes that good spellers tend to be fluent handwriters.

The conviction that spelling is overridingly a visual skill has lead to systematic strategies which approach correct spelling along the visual route. The result has been the accepted strategy, referred to in the National Curriculum itself, as Look–Cover–Write–Check. The first element is defined as follows:

✎ **LOOK – COVER – WRITE – CHECK** is a strategy for learning spellings which routes the processes almost exclusively through the visualization process. Bentley (p. 4) summarizes as follows:

LOOK at the word carefully and in such a way that you will remember what you have seen.

COVER the word so that you cannot see it.

WRITE the word from memory, saying it to yourself as you are writing.

CHECK the word. If it is not correct then go back and repeat the steps.

LOOK at the word in such a way that you will remember what you have seen.

This is understood to mean 'looking for words within words.' This might at first sight be taken to refer to the morphemic structure of words – and very sound that would be too. But examples given show this not necessarily to be the case. For instance, it is suggested that ***hat*** should be seen in *what*. Yet the connection between these two words is tenuous in the extreme, relying on a coincidence of a three-letter sequence which is not a string with any morphemic or even phonetic consistency; more seriously there is absolutely no connection of *meaning* between the two words; finally the association of these two words does not represent or consolidate a word attack strategy which is specifically relevant to word building as a whole. The real way to 'look' at the orthography of ***what*** is twofold: first associate it with the family of 'question words' which do begin with the digraph <wh->: *when, which, why, where* and even *who*; secondly refer to the phonological pattern shown later (page 71) that >a< following /w/ behaves like >o<.

'COVER the word so that you cannot see it' is the way the next step is described.

The recommendation is that children should never copy words, but always be encouraged to write them 'from memory'. This calls for caution for the following important reasons.

Experience of language is simultaneously aural, oral, visual and tactile. Engagement with a target word involves its structure in terms of meaning, what it sounds like, what it feels like in the mouth, what it looks like, and what it feels like when it is written. That is how we experience words and it is how we *learn* them – in a holistic way. The insistence that children should never copy words ignores this intersensory nature of experiencing words. It establishes a (false) impression that memory of word formation is all about visual recall and that writing is merely the written representation of that visualization. The search for these inner visualizations also gives rise to a habit of looking around in the air as if holograms of whole words float about waiting to be identified.

A copying ban routes word recall through a single isolated sense, and one at that which is not the most powerful in reproducing the correct spelling of a target word. This is difficult enough for mainstream learners; it can be a catastrophe for those, like many dyslexics, for whom the visually sequenced memory is virtually non-functional. And the copying ban is unnecessary anyway since writing 'without looking' will happen automatically when the writer feels safe; confident writers are unlikely to spend time copying when they don't need to, while one who needs to reference will do so as necessary and consolidate that skill in the process.

Children who are coping with any difficulties in their engagement with language may have their difficulty converted into a problem if they have to concentrate learning to spell on the isolated sense of visual recall - their 'mind's eye'. Far from being banned from anything that may be construed as 'copying', children should be encouraged to search for and recognize what will enable them to represent the target word. This basic process of 'scanning' is an early stage of the crucial learning strategy of **referencing** which will achieve a higher level with formal reference tools like the dictionary, the lexicon and the thesaurus.

While LOOK-COVER-WRITE-CHECK has become an orthodoxy, its adoption as a standard procedure can have unhelpful consequences:

- Even when 'words within words' are sought these are liable to be irrelevant to the real meaning and structure of the target word.

☞ **By all means acquaint children with LOOK-COVER-WRITE-CHECK as *one* sort of spelling game but do not give it high status or authoritative standing. Be particularly sparing in its use with children with special learning needs in language.**

- It is not a generative strategy which will enable the representation of a previously unmet and unlearned target word.
- By banning 'copying' a climate of testing, and therefore of threat, is creeping in.
- By actively hiding a target word opportunities for developing and practising referencing are lost.

We learn the *spelling* of words because we know *how they are constructed.*

Avoid the over-concentration on visualization as a route to orthographical competence of the LOOK-COVER-WRITE-CHECK orthodoxy with something like the following: **SEGMENT** the target word; **WRITE** the word segment by segment, spelling out each segment as you do so; **CHECK** the word by spelling out loud segment by segment what you have written, using the letter names. **CONNECT** the word to its relatives by making a word web; connect its morphemes to words of related form or meaning.

Recourse to 'Sight Vocabulary'

Some will say that, while they realize that spelling is much more than mere phonics, they want to base their teaching of early learners on sounding out because they regard that as straightforward. It is reasoned that phonics at least lies at the base of early reading and writing and so avoids complicating the process unnecessarily.

☞ **The 'sight vocabulary' theory *may* have some application to learning to read; it is of little help with spelling and may even be a hindrance to children with special learning needs. Concentrate instead on learning by segmental writing.**

Since not even the simplest vocabulary is susceptible to consistent phonic representation an exclusively phonic approach has to come to terms with those frequent words which don't 'build' or 'blend' on phonic tramlines. They are then classified as needing to belong to a 'sight vocabulary'. These basic words include such very common words as the following, all of which would be needed for early writing:

of	was	all	one	they	their
about	the	a	an	eye	come
people	buy	four	know	sugar	water
any	some	says	said	high	who
walk	would	could	should	enough	love

Such teaching is effectively saying to children, 'Spelling is phonic, except when it isn't; you just have to learn the other words only by remembering what they *look* like before you write them.' And we know that learning words by sight alone is inefficient and unreliable.

The 'sight vocabulary' idea as a route to spelling has an element of confusion between the spelling and the reading process. Adherence to the 'learning spelling by sight' approach makes the assumption that if you can recognize a word in a text when you see it then you should be able to reproduce it in writing too. This canard has been disposed of earlier in this book.

CHAPTER 5: BASIC WORD ATTACK SKILLS

Priority for Morphemes

From their earliest learning, children should know that the written form of a word is a representation of its meaning. Everything else they will learn about writing – phonics, handwriting, spelling rules and patterns – is helping to make meanings clear. The sort of thing that can be said to them is, 'When you have written a word make sure that the way you have written it helps you, me or anybody else to know what it *means*.'

☞ **Teaching the recognition and management of morphemes ought to be at the forefront of our priorities for children's word building.**

Our understanding that the mind stores the significant elements of meaning from which we assemble words is the key to our understanding of how the learning of spelling can take place. The central theme of the way we help children towards word building should be the concept that the lexicon operates with morphemes and their representation.

Using Word Matrices

Matrices should be used from the earliest encounters with word building. They are valuable for the following reasons:

- They direct attention to the essentials of word structure – morphemes and the letter-strings which make them up.
- They can provide a basis for handwriting practice by linking movement patterns with word structure.
- They are an accessible early form of reference for spelling.

look sleep kiss play buy box hold plant draw say	ing

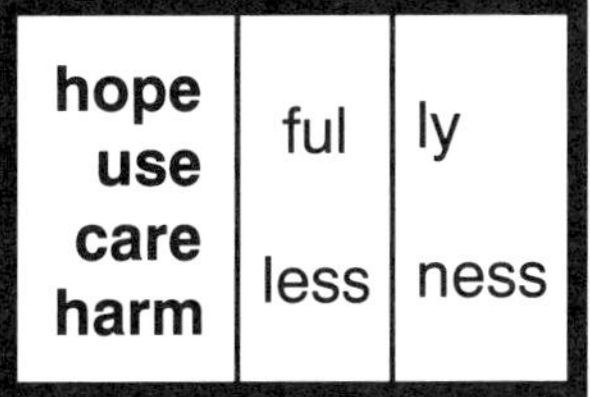

This first pair of examples is from my work with five- and six-year-olds. They followed some initial work on practising writing the five suffixes contained in the matrices, and some reading practice in recognizing the various base words listed. When they had spent some time writing as many different words as they could generate from the matrices (a possible twenty from the first and twenty-eight from the second if you include the base words as separate items) they then asked partners to spell out a given target word by locating it and reading out the spelling from the matrix. That was a two or three day project with early learners.

Even with experienced writers matrices should still be prominent. Here are two rather more complex examples from my work with Year 5. They were part of a word project which was looking at the common letter string <-igh>.

✎ **Matrix**: A word matrix is an arrangement of morphemes in columns in such a way that, by taking a single element from each column, complete words can be generated.

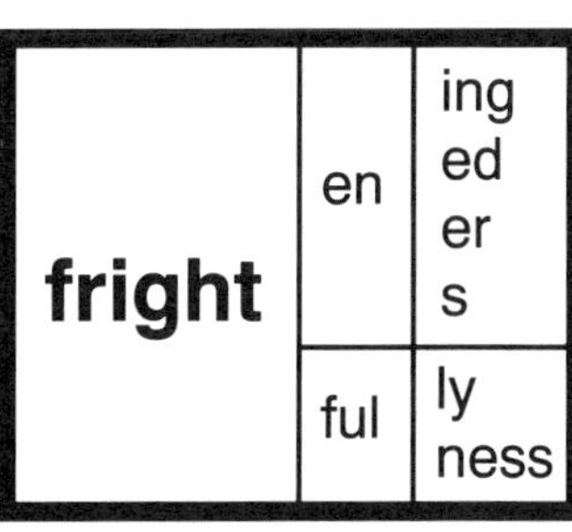

far- long- short- clear- fore hind	sight	ly ed	ness
		less s ing	
un		see	ing er

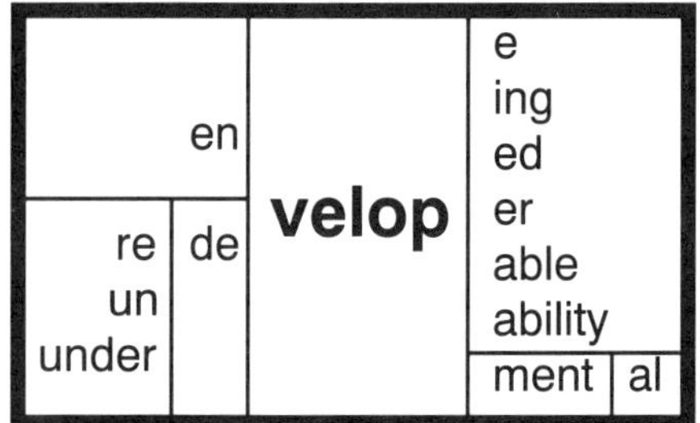

This next matrix was part of the follow-up to a study of the homophones *vale* and *veil*.

Since spelling is the representation of meaning there is a principle that where words sound the same ('homophones') but have different meanings then the different meanings will usually be represented by different spellings if that is possible. The word ***vale*** is related to ***valley*** while ***veil*** is related to the base element <-**velop**> which usually has some connection with a meaning of 'covering'.

Isolate the Base Word

We have seen that the central pivot of a word is its base element; that is why I usually underline it and ask children to do so too when they are word building. Since the identification of this hub of meaning is important in the process of word building we need to give children the skill of recognizing and isolating base elements. In order to reach a word's base element the affixes have to be identified and 'pruned' away, leaving the base element itself.

Keep morphemic structures at the forefront by using matrices at all stages of learning; matrices can be given by the teacher to illustrate points of orthography and constructed by learners to consolidate their own knowledge.

Recognizing Affixes

Compared with the number of *words* in the language (running into hundreds of thousands) the number of affixes is limited. It is, therefore, relatively easy to build a working vocabulary of prefixes and suffixes and attention should constantly be given to constructing and recognizing them. Here is one way you can set about it.

Working with Prefixes

There is a two-pronged test to verify a theory that you have identified a prefix:

1. When you remove it you should be left with a base element which you recognize or to which you can attach a different prefix to make a related word.
2. You should be able to identify the same letter-string as a prefix before base elements different from the target word.

To illustrate this test in action here is an example taken from work with a Year 4 class. The target word was ***mistake***; is the prefix <mis-> or <mist->? If you remove <mist> from ***mistake*** you are only left with ***ake*** which is not recognizable as a base element. If, however, you remove <mis-> from ***mistake*** you are left with <**take**> which *is* recognizable. The fact that the real prefix is <mis-> was quickly confirmed by the production of these words:

mislaid **mis**behave **mis**conduct **mis**fortune
mistrust and even **mis**chief.

It is clear, then, that the base element of ***mistake*** is <**take**>. The group produced the hypothesis that the prefix <mis-> meant that 'something is wrong with what the base word is about', so the word ***mistake*** means 'something that is *taken* wrongly'. The children then used the test of prefix substitution just to check that <**take**> is likely to be a base element and produced:

re**take**, over**take**, under**take**, in**take** and the compound word **take**away.

This small investigation had an interesting continuation when someone asked about the word ***mishap***. Her first observation was that the word had the letters

<sh> next to each other in a case where they do not represent the sound /ʃ/ – the word is spelled M-I-S (pause) H-A-P.

The second observation was that **<hap>** was probably the base element of ***happen*** and ***happy***. That turns out to be the case. The two suffixes in question are <-en> and <-y>; when they are fixed to the base element its last letter is doubled following straightforward patterns which we shall meet shortly.

Even very young learners quickly learn to recognize such basic prefixes as <un->, <dis->, <in->, <re-> and < mis->. It may be useful to have available some sort of reference list of basic prefixes so that each child can keep a copy with any personal reference book in which they collect the words they need to use. This simplified list can be the basis for your own selection of prefixes for the use of early learners.

A basic list of prefixes such as this should be available for reference for young writers. The actual selection should be determined by the teacher's professional judgement of the current needs and abilities of the class or group.

The result could be presented in the form of a class reference poster, a personal copy added to reference books, or both.

A comprehensive list of prefixes and their variations is provided in photocopiable form at the end of this chapter.

It is the form of these prefixes that is the most important element of their predictability. Where they do have clear and unvarying meanings it may be appropriate to share these with the children. Examples include: <circum->, <contra->, <ex->, <extra->, <fore->, <micro->, <mis->, <re->, <sub->, <tele-> and <trans->.

Some Prefixes

a-	de-	in-	per-
ab-	di-	inter-	pre-
ac-	dif-	intro-	pro-
ad-	dis-	ir-	
af-	dys-		re-
an-		maxi-	
ar-	e-	mega-	sub-
at-	ex-	micro-	suc-
	extra-	mini-	suf-
be-		mis-	sup-
	for-		
circum-	fore-	ob-	tele-
co-		of-	trans-
com-	hyper-	om-	
con-		over-	un-
contra-	il-		under-
cor	im-		

Prefixes: Some Technicalities

As the prefixes that are recognized are being collected on the class poster it may not be long before someone suspects that groups of what appear as separate suffixes are actually variations of each other; and they will be right. For instance, <ac-> (as in *a<u>cc</u>ept* and *a<u>c</u>knowledge*) as well as <ad->, <af-> and <as-> are all variations of the basic suffix <ad->. In a similar way <im->, <il-> and <ir-> are variations of a basic <in->.

It is a useful idea to install a poster in the classroom headed PREFIXES and to add to it, with some sort of appropriate ceremony, each time a new prefix is identified by someone in the class; this forms a corporate reference tool.

In order to help you to prepare an appropriate response, I include here some technical details of the formation of prefixes. Clearly these technicalities are only for more confident and experienced spellers. A good dictionary will provide most of this information.

Some prefixes are modified according to the first letter of the base word to which they are prefixed. For example the prefix <ob-> changes in the way shown in the diagram at the top of the next page.

Prefix	Before a base element beginning	becomes	Examples
ob-	**c...** **f...** **p...**	**oc-c...** **of-f...** **op-p...**	occur (ob + cur) offer (ob + fer) oppose (ob + pose)

Before any other letter <ob-> does not change (as in *object, observe, obdurate, oblation, obnoxious, obstinate, obtain* and *obverse*).

There is an entertaining plurality of meaning of this prefix which makes an excellent investigative theme for upper primary children. Frequently it means '*not* —' as in *inexplicable* (= not explicable), *imperfect, illiterate*, and even *inept* (= not apt). But it can also mean '*in(to), towards* or *within* —' as in *inherent, infiltrate, immigrate*. The prefix can also be an *intensifier* as in *inflame* or *imperil*.

Another example is the prefix <in->, which makes the following changes.

Prefix	Before a base element beginning	becomes	Examples
in-	**b...** **m...** **p...** **l...** **r...**	**im-b...** **im-m...** **im-p...** **il-l...** **ir-r...**	imbalance immature impose illogical irrational

Before any other letter <in-> does not change (as in *inactive, incoherent, indirect, inedible* and so on.)

Categories of Suffix

We have already met several common suffixes in the various matrices which have been given. The concept of suffixing can be present in the earliest learning of word building; we met <-ly> and <-ful> in the last chapter. There are more suffixes than prefixes but they behave in a predictable manner according to clear patterns.

Suffixes fall into two broad categories and the distinction is important for reasons that will be made clear. The categories are:

1. Suffixes which begin with a consonant, such as <-ly>, <-ful>, <-ness> and <-less>. These are called the *consonantal* suffixes.
2. Suffixes which begin with a vowel, such as <-ing>, <-ed>, <-er>, <-est> and <-ish>. These are often called *vocalic* suffixes.

Early teaching of word building should concentrate (though not exclusively) on *consonantal* suffixes since they do not affect base words and are therefore more straightforward to use than the vocalic suffixes.

Some of the commoner consonantal suffixes.

Some Consonantal Suffixes

-dom	-like	-ship
-ful	-ly	-some
-hood	-ment	-ster
-ledge	-most	-ward(s)
-less	-ness	-wise

The vocalic suffixes are more 'active' than the others because they can affect the spelling of the base word to which they are fixed. Here are two examples of their patterns of operation.

1. A single silent >e< at the end of a base word is dropped before a *vocalic* suffix. For instance <**love**> + <-ing> ➔ ***loving***. But a *consonantal* suffix does not affect the base word at all, so <**love**> + <-less> ➔ ***loveless*** and <**love**> + <-ly> ➔ ***lovely*** with the final >e< retained.
2. A base word which ends with a consonant can double that consonant when a *vocalic* suffix is attached to it. For instance <**forget**> + <-ing> ➔ ***forgetting***. But a *consonantal* suffix does not affect the base word at all, so <**forget**> + <-ful> ➔ ***forgetful***, with the final >t< undoubled. Doubling before a vocalic suffix does not always happen (for instance, <**cook**> + <-ing> ➔ ***cooking***).

The patterns which determine all these processes are systematic and absolutely regular and will be given in detail later (pages 64 and 109).

Enjoying Compound Words

Another way of establishing the concept of base elements is to work with compound words (see page 26). Look at the following three words and identify which one is *not* a compound word.

snowdrop snowing snowball snowman

The answer must be ***snowing*** because <**snow**>, <**drop**>, <**ball**> and <**man**> are all base elements and can stand as separate words in their own right; they are all free morphemes. The suffix <-ing>, however, cannot; it is a bound morpheme.

Spelling is the representation of meaning and sense, so when compound words are written **each base element is written in full in the same way as it is when it stands as a word on its own**. This is why the compound word *slowworm* must use the >w< twice because one of them belongs to one base element and the other belongs to the second base element. Here are more examples of compound words:

<**lamp**> + <**post**> ➔ ***lamppost*** <**bath**> + <**house**> ➔ ***bathhouse***

<**hot**> + <**head**> ➔ ***hothead***

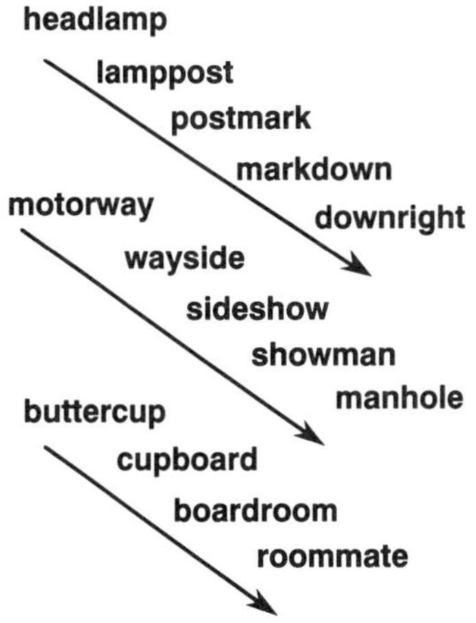

Building Compound Word Chains

The context for this activity can be oral or written, individual or co-operative. The object is to build a continuous sequence of compound words in which the second base element of one word is the first base element of the following compound word. Some examples are shown here.

Building compound word chains allows dictionary skills to be practised to good purpose. When looking for a sequel to a compound word the second element can be looked up in a dictionary and a suitable new compound found. If you are aiming to produce the longest chain you can, do not necessarily use the first compound that you come across but go for one with a second element which has promising possibilities for continuation.

Many compound words are 'solid' which means that both elements are written as one complete word. Some compounds, however, separate the elements with a hyphen. This is not the place for a full treatment of that pattern; get into the habit of consulting a good dictionary for hyphenated compounds.

Some compounds are written as two completely separate words, for instance *washing machine.* Modern dictionaries list these as a single lexical item.

Segmenting at the Forefront

☞ **It is an early priority that children should learn the habit of segmenting their target word and checking whether they recognize any of the resulting segments.**

Segmentation is the process of expressing words as a sequence of their parts; it lies at the heart of the spelling process. Without facility in segmentation, maturity in spelling is impossible. Here are some examples of word investigation in which segmenting provides the key to a correct understanding of a word's structure.

Take the target word ***designation*** as an example. Start by looking for possible suffixes. A good candidate could be <-ion>, so try removing it to see what you are left with. The result is ***designat***(e). Now <-ate> looks like a suffix; remove it, and you are left with ***design***.

What about prefixes? The opening <de-> looks like one, so remove it and you are left with **<sign>**. That cannot be further subdivided into anything that makes sense, so it must be the base element. Our original word, then, can be shown as

<de-> + **<sign>** + <-at(e)> + <-ion>

Now try building new words from this base element using different prefixes and/or suffixes. You might come up with a web such as the one based on ***sign*** which we saw on page 24.

Here is another example from early learners in a Year 2 class where the combined handwriting and spelling theme for that week was the letter-string <-tion>. I was offered the word ***celebration***. The process that followed illustrates clearly how the learning and teaching processes I am describing in this book operate.

☞ **Segmenting should be done orally by 'chanting' the target word while tapping out the resulting rhythm with the finger of one hand on the palm of the other.**

Our first job was to segment the word. There are four segments and we already knew the last one so we started by writing this:

The segment before that was easy, so our building of the word now looked like this:

| | | bra | tion |

The opening segment seemed quite straightforward, the representation of the sound /sel/. The first suggestion was S-E-L. This is where I intervened to say that if they looked for the word under the opening letter >s< they wouldn't find it, so they would have to use a different letter to start. No problem! They knew that the sound /s/ can be represented by >c< as well as >s<. The word now looked like this:

| cel | ? | bra | tion |

There only now remained the question of the second segment. In ordinary speech the vowel is indeterminate, sometimes called a collapsed vowel. It's the same sound as the first >a< in ***banana*** and in ***majority***, the >o< in ***collect***, or the >e< in ***problem***. I was prepared just to tell them on this occasion that the vowel they were looking for was >e< – they were, after all, only Year 2! But before I could do so I was offered the word ***celebrity*** and that, of course, solves the problem; in this related word the vowel of the second segment is pronounced distinctly.

The children were well used to the idea that when spelling a word they need to think about other words related to the target word; I just wasn't expecting them to know ***celebrity***. 'How do you know that word?' I asked. 'Easy,' came the reply; 'Hear it all the time on the television.' I was suitably chastened. We had now completed our word building.

☞ Children who *write* in strings which correspond to segments are likely to *look for* segments in reading; awareness of segmenting rather than whole-word or single-letter identification is an important strategy for constructing meaning in reading.

All the elements of orthography had come together in this episode.

- The initial segmenting was morphological, as was the representation of <-tion>.
- There was a strong phonological element *within* the structural units of the word.
- Etymological strategy led us to the identity of the vowel of the second segment.
- The spelling of the string <-tion> had been established through handwriting.

Most important, although our concentration had been on the construction of a single word *the processes with which we engaged were all relevant to word building as a whole*. With traditional learning of individual words in isolation by memorizing they are relevant only to the target word.

Beware of Syllables!

Segments are not necessarily the same as *syllables*. Segmenting divides words mainly according to meaning whereas syllabification divides words entirely according to sound with no reference to meaning. The rules for dividing into syllables are extremely complicated and even students of linguistics disagree about the precise syllabification of many words. Examples will illustrate the difference between the fairly straightforward segmentation and the often unhelpful syllabification. Note how when the word is *syllabified* the division takes no account of the morphemes.

WORD	SEGMENTS	SYLLABLES
accepted	ac—**cept**—ed	ac—cep—ted
intended	in—**tend**—ed	in—ten—ded
windy	**wind**—y	win—dy
faster	**fast**—er	fas—ter
jumping	**jump**—ing	jum—ping
keeper	**keep**—er	kee—per

In many words the syllables do coincide with the segments, but where there is a difference it is the segmenting which learners should opt for. Here is an example which illustrates the need to give priority to morphemes as segments.

A group of Year 6 children were segmenting ***dentist***. The first task was to identify any possible suffixes. If you syllabify it rather than segment it the result is ***den—tist***. ***Den*** is certainly recognizable as a word in its own right but its meaning has absolutely nothing to do with ***dentist***, so it cannot be an appropriate base element for our purposes here. Neither is ***-tist*** a likely suffix; perhaps <-ist> seems a better candidate. They tested the theory by trying to find other words with this same suffix. They came up with:

sex**ist** commun**ist** solo**ist** motor**ist** social**ist** typ**ist** environmental**ist**

They then suggested a theory that **-ist** carries a meaning like 'someone who engages with...' Clearly, the correct segmentation of ***dentist*** is **dent–ist**.

When you remove the suffix from ***dentist*** you are left with <**dent-**>. The question was whether this is a complete base element or whether it can be split up into any further units of meaning. Perhaps you suspect that ***de-*** is a prefix here (as it is in **de**cide, **de**pend, **de**crease, **de**fault, **de**finite or **de**form). They tested this idea by removing the ***de-*** from ***dent*** and were left with < **-nt-**> which can make no sense, so the ***de-*** must be an integral part of <**dent**>. They now knew that <**dent**> must be a unit of sense and meaning; it is the base element. They knew from the meaning of ***dentist*** that it is likely to carry a meaning which is *something to do with teeth.*

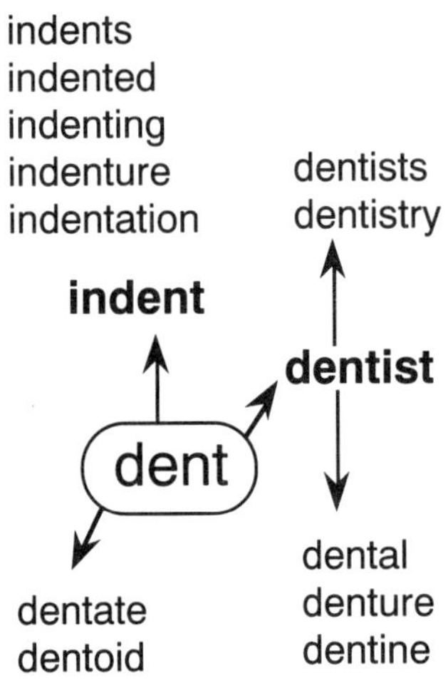

I gave them the task of adding different suffixes to the base element, but making sure that in some way the resulting word had *something* to do with teeth. They came up with the following words:

dental **dent**ure **dent**ine **dent**istry.

This knowledge also helped them to understand what a botanist means when he talks of leaves being ***dentate***, or what shape something is when it is ***dentoid***.

What about prefixes? I asked them to suggest a combination of prefix + <**dent**> which will still have some connection with teeth. I suggested that they should investigate ***indentation***, a line which led to a mini-project on paragraphing.

Finally the whole experience should be consolidated by building a word web. Something like the one given here was the result.

indents
indented
indenting
indenture
indentation
indent
dent
dentist
dentists
dentistry
dental
denture
dentine
dentate
dentoid

Summary of Word Attack Skills

This diagram summarizes the main structures of the word attack process. It should both inform our teaching of word building and also be in the ownership of all learner writers. It will be useful to compare this diagram with the summary of the segmenting strategy which is given on page 33.

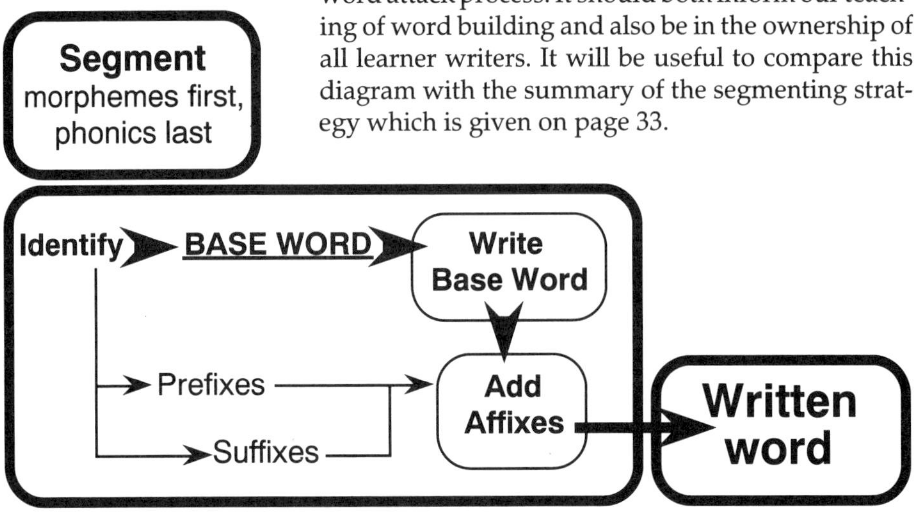

Segment
morphemes first,
phonics last

Identify → **BASE WORD** → **Write Base Word**
→ Prefixes
→ Suffixes
Add Affixes → **Written word**

✎ **Word attack** is the process of committing a target word to writing according to established orthographical conventions and in such a way as to represent its meaning. It is the operation of a system of consciously known skills.

Prefixes
and their variations

a-
an-

ab-
abs-

ad-
a-
ac-
af-
ag-
al-
an-
ap-
ar-
as-
at-

ambi-
ana-
an-

ante-
anti-
ant-

auto-

be-
bene-
bi-
bin-

by-

cata-
circum-
com-
co-
col-
con-
cor-

contra-
counter-

de-
dia-
dis-
dif-
di-

dys-

en-
em-

eu-
ex-
e-
ef-

extra-

for-
fore-

homo-
hyper-

in-
il-
im-
ir-

inter-
intro-

macro-
male-
mal-

maxi-
mega-
micro-
mini-
mis-

neo-
non-

ob-
o-
oc-
of-

out-
over-

para-
per-
post-
pre-
pro-

re-
retro-

se-
sub-
suc-
suf-
sug-
sum-
sup-
sur-
sus-

super-

tele-
trans-
tra-
tran-

un-
under-

with-

A good dictionary should list prefixes as separate entries.

CHAPTER 6: CONVENTIONS AND PATTERNS

Rules and Exceptions

Traditional teaching of English spelling has usually been of rules which are honoured mainly in the breach. The result has been a somewhat odd situation in which the burden of learning is the memorization of lists of *exceptions* to rules! This state of confusion should not continue. The impression of widespread inconsistency is an injustice to the real nature of English spelling. More important, our children deserve better than to be fed misleading and contradictory information. Consistency and order characterize the spelling system and the same qualities need to be brought to our presentation of the patterns of orthography.

☞ **It is probably best to avoid talking of '*rules*' of spelling, partly because 'rules' are often thought of as being proved by the exception, and partly because many so-called 'spelling rules' are bogus.**

The National Curriculum of 1990 makes a start. It does talk of *patterns* and *conventions*. Unfortunately it offers only sketchy examples without help as to what those terms actually mean or what might be the distinction between them.

This chapter will serve as an introduction to the patterns and conventions of orthography. It is not comprehensive – a full account of English orthographical conventions would need a separate book – but it will give sufficient examples and illustrations to establish the principles and operation of these patterns.

Orthographical Consistency

It is crucial to understand that ***structures of our orthography have evolved to serve the needs of consistency***. A coherent and consistent system of representing meaning is necessary both for writers, for whom fluency is retarded if each word becomes a conscious encoding problem, and for readers who will be similarly hampered by having to decode idiosyncratic representations of every word. The principle, met earlier in this book, is overriding: **words or parts of words with similar *meanings* or functions will usually be *spelled* similarly**.

I will use the terms **law**, **convention**, **principle** and **pattern.** The diagram summarizes what these terms mean in a form which can constantly be referred to as the chapter progresses. In order to make clear the nature of laws and conventions we will look at a selection from each category with examples of their application. Sufficient will be offered to illustrate the conventions in operation and also to give some structures for teaching.

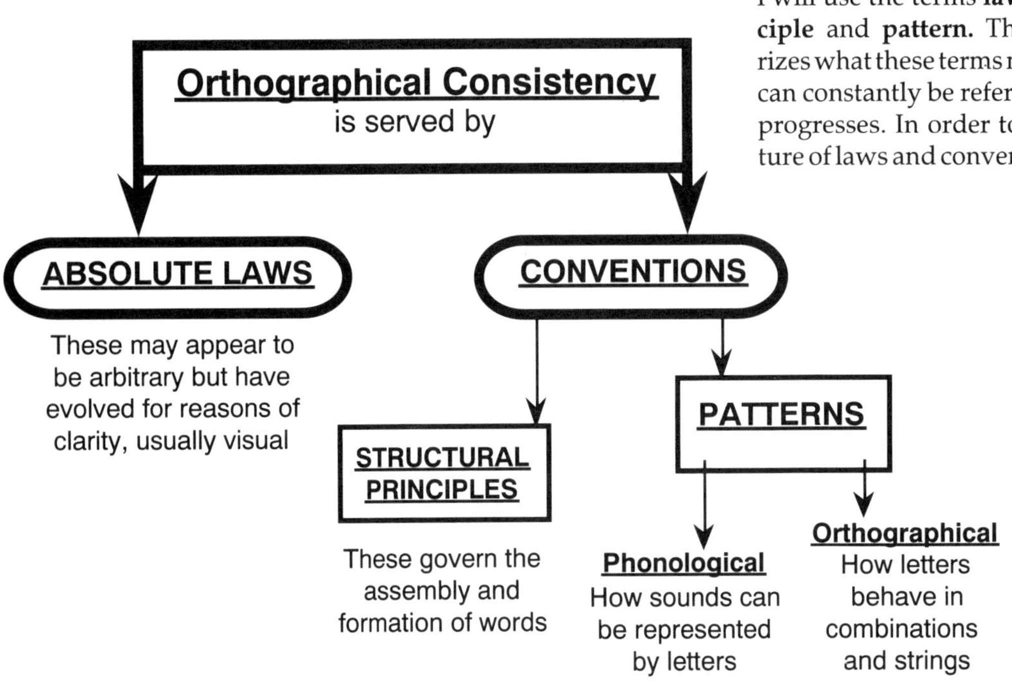

Orthographical Consistency
is served by
ABSOLUTE LAWS
These may appear to be arbitrary but have evolved for reasons of clarity, usually visual
CONVENTIONS
STRUCTURAL PRINCIPLES
These govern the assembly and formation of words
PATTERNS
Phonological
How sounds can be represented by letters
Orthographical
How letters behave in combinations and strings

This chapter contains much material that will best serve as reference. But it is worth reading through to get the flavour of our orthographical conventions and patterns and to acquire a 'feel' for them.

Laws of Spelling

If you do use the term 'rules' do so only of absolute conventions and assure children that when you give them such a rule, they can be certain that it always applies; there are no 'exceptions'.

Consistency in spelling English is achieved by interweaving and interaction between laws and patterns. In this system it is the laws which have priority.

Laws of spelling will be indicated by this icon.

There are relatively few orthographical structures which apply without exception; because they will always override any other convention the term *laws* can safely be applied to them. They should all be familiar to learners by a fairly early stage.

These laws may *appear* to be arbitrary, but they have usually evolved in order to serve the purposes of visual clarity and ease of reading. We will now take examples of these laws and look at how they operate.

A Simple Example: The Three Letter Law

The same letter cannot occur three times in a row; use just two instead.

When the suffix <-ed> is added to the base word <agree> the result would at first need to be ******agreeed*. It is clear that this string of the same letter is visually a little confusing, so the law about not having three letters the same in a row comes into action: <agree> + <-ed> → *agreeed → ***agreed.*** Try this process with the following:

<**free**> + <-er> / <-ed>; **referee** + <-ed>; <**see**> +<-er>.

Two Orthographical Topics About Laws

1. Classifying words that have a final >i<

No complete English word ends with the letter >i< (you usually use >y< instead).

The law that no complete English word ends with the letter >i< can provide an entertaining investigative theme for a class, group or individual. The object is to start a collection of words that do correctly end with >i< and to relate them to the law. One way of classifying them is to use a Venn diagram. Here is an example of how it might start. Set **A** contains words that are not complete – **A**bbreviations – and set **NE** contains words that are **N**ot **E**nglish.

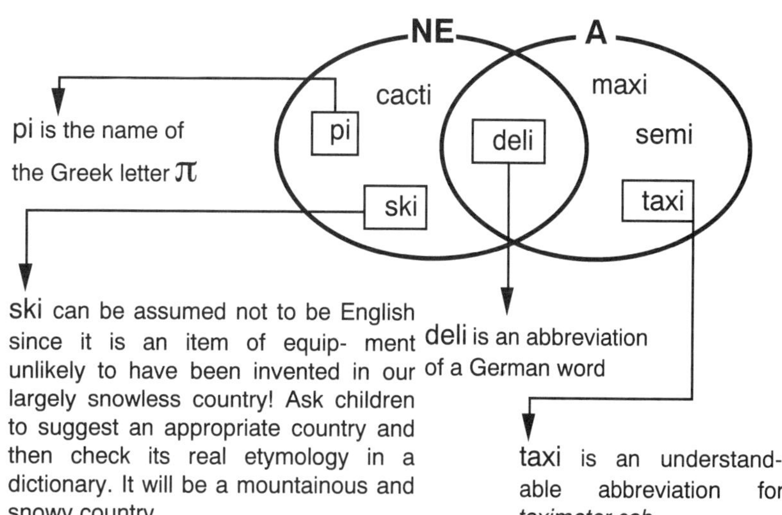

2. Investigating the letter >v<

There are two laws which are concerned with the letter >v<. They too can make an interesting orthographical topic. During the course of it children (and possibly even you!) will discover the reasons for the spelling of what is often one of the earliest words that children learn to write – *love*. There are two questions which arise from this spelling. (i) What is the >e< doing at the end of the word? After all the word doesn't rhyme with *clove*. (ii) Why is an >o< used? The sound of the word would suggest that a >u< would be more appropriate.

❒ No complete English word ends with the letter >v<; use <ve> instead.

The law easily accounts for the presence of the >e<. It is not there to act as what is sometimes called the 'magic' >e< making the >o< long; it is needed to obey the law that English words don't end with >v<.

Here are a couple of other examples of the operation of this law. The adjective ***live*** – /līv/ with a 'long' >i< – has a so-called 'magic' >e< at the end to show that the >i< is long; the verb ***live*** – /lĭv/ with a 'short' >i< – has an >e< at the end to prevent the word ending with >v<. The result is that both words are spelled the same though the final >e< is fulfilling different functions. A similar thing has to happen with the basic word ***have***. After all it doesn't rhyme with ***brave*** or ***shave***, or even ***behave***. Here are some more words you could give to children to practise this pattern.

native delve leave brave relative give

❒ There is no such spelling as <uv>; use <ov> instead.

Why, then, will *love* need to be spelled with >o< when the sound is clearly /u/? The other >v< law accounts for that, since the spelling l<**uv**>e would be impossible. Other examples of the operation of this law can be collected by children. Here are some of them. Use the matrix too.

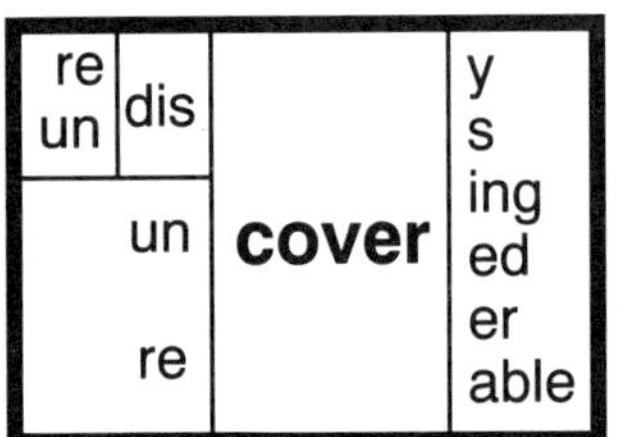

re
un
dis
un
re
cover
y
s
ing
ed
er
able

/uven/ → *uven → ***oven*** /kuver/ → *cuver → ***cover***
shove dove above shovel glove

The reason for the evolution of this law makes an interesting investigative task for a small group of researchers to prepare and present to the rest of a class. Here are some notes to start you off. It lies in the history of print and the need for clarity in presentation for ease of reading. Other evidence can be assembled from reproductions of medieval manuscripts.

n m u i

In this script the letters >u< and >v< were represented by the same shape, the third one in this row.

At about the time that printing was establishing itself the letter forms in use were very angular, based almost entirely on straight, thick downstrokes. This style is often popularly referred to as 'gothic'. Letters resembled each other very closely.

It will be clear that with the letter forms so similar it can sometimes be quite difficult to distinguish them when they are in close proximity in a word. For example, what is this word?

minim

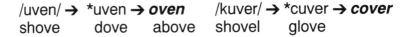

It is ***minim***! Clearly it would help if the single stroke which represents >i< could be singled out in some way; accordingly the dot was invented for just this purpose – well, not a dot exactly but a small stroke. To illustrate this the word ***minimum*** in this script is shown in the margin, with each >i< appropriately marked.

The 'dot' on the >i< was one invention of the period to aid ease of reading. Another was an inevitable result of the fact that >u< and >v< used to be written identically. Printers did develop two versions of the letter – v and u – but choice between them

uu ou

was dictated by their position in the word; for instance **vse, vnder, haue**. The confusion was resolved by an increasing tendency to use >o< instead of >u< if that helped to make the word clearer. In the examples in the margin, first <uv> is written in the script of the time, then <ov>. The contrast in clarity is obvious. This is thought to be the origin of the law that you always write <ov> for <uv>.

The other law about >v< was also growing at about this time; probably influenced by French spelling conventions, a final >v< was distinguished by joining it to a following letter >e<. The contribution of this practice to clarity can be illustrated by looking at the history of the spelling of the word *love*; the earlier spelling is visually more difficult than the established form.

luu → lou → loue

Such investigations of the history of our writing system should be a feature of children's learning about language. For instance, this investigation may lead children to understand why in some words the sound /u/ can be represented by the letter >o<. Offer them these words:

among	come	mother	other	ton	won
some	none	honey	front	monkey	month

Conventions of Spelling

Structural Principles

These are the conventions that govern the structure of segments and morphemes – how they must be represented. Structural principles also govern how the segments are sequenced to form whole words. As with laws, there are not many of these principles. We will look at three representative principles in turn in order to see how they operate.

Structural principles will be indicated by this icon.

The Vowel Principle

Every English word must contain at least one vowel.

Vowels are important elements of the way English determines meaning – change a vowel and you change meaning. Children can investigate this aspect of language for themselves by collecting such sets of words as **bag beg big bog bug** and **lack lick lock luck** where the connection between vowel change and meaning is clear.

Not surprisingly the alphabetic signs for the vowels are the most frequently used letters in our writing system and this results in the structural principle that every word must contain at least one vowel. The prominence of the vowels suggests that there is a case for making them the first letters children learn to recognize and to write. From earliest encounters with the written language children should know that the vowel letters are

A, E, I, O, U – and sometimes **Y.**

A powerful spelling strategy is the knowledge that every segment of a word must contain a vowel. It should be the first thing that is checked when editing a word's spelling.

Identifying Vowels

A text-scanning activity for very early learners can be the identification and naming of the vowels in words, and for this purpose all sorts of texts can be used

– reading books, novels, posters, newspapers, magazines, and handwritten documents from teachers and other children.

Early learners who know this principle will soon know that words like ***be*** and ***see*** or ***jay*** or ***pea*** or ***cue*** or ***are*** or ***tea*** cannot be written just as **b** or **c** or **j** or **p** or **q** or **r** or **t**; they need a vowel to give them the status of a word.

✠ Every English word must contain a vowel, **and so must every *segment* of every word.**

The vowel principle is actually more comprehensive than the form that has been given so far; it extends to the requirement that every *segment* of every word must contain a vowel. This now empowers children to know why such a spelling as ****njoy*** is impossible – the first segment does not contain a vowel, so it must be spelled ***enjoy***. Similarly, the word ***empty*** cannot be spelled as ****mt***!

The knowledge that >y< can also be a vowel does not seem to be very widespread. When the vowel principle is known it is clear that >y< needs to be a vowel in such words such as ***my***, ***try***, ***only***, ***copy*** and ***mystery***.

a e i o u
y

From their earliest writing experiences children should write the vowels in the arrangement shown in the margin. It has the advantage of showing on one level the five letters that *always* represent vowels as a separate group, while also indicating the close relationship between >i< and >y<. How the vowel letters >i< and >y< often represent the same sounds and, in certain circumstances, can swap places with each other is dealt with on page 72.

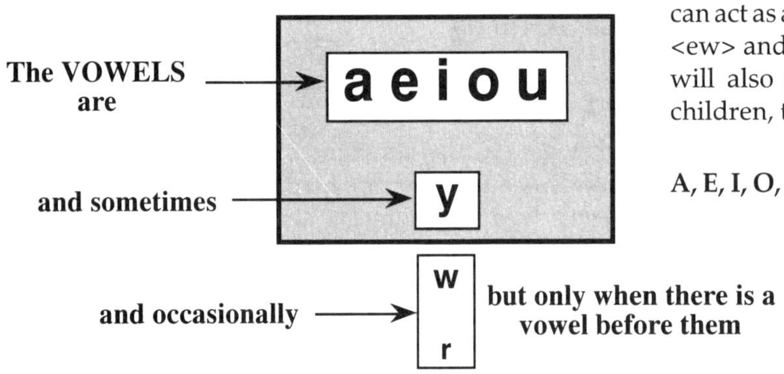

The VOWELS are → **a e i o u**

and sometimes → **y**

and occasionally → **w r** **but only when there is a vowel before them**

As children progress they will discover that >w< too can act as a vowel, but only in the combinations <aw>, <ew> and <ow>. The name of the letter ('Double U') will also indicate that it is a sort of vowel. Older children, then, will know that the vowel letters are

A, E, I, O, U – and sometimes **Y** – and occasionally **W.**

Further vowel sounds can be represented by using the letter >r< in combination with the main vowel letters. The diagram summarizes what children need to know about the letters which represent the vowels.

If you know the vowels it is a simple matter to recognize the *consonants*: they are the sounds, and the letters used to represent them, which are not vowels. Knowing the vowels, and therefore the consonants, is fundamental to many of the patterns and principles of the English spelling system.

The Homophone Principle

✠ Wherever possible homophones will have different spellings to reflect their different meanings.

Homophones are pairs of different words which sound the same. The overriding characteristic of English orthography that spelling represents meaning gives rise to the homophone principle. Where two words *sound* the same but have *different meanings* then those different meanings can be represented by different spellings. Children should be familiar with the term homophone and collections of them should be part of every class's lexical life.

Here is a starter collection of homophones which are distinguished in their spelling by alternative ways of representing long vowels.

Make sure that even the youngest learners know that when words *sound* the same but *mean* something different, then if you *can* spell them differently, you do.

male mail	pane pain	plane plain	mane main
made maid	pale pail	sale sail	tale tail
ale ail	rows rose	mown moan	grown groan
lone loan	row roe	slow sloe	tow toe
might mite	right rite	sight site	higher hire
sighs size	dies dyes	days daze	tee tea
been bean	beet beat	meet meat	reel real
week weak	heel heal	seen scene	blue blew
due dew	flue flew	cue queue	threw through
towed toad toed	choose chews	throws throes	thrown throne
rode road rowed			

Don't present homophones as a problem (a spelling book I know calls them *Double Trouble*) – celebrate them as showing the brilliance of English spelling.

The different spellings of homophones can sometimes be accounted for by etymology. For instance ***real*** is related to the words ***reality*** and ***realize*** in which the >e< and the >a< are in different segments and pronounced separately. Similarly in the homophones ***sighs*** and ***size*** only one of them can be related to the base word <<u>sigh</u>>. It is always worth being on the lookout for this etymological dimension of the variant spelling of homophones. **The ability of the orthographical system to spell homophones differently is an indication of its sophistication and power.**

Homophones and Puns

Homophones can be the basis of much *punning*. Puns have had a bad press in recent decades, but they are not only an excellently entertaining way of playing with words and meaning, but they also lie behind much of our best literature. Even the pop world treats itself to puns at times. Just look, for instance, at the spelling of THE BEATLES; the insect is spelled *beetle*.

Quite young children enjoy puns, and will soon be generating some of their own. Such prize examples as the following have come my way from infant classes from time to time:

- When you break a window with your head it is **paneful**.
- What do you call Prince Charles inside a post box? – The Royal **Male**.

Lexical and Grammatical Homophones

The National Curriculum of 1990 talks of *lexical and grammatical features of language* (for instance on page 40 in Programme of Study 28). It obviously expects its readers to understand these terms so the following section investigates a structural principle which deals with them.

Where possible a lexical word will be longer than a grammatical homophone.

A *lexical* word is most simply described as a unit of vocabulary, one which can stand on its own with a specific meaning (e.g. ***bucket, eat, five, you***). A *grammatical* word cannot occur on its own but is used to contribute to meaning by being attached to a lexical word. In the following sentence the lexical words are printed in **bold** type and the grammatical words in *italics*.

Once *upon a* **time** *a* **prince went** *to the* **forest** *with* **his horse** *in* **search** *of a* **happy ending**.

There is a feeling that the lexical words are more 'weighty' because they carry specific meaning, while the grammatical words are less so because they only indicate relationships. Where, then, a grammatical and a lexical word are homophones it is the 'weightier' lexical word that is written with more letters, if that is possible. Here are some examples of grammatical words with their (longer) lexical homophones. It is a useful ongoing class project to collect these as they are encountered and recognized.

Grammatical Word	**Lexical Homophone(s)**
or	oar ore (awe)
to	two too
in	inn
for	fore four
by	buy bye
so	sow sew

An Etymological Principle

✠ Orthographical conventions of a source language will be reflected in the spelling of the English form of the word.

Part One established that etymology is one of the three pillars of the English orthographical system. This principle relates to that. It is the sort of subject which would be an ideal long-term spelling topic for a class. Here are some examples to start you off.

Greek does not use the letter >f<; the digraph **<ph>** is used to represent the Greek letter ϕ (phi). If, therefore, /f/ is represented by <ph> then the word is of Greek origin. Similarly children will know to represent /f/ as <ph> in a word that they have been told is of Greek origin. Contrast ***frays*** – the Old English base word <**fray**> with the suffix <-s> – with its homophone ***phrase*** – a base word from Greek.

☞ **Older juniors will enjoy investigating other alphabetic systems. The Greek alphabet is particularly suitable as many of its letters crop up in other subjects too such as maths and science.**

Another indicator of Greek origin is the use of the digraph <ch> to represent the Greek letter χ (chi). Thus the words ***echo*** and ***school*** in which <ch> represents the phoneme [k] can safely be assumed to have come to us from Greek.

This digraph <ch> is entertaining because it represents different phonemes depending on the etymology of the word in which it finds itself. In the French spelling system <ch> represents the phoneme [ʃ] so words which have come into English from or through French are likely to represent [ʃ] as <ch>. Here are three:

brochure chef machine

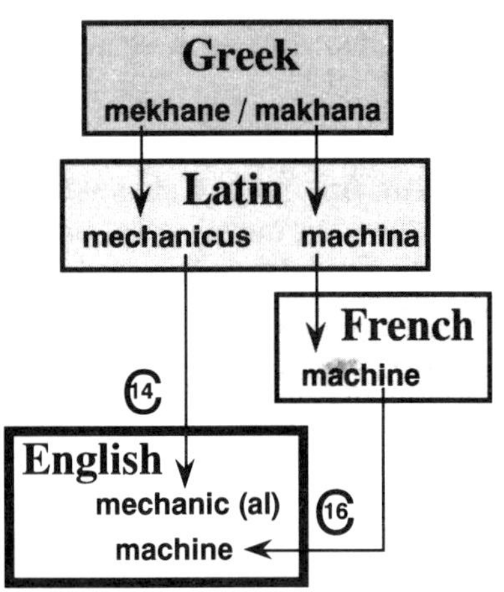

The etymology of ***machine*** is interesting. It is clearly related to such words as ***mechanic***(al) in which the <ch> represents /k/. The representation of /k/ by <ch> is a characteristic of words of Greek origin (like ***orchid, Christ,*** and the like), so how do we reconcile the apparently conflicting clues that ***machine*** came to us from French and ***mechanic*** from Greek?

The subject will provide an interesting project for upper juniors; they will discover that all these related words can be traced back to the original Greek word μηχανη (mekhane) with a variation μαχανα (makhana). In Latin the word appeared as ***mechanicus*** and ***machina. Mechanic***(us) came straight into English in the fourteenth century as ***mechanic***(al), but ***machine*** only came to us in the sixteenth century *through* French, acquiring the French pronunciation of <ch> as /ʃ/ on the way. The diagram represents the history of these words.

The other sound, of course, that is represented by <ch> is the phoneme /tʃ/ found in ordinary words of Old English origin such as *each, chin* and *chop*.

Patterns

Patterns will be indicated by this icon.

The bulk of spelling processes fall into this category. We will look at just a few examples of these patterns in order to illustrate how they interact with each other and support the conventions we have just been looking at. The patterns are often closely linked with the phonic dimension which is why they are always subservient to the laws and conventions which control more important structures of word formation.

Phonological Patterns

Phonological patterns are concerned with how letters are selected to represent sounds. Several (though not as many as the partisans of the primacy of phonics would have us believe) are quite straightforward. The sound /m/ is almost always represented by >m< and /h/ by >h<. But it is important that children should know from the start that the reverse is not necessarily true; >h< represents no sound in such words as ***honest*** and ***oh!***, and when it forms parts of grapheme strings like <ch> <th> <sh> <igh> and <ugh> it is certainly not representing /h/. Phonological patterns, then, must be thought of as not necessarily acting in both directions.

Here are a few examples of these phonological patterns and examples of how they translate into the writing of words.

The letter >q< must always be followed by the letter >u< as the digraph <qu>.

A pattern about >q<

This one concerns the use of the letter >q<. The earliest learners will know the law that whenever a >q< is written a >u< will be written immediately after it. A phonological pattern indicates that when it is necessary to represent the sound /kw/ then the digraph <qu> will be used.

/kwĭt/ → ***quit*** /kwōt/ → ***quote*** /rĭ kwest/ → ***request***

The digraph <qu> is used to represent the sound /kw/ only when it is entirely within one segment of a word.

The pattern also stipulates that the /kw/ that is being represented must be entirely within one segment of a word. Here is a case in which /kw/ is not represented by the digraph <qu>.

<**back**>+ <-ward> → *backward*

Note how this pattern is subservient to the morphological nature of spelling.

The letter >j< cannot be used at the end of a word or base element; use <ge> instead.

A pattern about >j< and >g<

The letter >q< does not occur frequently in English; nor does >j<. The reason is that it shares the job of representing [dʒ] with >g<, but >j< is almost always used only at the beginning of a word or base element, almost never inside it and never at the end of it. Here are some examples of the operation of this phonological pattern.

job just jam

<ob-> + <**ject**> → ***object*** <ad-> +<**just**> → ***adjust***

BUT ***cage*** (/kādʒ/) and ***large***

One of the few English words children are likely to meet which has >j< inside it is *major*, and it is worth making a point of their knowing it. It is also useful as an illustration of the principle summed up in the National Curriculum as '**the spelling of unstressed syllables can often be deduced from the spelling of a stressed syllable in a related word**' (AT 4/5, Level 6).

In the case of *major* where the second segment is unstressed it is not clear from ordinary pronunciation what the vowel is – from sound alone it could, for instance, be *maj<u>er</u>. But add the suffix <-ity> to the base word <**<u>major</u>**> to form *majority*, and the identity of that indistinct vowel becomes clear; it has to be >o<.

The trigraph <igh> represents /ī/ when preceded by a consonant. Preceded by a vowel the combination represents /ā/.

Teach the trigraph <igh> as a single written unit, dotting the >i< only after the >h< has been written; in this way its unity will be consolidated and its difference from <ugh> established.

A pattern with the string <igh>

The letter combination <gh> has achieved notoriety as some sort of inexplicable bugbear. Yet the patterns of its use are hardly complicated. Instructions and materials for a fuller spelling topic on <gh> appear on page 107. In the meantime we will look at a couple of the patterns in which <gh> appears.

One cause of the problem over <gh> is that people commonly get the string wrong; ***it is not*** **<ght>**. The >t< is always a separate phoneme unaffected by and not affecting a preceding <gh>. Only two strings contain <gh>: **<igh>** and **<ugh>**.

The trigraph <igh> most commonly represents the sound of the 'long' >i< – the sound of the pronoun ***I*** and the word ***ay***, the synonym for *yes*. *It does so when the letter immediately preceding it is a consonant.*

The margin gives a structural matrix from which most of these words can be built. Give a copy to your children and see how many words they can construct from it. The first use of this matrix will produce such words as these:

sigh high bright fight flight light might night right sight tight

If they then also add prefixes and suffixes and make compound words the result could surprise you – and them – by the high number they find. Such words as the following might arrive:

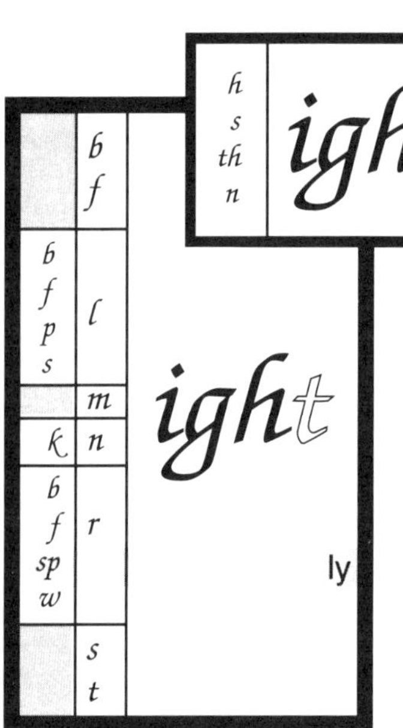

sighing	sighed	higher	highly
brighten	brightening	fighter	dogfight
flightless	lighten	lightened	lightening
delight	delightfully	mighty	almighty
nightly	midnight	right	aright
rightly	righteous	outright	unsightly
sightseeing	tightly	tighten	sprightly

When this same string <igh> is preceded by a vowel (in practice only >a< or >e<) then the resulting combination (<aigh> or <eigh>) represents the 'long' a sound like the last sound in the word *say*. This is a rarer use of <igh> than when it is preceded by a consonant and produces only few base words, but, again, the use of affixes and compounding will generate a fair crop of words, such as the following:

eight	eighty	neigh	neighing
neighbouring	sleighbells	weigh	weight
weighty	weighted	straightforward	unneighbourly

A pattern about how to represent the sound /k/

Now we look at a group of phonological patterns concerned with the related letters >c< and >k<, each of which can represent the sound /k/.

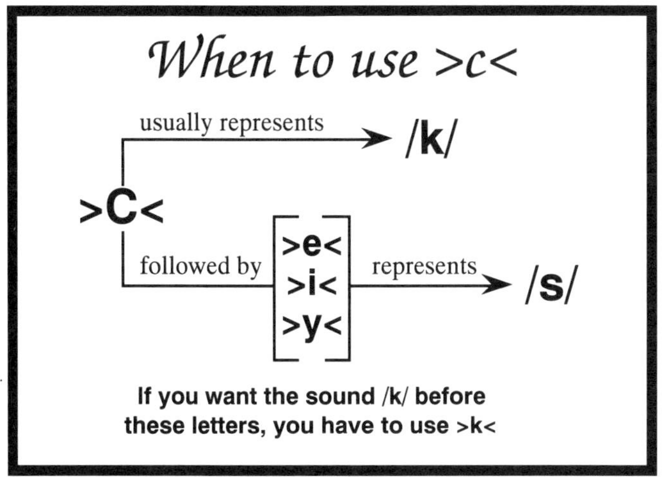

We start by noting that >c< sometimes represents /s/ and in words such as ***circus*** and ***cycle*** it can represent both /k/ and /s/ in the same word. Decisions as to whether to use >c< or >k< fox many children, who are abandoned to discovering it for themselves; yet the patterns which govern their use are straightforward and consistent.

Look at the basic phonology of >c<. Children in the early stages of word building should know this pattern. The diagram is one which I use to help children to check through it. A copy of it would be a useful component of children's own spelling reference books. It follows from this pattern that if you want to represent the sound /k/immediately before >e<, >i< or >y< then you *have* to use >k< since >c< is not available.

Teach children that they should always choose >c< in preference to >k< unless they know of a reason why >c< cannot be used.

[k] + -at → ***cat*** [k] + -og → ***cog*** [k] + -eg → ***keg***
[k] + -id → ***kid*** [k] + -ub → ***cub*** [k] + -ing → ***king***

[k] + -urb → ***curb*** — **BUT—** [k] + -erb → ***kerb***

There are further patterns which concern choices about whether to use >c< or >k<; they will conveniently take us to the next section.

Orthographical Patterns

In general, represent /k/ with >c< at the beginning or anywhere inside the word and >k< at the end of the word.

>C< cannot be the last letter of a complete word unless it is the segment <-ic>. Otherwise final /k/ is written as >k< or >ck<.

Orthographical patterns are concerned with what happens to letters in the various combinations in which they find themselves as the word is built.

Patterns make >k< an uncommon letter, which means that writers must always try to represent /k/ with >c<, only using >k< when it is not possible to use >c<.

When you are representing the sound /k/ then first opt for >c< if it is at the beginning or anywhere inside the word and >k< if it is at the end of the word; only use the other letter if you know of a good reason why.

If /k/ is the last sound of an English word then the last letter will always be >k< **unless the last segment is <ic>**. Here are some examples of such words:

topic	logic	magic	music	attic	antic
public	comic	frolic	basic	sonic	critic
frantic	elastic	plastic	drastic	metric	electric
athletic	arctic	fantastic	gigantic	cosmetic	tragic

Note that the <ic> is referred to as a *final* segment; the pattern, therefore, can only apply to words which have more than one segment. Words such as ***pick, sick, wick, trick*** and ***slick*** do end with /ik/, but it is not a final segment since each of those words has only a single segment.

A further pattern which occasionally foxes writers is whether to use <ck> at the end of a word, or just to write >k< alone. Again the pattern is straightforward. The accompanying diagrams, copies of which I usually give to children I work with, represent patterns which govern the choices between >c< and >k<.

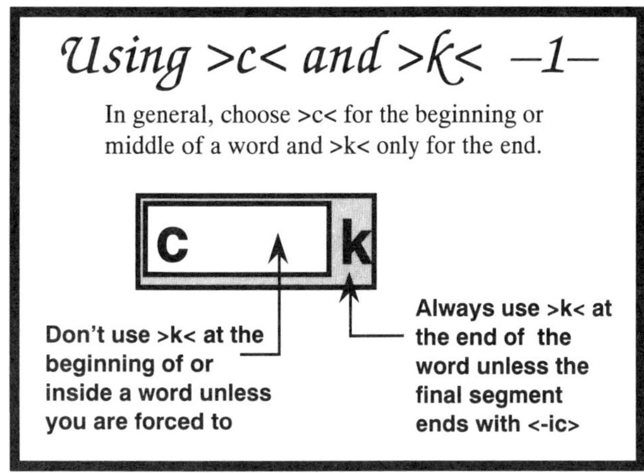

Using >c< and >k< –1–
In general, choose >c< for the beginning or middle of a word and >k< only for the end.
c
k
Don't use >k< at the beginning of or inside a word unless you are forced to
Always use >k< at the end of the word unless the final segment ends with <-ic>

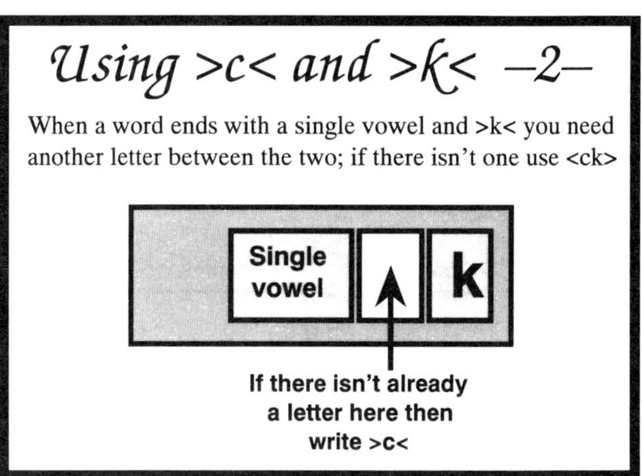

Using >c< and >k< –2–
When a word ends with a single vowel and >k< you need another letter between the two; if there isn't one use <ck>
Single vowel
k
If there isn't already a letter here then write >c<

When a word has one segment and one vowel there must be another letter between that vowel and the final >k<; if there isn't write <ck>.

Here are examples of single segment words on which to practise these patterns.

back	bank	bark	black	blank	crack
crank	pack	quack	rack	rank	dark
tack	tank	talk	deck	neck	peck
speck	spark	brick	brink	chick	lick
link	pick	pink	perk	quick	quirk
sick	sink	stink	stick	thick	think
tick	block	clock	clonk	flock	lock
rock	shock	sock	stock	stork	pork
buck	bunk	bulk	cluck	clunk	duck
dunk	luck	lurk	muck	suck	sunk
sulk	work	walk	tuck	lark	cook
week	soak	look	speak		

This collection of patterns concerning the use of >c<, >k< and >ck< make an ideal basis for a spelling topic that can be used as a theme for a couple of weeks or more.

Older children could then follow it up with an investigation of other graphemes which are used to represent the sound /k/, such as <ch> (in such words as *echo* and *chemist*) and <que> (in such words as *unique, cheque* and *discotheque*).

An Important Orthographical Pattern about Doubling

Here is another example of an orthographical pattern, the need for which crops up frequently in writing, even at early stages. The pattern in question is the one which controls whether or not the last consonant of a base word doubles when you add a suffix to it. For instance with **get** + -ing ➔ *getting*, the >t< doubles, yet with **belt** + -ing ➔ *belting* the >t< does not. Similarly, in **mad** + -er ➔ *madder* the >d< doubles, but with **mad** + -ly ➔ *madly* it does not. The pattern is actually quite straightforward. First you will need to be sure that your children understand—

Vocalic Suffixes

The majority of the suffixes of English have a vowel as their first letter. They are called the 'vowel' suffixes or, more properly, the *vocalic suffixes*. The most common of these are <-ing>, <-er>, <-est> and <-ed>. A fuller list of these vocalic suffixes might include:

-al	-ity	-ing	-ed	-en
-er	-est	-ee	-ie	-ish
-ism	-ist	-ic	-y	-ion
-ure	-ive	-ate	-ite	-ant
-ent	-or	-ar	-ous	-age
	-able	-ably	-ability	
	-ible	-ibly	-ibility	

What the Vocalic Suffixes Can Do

The vocalic suffixes are interesting because when they are fixed on to a base word, they frequently affect the ending of that base word. Here are some further examples; when you add the vocalic suffix <-er> to the base word <**big**>, the final >g< will double:

<big> + <-er> ➔ *bigger*

Yet if you add the same suffix to <**bang**>, the final >g< will not double:

<bang> + <-er> ➔ *banger*

Similarly add the vocalic suffix <-ed> to the base word <**fit**> and the final >t< doubles:

<fit> + <-ed> ➔ *fitted*

Yet add the same suffix to the word ***benefit*** (and this is an old chestnut!) and the final >t< does not double: <**benefit**> + <**-ed**> ➔ ***benefited.***

Compare also **<sip>** + <-ing> ➔ ***sipping*** where the >p< does double, yet ***<gossip>*** + <-ing> ➔ ***gossiping*** where it does not. (The reason for this is explained on pages 110–111.)

There is a set of basic orthographical patterns which determines all this, and they are simple. Yet they are often presented to children as difficulties, usually because teachers are unaware (as I used to be) of the way they operate and the impression is given that they are inconsistent and awkward. They are not. Indeed it is far better to present the behaviour of the vocalic suffixes as an *entertainment,* a process which children can easily learn and *enjoy* operating.

I find that it is useful to establish the principles of the use of these vocalic suffixes by operating only with <-ing> and <-er> at first. These two suffixes are extremely common and illustrate all the principles of the operation of vocalic suffixes very clearly. I then extend the activity to include several more. But the same principles will apply to any suffix which begins with a vowel.

Base Words Ending with a Consonant

We will look here at the effect that vocalic suffixes have on base words which end

✎ **Monosyllable:** A word which consists of only one segment; the opposite of *polysyllable*, a word which consists of more than one segment.

with a consonant; they sometimes double that last consonant letter when a vocalic suffix is added. The decision whether or not to double that last letter depends on the structure of the base word. Make sure that children encountering this pattern know the vowels, and therefore the consonants.

In the early stages of getting used to this pattern it is best to confine your work to monosyllabic base words. The pattern is at its simplest with monosyllables and will therefore help young learners to get used to the processes in their simpler form.

☞ **There is no need specifically to teach the consonants as long as children know the vowels; consonants are simply letters and sounds that are not vowels!**

To Double or Not? Two Questions

To decide whether or not to double the last consonant of the base word you ask two questions. If the answer to *both* questions is YES, then YES, you do double the last consonant of the base word when you add a vocalic suffix. Those questions are:

1. **Does the base word end with a *single* consonant?**
2. **Is there a *single* vowel before that last consonant?**

You will need to discuss the meaning of the word *single* in this context. Basically it means *not double*, but it can also be extended to mean *not more than one* of them.

Does the base word end with a **single consonant?**

YES

pl o d

Is there a **single vowel** before that?

YES— so you do double

plod + ing → plodding

This example of this process combines **<<u>plod</u>>** + <ing>. First you check that we are dealing with a vocalic suffix and that the base word ends with a consonant. Then ask the Two Questions. In the early stages these questions should be asked aloud (remember that the voice generally has a better 'memory' than just sight and hearing). Both answers are yes, so you do double the last letter of the base word before adding the suffix. If the answer to either question had been NO, then there would have been no doubling.

The process is systematic; make sure that children apply it in a step-by-step way.

Another example, using the base word <**<u>look</u>**>, is given where the answer to one of the questions is 'no'; so you do not double the last letter of the base word before adding the suffix.

Does the base word end with a **single consonant?**

YES

l oo k

Is there a **single vowel** before that?

NO— so you don't double

look + ing → looking

Here are some base words with which to try the process. Add appropriate vocalic suffixes after asking the two questions.

sad	sip	sing	fit	boss
drag	put	teach	plug	mark
land	dim	drop	gun	rest
ship	bath	jam	fast	buzz
meet	tramp	farm	heal	wish
lift	boat	peel	sleep	weak

Making a Flow Chart

Since such orthographical patterns follow a systematic process one way of consolidating them is to reformulate them as a flow chart. This activity will also confirm for your learners that spelling processes have predictability and consistency because they are susceptible to the rigours of flow charts.

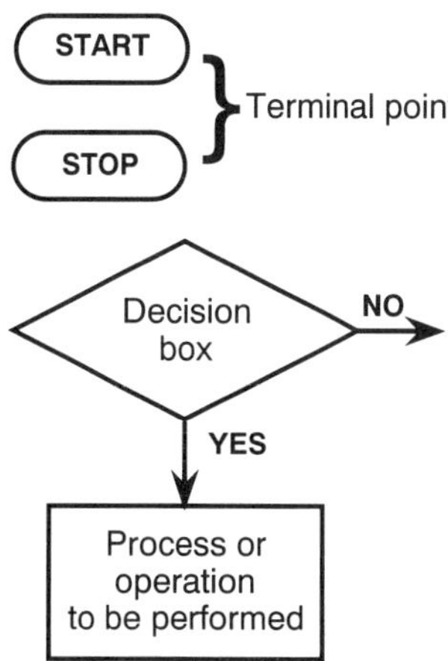

Work on word building does not have to be confined to timetable slots labelled 'English'; here is an example of how its processes can inform a maths theme.

The conventions of flow charts are shown in the margin. You could set this task as a maths activity. The questions for the decision boxes must be worded so that they require only YES/NO answers.

Older children might like to have a go at constructing their own flow chart. For younger or less confident learners you might offer them something like the chart given here; it is an attempt to formulate the patterns so far encountered and was produced by a group of top juniors. You will see that it is not entirely comprehensive; we need to look at >w< and >x<.

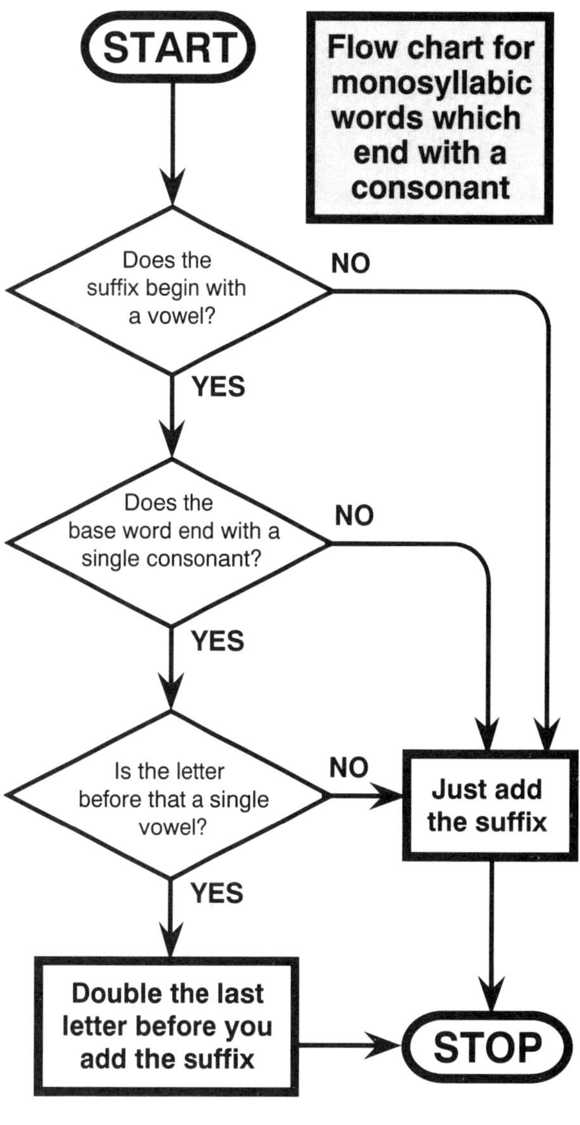

>W< is double and probably a vowel!

Someone may observe that, for instance, **<<u>blow</u>>** + <-ing> → ***blowing*** (not ***blowwing**) and will ask why the final >w< does not double. Call attention to the fact that the name of that letter is 'Double U'. The clue to why >w< does not double is in that name: it is 'double' already! The name also suggests that >w< is a sort of vowel since it is a 'double >u<'; that would be another reason why the answer to your first question would be NO. When the letter >w< appears at the end of a word it is always in one of the combinations <aw>, <ew> or <ow>, all of which are actually *vowel digraphs*. In short, then, **a final >w< is not 'single' and it may not even be a consonant.**

Other alphabets sometimes contain such letters. Greek, for instance, has a single letter ψ to represent the combined sounds /ps/ (which accounts for such words of Greek origin as psychology*) and the letter ξ, an equivalent of our >x< which represents the combined sounds /ks/.*

Two Sounds in One Letter – X

The case of>x< is also interesting. Children will have noticed that, for instance, **<<u>box</u>>** + <-ing> → ***boxing*** (not ***boxxing**). The letter >x< is unique in the English alphabet in that it represents a combination of two consonantal sounds; there are two sounds packed inside one letter. Our letter >x< represents the combination of the sounds /k+s/ (as in ***expect***) or/g+z/ (as in ***exact***). Because it has two consonants in it, it fails the first question: is it a *single* consonant? No, because though it is only one *letter* it represents two consonants together. Try out these processes by affixing appropriate suffixes to the base words given over the page.

box fox few slow stew fix stow bellow mix flaw flow chew

We have only examined this doubling pattern as it applies to base words which are monosyllables and which end with a consonant. The pattern has further elements to enable it to apply to base words which are polysyllables or end with a vowel. The full patterns are given later (pages 109–114). What will be clear from what has been seen is that patterns are systematic, orderly, predictable, and even entertaining.

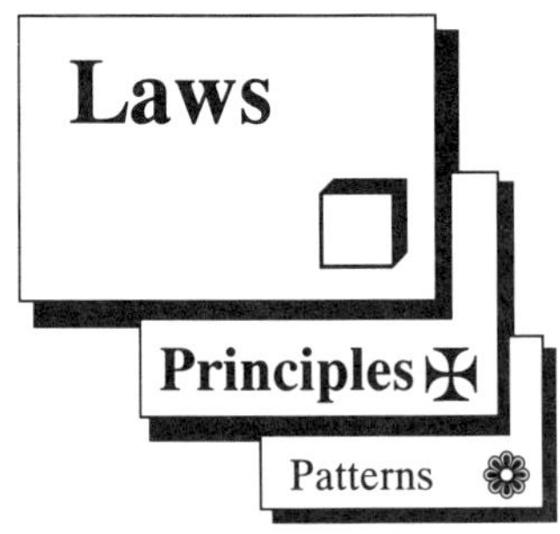

Priorities

Patterns are lowest in orthographical priorities. Phonological patterns can combine with each other but all patterns must conform to structural principles. Laws are absolute and unchangeable and override all other principles and patterns. It is important too always to remember that all patterns, principles and laws serve the fundamental need to represent meaning consistently.

As an example of priorities in operation take the target word / wā / which means 'path or route' as in 'Show me the / wā / to go home'. The word is made up of two phonemes, / w / + / ā /. The first of those phonemes can be represented by >w<. The second phoneme can be represented in a number of ways; the pattern which gives them is in the margin. We cannot use 1. in the pattern because we need a consonant sound between the >a< and the final >e< and we do not have one in / wā /; we use 2. instead which gives us ***wai**. This will still not do because of the law that no complete English word can end with >i<. We obey that law and ***wai** becomes ***way***.

The 'long a' sound /ā/ can be represented by:

1. single >a< + consonant + single, silent >e<;
2. the digraph <ai>;
3. the strings <aigh> and <eigh>;
4. the digraph <ey>;

The word ***way*** has a *homophone* which means 'find the heaviness of something' as in 'How much does that piece of cheese / wā /?' Homophones should be spelled differently from each other if that is possible, so phonological patterns must be subservient to this principle; we need a different pattern from the one we used for ***way*** to serve it. The strings <aigh> or <eigh> are alternative representations of / ā /, so we can use one of those. It is etymology that will decide which of the two we use: the word we want is from the Old English *wegan*, in which the >w< is followed by an >e<, so we select the string <eigh> because that will allow us to use an >e< after the >w< and spell this homophone ***weigh***.

There is a less common third homophone of / wā / – what Miss Muffet ate with her curds. The principle of homophones being spelled differently if possible compels us to look for yet another means of representing the phoneme / ā/. We find from 4. in our pattern that we can use <ey>; this gives us ***wey**. One further adjustment needs to be made to take account of etymology. Our word derives from an Old English word which began with an >h< (*hwæg*), so we use the other digraph which is available to represent / w / – <wh> – which gives us ***whey***.

Similar principles govern the homophones /wāt/, one of which means *heaviness* (as in 'Guess the /wāt/ of the cake') and the other *to hang around* (as in 'Please /wāt/ here for me'). The connection with ***weigh*** will mean that the one which means *heaviness* will be spelled as much like ***weigh*** as possible so the result is ***weight***. That leaves the other homophone to be spelled ***wait***, the simplest alternative to ***weight***.

I will end this introductory tour of conventions and patterns at this point in the hope that sufficient examples have been given to make clear what sorts of thing they are. We now go on to examine phonological and orthographical patterns which govern the letters of the alphabet.

CHAPTER 7: KNOWING THE ALPHABET

✎ **Case** In the early days of printing the capital letters were stored in a separate wooden tray, called a 'case'. Since the capitals were needed less frequently the case which contained them was stacked above the case of ordinary letters, which was level with the composition board.

☞ **You and your children should use the correct terminology from the start of learning: *Upper Case* or 'Capital' letters, and *Lower Case* letters.**

☞ **Make it a principle that capital letters are never used by children unless the convention compels them to do so in the particular piece they are writing; in this way the upper case will always be used as a matter of informed intent rather than by whim.**

Often it is assumed that once children have learned to recognize the twenty-six letters in upper and lower case and know their alphabetic order that there is little else to know about the alphabet. In fact the alphabet and its conventions will need constantly to be revisited and the repertoire of knowledge about it expanded.

Upper and Lower Case

We have already noted that calling letters 'big' and 'little' is as inappropriate as it is patronizing; the distinction between upper and lower case is not one of size; this upper case A is smaller than this lower case a!

Using the Upper Case

It is only when early learners have developed facility with the writing of words in the lower case that they should start learning about the uses of the upper case. They will, of course, have seen it around them all the time, will almost certainly have used upper case letters for the initials of their own names, and will have deduced something about its use. What children should be told from the beginning is that case *can affect meaning* and is therefore an aspect of orthography. Look, for instance, at the following pairs of sentences.

The man who had a holiday was brown. The man who had a holiday was Brown.

We always loved swedes. We always loved Swedes.

Introduce learners to the word ***initial*** since upper case letters are almost always only used as initial letters. The usages which should be introduced first and consolidated are the initial letters of names of *people* and *places* and of *sentences*.

Other conventions should be introduced gradually. Here is a summary of the occasions on which upper case letters are properly used.

1. **An overall convention**
   If a word does not *begin* with a capital letter, it cannot have a capital letter anywhere else in it. To put it another way, a capital letter can only be used *either*
   • at the beginning of a word *or* • for the whole word.
2. **Sentences**
   Use a capital letter to signal that a word is the beginning of a new sentence.
3. **Names**
   Use an initial capital letter for the names of:

People	e.g. Jack and Jill; King John
Groups of people	e.g. Muslims; Swiss
Countries and places	e.g. France; Devon; Toytown
Languages	e.g. Hebrew; Esperanto
Days of the week	e.g. Wednesday
Months	e.g. August
Holidays	e.g. New Year's Day; Good Friday
Institutions	e.g. The Labour Party; Oxfam

4. **Titles of Works**
   This includes: books, newspapers, magazines, plays, films, music, paintings, poems, short stories, songs, chapters in books, and television programmes.
5. **Poems**
   Start each line of a poem with a capital letter (unless you are e.e. cummings!).

The Alphabet and Phonology

We know that for orthographical purposes any supposed phonetic functions of the letters are subservient to the overall need to represent meaning. In particular the sound values assigned to the letters by the 'phonetic' alphabet are trite and often misleading. But the alphabet is a versatile tool; it is capable of serving a phonetic purpose where it might be appropriate or useful to do so.

Slash Brackets (/ /)

☞ **Encourage children to use the slash bracket convention; it is a helpful editing tool for the learner and also gives teachers useful indications of the writer's orthographical awareness.**

This book uses the convention of slash brackets to indicate that what is enclosed in them is only intended to be a general phonetic representation.

This convention is a useful one for the classroom too because it allows writers to indicate that they know they have attempted only a phonetic representation of a word, and they want it only as a 'holding' form before they attend to the proper orthography in later editing. By using them a learner can send the message,

> 'I know that what I have written between these slash brackets is only about sounds. The real spelling may be different but I'll attend to that later when I'm editing.'

In this way they need not be held back in an early draft of a longer piece of writing by fear of the teacher's correcting pen. Thus, for instance, you might see an early draft of a sentence such as this:

It was time to pro/seed/ with the work.

The learner writer indicated by using slash brackets that he knew that the spelling of the fifth word needed further attention, but was concentrating at this point on the need to get the whole sentence down on paper.

The International Phonetic Alphabet

✎ **International Phonetic Alphabet (IPA)** First published in 1889. A series of signs based on the Latin alphabet and supplemented with signs from other writing systems, used to transcribe the signs of a language.

From a phonetic point of view alone the letters of the alphabet are quite rough and ready symbols. There is a highly specialized alphabet of over a hundred signs which has been developed specifically for recording and representing the sounds of any language; it is called the **International Phonetic Alphabet** (IPA). Teachers need to be aware of the IPA because modern dictionaries tend to use it to represent the sounds of words they list. The full IPA is, however, far too complex for any but serious students of linguistics, but some of its symbols can be of use to us in teaching. One of them – [ʃ] – is the IPA symbol for what could be represented as /sh/. Another pair of symbols that can be of use are [θ] and [∂]. They are the two sounds represented by the digraph <th> – as in thick (/θĭk/) and those (/∂ōz/).

Real Alphabetical Phonology

The 'phonetic' names of the letters are inappropriate; the alphabet performs a fuller function than mere phonology. Even when letters do have a phonological function almost all are available for representing more than one sound – or even silence. To attribute a single phonic value to each letter is misleading.

While children should not be burdened with the 'phonetic names' they *do* need to know what are the real phonological functions of the letters of the alphabet. This repertoire of knowledge should be built up from their earliest learning.

☞ Children should know the names of the letters and the sounds they sometimes represent; they should also know that letters sometimes represent no sound at all because they are doing something more important.

☞ When indicating the sounds that can sometimes be represented by letters don't add the sound 'uh' to how you say them.

When you are helping children to learn some of the consonantal sounds represented by the letters don't add the sound 'uh'. For instance the sound often represented by the letter >m< is not 'muh'; it is more like the 'mmm' of anticipated pleasure of eating something good. I remember one Year 1 learner, confronted with the word *am*, trying to read it as 'ă-muh' and coming up confidently with '*hammer*'. Another early learner, told to call the letter >d< 'duh', read *lad* as 'lă-duh → ladder'.

An eight-year-old's spelling of the word ***teacher*** showed how confused or non-existent his learning of real alphabetic phonology had been; he wrote ***teacher*** as ***Tch** – 'Tee-chuh'! He had clearly been confined to the broken reed of phonic strategies in word building. I spent only a few minutes with him asking first what a teacher has to do. 'Teach' was his immediate answer. 'So write that first,' I told him, 'and if you know how to write -er write that after it.' The resulting spelling was immediate and correct. I then asked him to try ***cooker*** and ***helper***, and he got them right first time. The light in his face was reward enough for the fact that in just a minute or two he had consciously engaged in the *morphology* of spelling and been rescued from debilitating dependency on false phonics.

Another problem is illustrated by the fact that >d< does not always represent [d] anyway. The very common suffix <-ed> has three pronunciations depending on where it occurs. In ***planned*** it sounds /d/; in ***landed*** it sounds /ĭd/; in ***cooked*** it sounds /t/.When it is followed by /ū/ it is now almost always pronounced /j/: ***due*** and ***Jew*** and ***do you...?*** are effectively homophones in the ordinary spoken language. In words such as ***handkerchief*** and ***handsome*** the >d< represents no sound at all; it is there for etymological reasons.

What children should know about this letter is its name, the sounds it sometimes represents in sample words where it is not always in initial position (***dam*** and ***mad***, for instance), and that sometimes it doesn't stand for a sound at all.

Examples of the Phonology of Some Consonants

It will be useful to look at the patterns of just a few letters in order to reinforce a feeling for real alphabetical phonology.

The Phonological Influence of >w<

Choices have to be made from this matrix to ensure that words constructed from it are known and usable; e.g. ***unwatching*** *is suitable while* ***unwatcher*** *is unlikely. On the other hand words which are officially unattested may nevertheless be completely understandable and usable, e.g.* ***unwantable***.

un	**want** **watch** **wash**	s ing ed er able

A phonetic characteristic of >w< is that when it is followed by >a< the combination <wa> often sounds like /wŏ/. This has probably arisen because the formation of the >w< involves pursing the lips and that has affected the pronunciation of the following >a<. Try pursing your lips while you say a short >a< and you will find that it turns into /ŏ/.

Your children will now know why the simple and common word ***was*** is spelled as it is. Here are some further words you can use to consolidate this pattern or form the beginning of a class collection of words which contain this characteristic.

was	wasp	want	wash	wand	wander	wad
watch	swan	swamp	swap	swat	swab	swallow

You will note that the family contains several very common words which must feature in early writing; even very young writers need to know this pattern. Such very common words as ***want, wash*** and ***watch*** can be further consolidated with a word matrix such as the one given here which I use with Year 2 and 3 children.

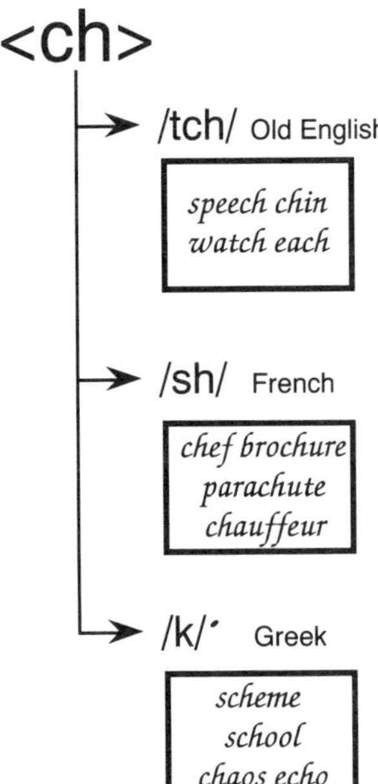

The pattern not only applies to the *letter* >w<, but also to the *sound* / w / . So it applies when the >a< is preceded by <wh>, and even by <qu> which, of course, represents the sound / kw / . Here are further words for your growing collection.

whatever	what	quad	squad
squat	squash	squadron	squabble

The Phonology of Some Digraphs

As always, attention should never remain exclusively on single isolated letters; combinations of letters are important too. Some digraphs should feature in children's learning at all stages.

The Digraph <ch>

This digraph can represent three distinct phonemes: [tʃ], [k] and [ʃ]. These phonological differences are indicators of etymology. If <ch> represents [tʃ] the word is Old English, if it represents [k] then the word is of Greek origin, and if it represents [ʃ] then the word has come from or through French. This diagram gives representative examples to illustrate this principle.

The Digraph <ph>

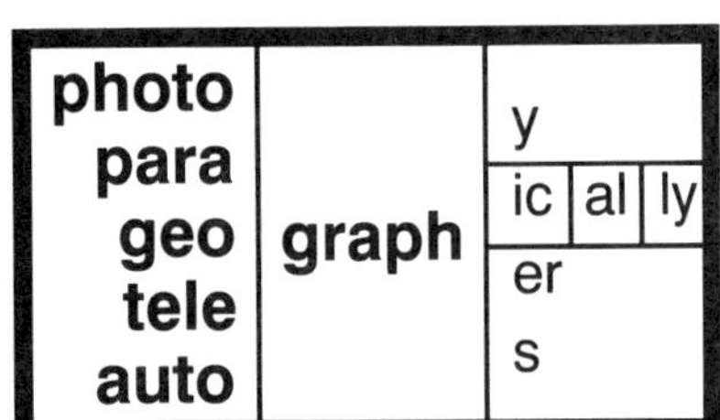

photo
para
geo
tele
auto
graph
y
ic
al
ly
er
s

Words which have come into English directly from Greek do not use >f<; instead / f / is represented by the digraph <ph>, an equivalent of the Greek letter ϕ (phi).

Here are some examples and a matrix to start your collection of words whose origin in Greek is indicated by the use of <ph> for / f / .

phrase	emphasis	phonic	alphabet	prophet
elephant	sphere	telephone	phantom	physics

The Vowels

✠ Every English word must contain a vowel, **and so must every *segment* of every word.**

The alphabetic signs for the vowels are the most frequently used letters in our writing system as a result of the structural principle about vowel presence that we met on pages 56–7. That section should now be reread.

Knowing >y< as a Vowel

It is important to know that >y< is not used as a consonant very frequently; it is usually used as a vowel. In that case it shares functions with >i<. The letters >i< and >y< are closely related. They rhyme and each can represent the same sounds. They also relate to each other in the orthographical law that no complete English word can end with >i<; you usually use >y< instead.

✠ >Y< will only appear at the beginning or at the end of an English word, but not inside it unless there is a specific reason otherwise.

There is also an important set of orthographical patterns concerning >y< which should be learnt by young writers.

❒ Never write < ii > in an English word: write <yi > instead.

>Y< is only found as the first or last letter of a word unless:

(i) it has another vowel immediately before it (e.g. play + er ➔ ***player***)
(ii) it is used to avoid writing two successive >i<'s (e.g. try + ing ➔ ***trying***)
(iii) the word is a compound (e.g. ply + wood ➔ ***plywood***)
(iv) the word has a Greek etymology (e.g. ***mystery; synonym***)

Here is a photocopiable resource sheet to practise and consolidate these patterns.

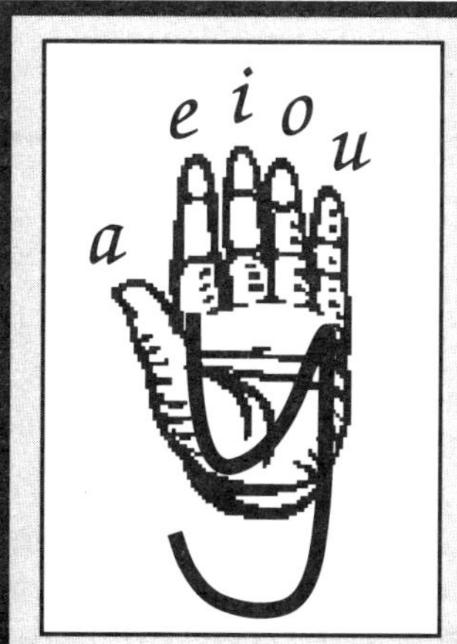

With very young learners teach them the vowels by using the hand. Touch each finger in turn as you say the appropriate vowel and finally trace the shape of >y< on the palm.

a e i o u
y

happy, pretty, easy, sleepy, greedy, clumsy	ly, ness

pity, fancy, plenty, duty, mercy	ful	ly

play, buy	er, s, ing

like, live	ly	hood, ness

lone, man, home, wool	ly	ness

try, reply, supply, fry, copy, cry, multiply, occupy	er, ed, es, ing

marry, carry	ed, ing, age

fury, glory, envy, victory, study, mystery	ous

employ, enjoy	ing, ment, ed

rely, copy, envy	able, ed, es, ing

☞ **Teach children the terms 'long' and 'short' when referring to vowels. Make a sort of catch-phrase of 'A vowel is long when it makes the sound of its name.'**

Long and Short Vowels

The five principal vowels (a, e, i, o, u) can – uniquely among the letters of the alphabet – represent the sound of their names. These words will illustrate this property: **gate compete pipe cone cute**. When vowel letters are representing the sound of their names they are said to be 'long'. It is useful to know and use the old convention of indicating that a vowel is long: write it with a macron (¯) above it. The words above would then look like this:

gāte compēte pīpe cōne cūte

These five principal vowels can also be 'short'. When they are, the sounds they represent are those which many people associate with twentieth-century infant schools – one case when the so-called phonetic names of letters can be of use. The sign used for a short vowel is a breve (˘). These words will illustrate its use:

căt mĕn pĭn cŏt cŭt

These signs (˘ and ¯) are useful as tools of word building and analysis, but they do not form part of our orthographical system. We have developed other ways of indicating vowel length which do not use markings above the letters; we use *combinations* of letters instead. It is this system of letter combinations which we should be sharing with children.

The Importance of Indicating Vowel Length

It is axiomatic that the English spelling system is principally the representation of meaning. The representation of sound is firmly subsidiary. Why, then, should we need a system of representing vowel length? The reason is quite simple: *in English, vowel length actually affects meaning.* If in French you pronounce vowels with the wrong length you will certainly sound odd, but your meaning will still be understood. In English, if you change vowel length *you also change meaning.* Take the following pairs of examples:

/hăt/ – /hāt/ (hat–hate)   /mĕt/ – /mēt/ (met–meet, meat)
/pĭp/ – /pīp/ (pip–pipe)   /cŏd/ – /cōd/ (cod–code)
/tŭb/ – /tūb/ (tub–tube)

So even something which at first sight appears to be only to do with phonology is really a consequence of a need to represent differences of *meaning* in words.

There were three possibilities in the evolution of the spelling system which could have coped with the need to represent vowel length.

1. Separate letters could have been evolved for each vowel; this would have meant, for instance, that there would be separate letters for /ă/ and /ā/. The problem here is that such a system assumes that there will be a one-to-one correspondence between phonemes and written letters. There are between 44 and 50 basic phonemes in English, 20 of which are vowel sounds. If we had a separate letter for each vowel we would then be lumbered with a huge alphabet.
2. Separate marks above the vowels (like the macron and breve illustrated above, and the accents that most people know from French) could have been introduced. This would slow down the pace of writing, and would still not necessarily cope with the many variations of vowel sound that exist in English.
3. **Existing letters could be used to form special combinations and predictable patterns which could define the vowel sound needed.**

It is this third system which has prevailed because it has many advantages over the others.

How to Indicate Long Vowels

Using a Single, Silent E

The commonest pattern for showing that a vowel is long is to write a **single, silent >e<** at the end of the word to say, 'Read that last vowel as long.' (Remember that a vowel is long 'when it makes the sound of its name'.)

VOWEL + consonant + SINGLE, SILENT E

☞ It has become fashionable to call this the 'Magic E'. There is nothing 'magic' about the function of this >e<. It is a completely regular part of the patterns of spelling. If you call it 'magic' you will reinforce the impression that much of spelling is about trickery and illusion!

It would be useful for you to build a collection of pairs of words which change meaning when the vowel is lengthened and that lengthening is indicated by the single, silent >e<. Here are a few to start you off. Use the list as the beginning of your own resource collection.

at/e gap/e hat/e fat/e mat/e
rat/e tap/e mad/e fad/e can/e
man/e pan/e cap/e nap/e scrap/e

pip/e rip/e pin/e fin/e din/e
(t)win/e spin/e bit/e spit/e rid/e slid/e
grim/e slim/e quit/e (s)trip/e

cod/e cop/e hop/e mop/e not/e
pop/e rod/e rob/e slop/e rot/e
tot/e cloth/e

cub/e tub/e mut/e cut/e plum/e
us/e

When children are playing with the building of these words encourage them to use the signs (¯ and ˘) to show whether the vowels are long or short.

Letter Combinations for Long Vowels

In single segment words a *combination* of vowels can be used as an alternative way of representing long vowels. These combinations are:

Long A <**ai**> and <**ay**>

Long E <**ee**> and <**ea**>

Long I <**igh**>; <**-y**> at the end of words; very rarely <**ie**>

Long O <**oa**> and <**ow**>; <**oe**> at the end of very few words

Long U <**ew**>, <**ue**> and <**oo**>

Our repertoire of different ways of representing the same sound is not an encumbrance; it gives us the versatility necessary for making distinctions of meaning. Having a range of spellings for the same sounds serves the etymological dimension of spelling.

CHAPTER 8: ETYMOLOGICAL CONVENTIONS

English is a vibrant mixture of ingredients. Our orthography echoes the cultural, historical and social changes which have affected our language; they have left their traces in words as reverberations, however faint, of former meanings and forms. The spelling of words contains a sort of inbuilt history, an aspect of the etymological dimension of spelling. The journey of a word through the centuries is of relevance to its meaning and relationship with other words which have had similar journeys. Words which share common histories are likely to share common elements of meaning or emphasis; they will also share orthography.

☞ **The history of our language affects the way it is written; knowledge of it empowers children to master orthography.**

Because etymology influences spelling, teachers must have an informed familiarity at least with an outline of the history of our language. So should learners, and there are excellent opportunities for linkage between orthographical themes and the teaching of history. This is not the place to give a full history of the English language. Any good dictionary should contain a useful summary of the language's history in its introduction. For a fuller treatment I recommend both **Burchfield** and **Claiborne** for readable and entertaining accounts of the subject. What I give here is a summary of the linguistic influences on English with representative examples of words which can be used to illustrate these influences to learners.

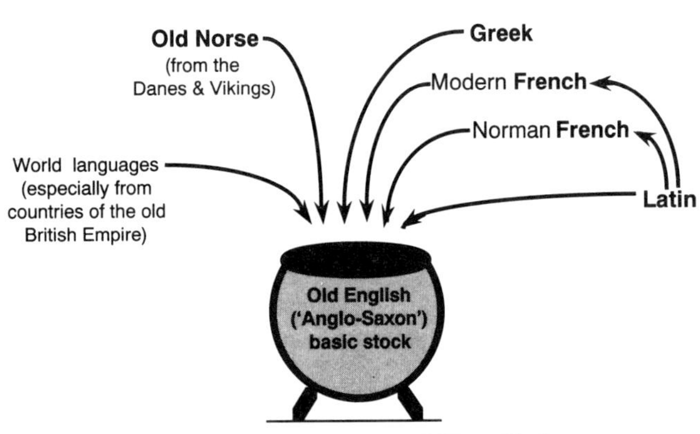

The Ingredients of English

Ingredients of English

I find it helpful to present children with the idea that English is a sort of soup. This linguistic broth has a basic stock to which over the centuries various lively ingredients have been added. All these have combined to produce an ever richer and more nourishing mixture. New ingredients are still being added.

First Phase: English until 1066

The main stock of the soup consists of **Old English** (often referred to as Anglo-Saxon), a Germanic language. The grammar and basic stock of our language, most everyday, basic and straightforward words are Old English. Here are some examples:

woman	man	child	winter	milk	eat	drink
sleep	tree	horse	land	house	field	finger
day	night	harvest	crop	summer	chin	father

The old British language (sometimes referred to as **Celtic**) survives as separate languages such as Welsh, Scots and Irish Gaelic, Breton and even Cornish, but hardly any words at all have found their way into English from the ancient Celtic. (***Hog*** is one of them; ***gob*** – usually assumed to be vulgar – may also be one of the few.) The 'Anglo-Saxon' invasion changed Celtic ***Britain*** to Germanic ***England***.

Other north Germanic invaders from Scandinavia, the Vikings and Danes brought words from their language, often referred to as **Old Norse**. Words beginning with <sk-> are likely to be from Old Norse. Here are some further examples:

sky	skin	skill	skirt	skull	skip
ransack	outlaw	window	fellow	snare	bag
anger	crook	awe	rotten	ugly	freckles

☞ Linking points of linguistic interest with the teaching of English history will benefit both the learning of history and the understanding of language.

Latin was reintroduced into England in 597 AD when the Roman Church brought Christianity back under St Augustine. The Church controlled bureaucracy and inevitably provided words to do with government, learning and medicine. Words which came into Old English from Latin at an early period include:

church priest monk candle master plaster fever

Previously unfamiliar objects brought into England brought their latinate names with them; ***lily, rose, pea*** and ***sponge*** are examples of these.

The Orthography of Old English

The ecclesiastical establishment made the transition from oral to a written Old English literature by using the Latin alphabet. That alphabet needed adaptations and modifications to cope with English phonemes which do not occur in Latin.

The Watershed of 1066

In 1066, the Normans (i.e. the 'Norse Men') took over the country under William the Conqueror. Long-settled in northern France they had adopted French, a language closely related to Latin. England was now governed and administered by speakers of this latinate language so Norman French introduced such words as:

castle	crown	state	judge	jury	palace
heir	tower	honour	beauty	prison	justice
treasure	battle	chapel	feast	pleasure	parliament

French orthographical conventions began to affect the spelling of English words. For instance, the Old English word ***hus*** was now spelled ***house*** to distinguish the French pronunciation of the vowel >u< from the English pronunciation. The Latin digraph <qu> arrived at this time to replace the Old English <cw>. So, for example **cwēn** ('wife, consort') became ***queen*** and **cwic** ('living, lively') became ***quick***.

Middle English

Throughout this time English developed into a new form, influenced by French in vocabulary, pronunciation and orthography. With the rise of English nationalism all classes of society began to speak and to write English (*Chaucer* is the big name here). In 1362 even the law courts began to use English as their official language. **Middle English** began to consolidate.

The French-educated scribes had now established much of the orthographical system of the language on Latinate lines. The arrival of printing at this crucial time meant that those orthographical conventions became the widespread norm. Middle English had wide regional variations and there were also new and far-spreading shifts in its pronunciation. This was a difficulty for the printers who, with an eye on mass circulation, needed to achieve consistency and uniformity in orthography. The instability of the pronunciation of the language meant that any attempt to tie orthography just to phonology was inappropriate from the outset since the sound of the language was varying from region to region and from decade to decade.

The Arrival of Modern English

Printing, political moves towards national unity, and the development of a new vibrant English literature brought a development of Middle English into a form of the language which we now recognize as familiar. The age of Shakespeare and the King James Version of the Bible consolidated what we can call Modern English.

The use of English in the great universities and the law courts increased the need for scholarly and precise vocabulary. Many learned words, often polysyllabic, came into English mainly from the classical languages. It was the second Latin invasion of English. As a result our language has a basic Old English, Germanic, grammar with a strong latinate element in vocabulary and style.

It is a creative mix. Dr Johnson represents for many the pinnacle of this latinate tendency; here is his splendid, entertaining and self-mocking definition of ***network*** from his famous dictionary of 1755; I have indicated latinate words with italics:

> Any thing *reticulated* or *decussated* at *equal distances*, with *interstices* between the *intersections*.

☞ It is well within the capability of primary children to become proficient at recognizing the origins of words. The clues are mainly orthographical so part of every class's experience of spelling should contain an element of detective work on word origins.

As English became an important European language it adopted words from every major European language. In particular French (this time the modern form of the language) again invaded English. As English was carried to more distant lands it has absorbed words from remoter languages. Many of these entered English as a result of the British Empire. In the examples for investigation given at the end of this chapter are several words which have come into English in this way.

Clues about Source Languages

Reference Material

Every class should have easy access to a real dictionary, that is one which contains etymological information for the words which it lists. Children need to know how to find etymological information about a target word when they have located it. The conventions vary between publications and you will need to check out for yourself how the dictionary that you use records etymologies. There are also dictionaries which deal exclusively with etymologies, but they tend to be complex and expensive. I can recommend the excellent Longman Pocket Companion: *Dictionary of Word Origins* by Brian O'Kill (Longman, 1983).

Signs of Old English

Two sorts of clue serve as indicators of an Old English origin. The first is to do with the meaning of the word; Old English words are only about basic materials, objects and ideas. Complex or technical meanings are not represented by words of Old English origin. Old English base words tend to be monosyllables and the ordinary grammatical words of the language.

The second sort of clue will be contained in the spelling of the word. Here is an example. We have met the trigraph <igh> as one way of representing the 'long' >i< sound /ī/. Children should also know that any word that contains this letter-string is Old English. In fact any word that contains the string <gh> is almost certainly Old English. Other strings which can point to an Old English origin include:

- The initial string <wh->.
- The digraph <ch> when it represents /tʃ/.
- The vowel digraphs <aw> <ow> <ew>.

You will find that you soon get the 'feel' of an Old English word.

An entertaining activity for individuals or, preferably, a co-operative group is to generate a short piece of writing in which every word is of Old English origin. Here is an attempt written by a Year 4 learner.

> A knight in silver plate is a frightening sight. He goes from one spot to another on his horse. When it rides quickly against its foe it meets a hail of arrows. Hundreds are killed and only a few ever get to their lines. When they get there they get their own back, killing off the bowmen.

There is still a little work to do on this passage. For instance, the writer originally began with *A knight in armour*. He checked the word ***armour*** in the Collins Dictionary and found the following etymological entry:

[C13: from Old French *armure*, from Latin *armatura* armour, equipment]

He had at first linked ***armour*** with the word ***arm*** which, quite rightly, he assumed to be Old English *but only when it means a part of the body*. Now he realized that when ***arm*** means *weapon* it is not Old English and that there was no necessary connection of meaning between ***arm*** when it means a limb and ***armour*** which is military clothing. He chose ***silver plate*** as a synonym. Though suspicious of the word ***silver*** he was delighted to discover that it is Old English. He will have to check ***plate***, though; he will discover that it's latinate! He will also have to check the word ***line***.

Incidentally, I made a discovery of my own through this passage; it is that the pronoun ***they*** is not Old English – it's Old Norse, and until then I had always assumed that the simple pronouns were all Old English!

This famous piece of English prose indicates the power that words of Old English can have; most are monosyllabic too. Words which are not Old English are in italics.

> In the beginning was the Word, and the Word was with God, and the Word was God. The same was in the beginning with God. All things were made by him; and without him was not any thing made that was made. In him was life; and the life was the light of men. And the light shineth in the darkness; and the darkness *comprehended* it not. There was a man sent from God, whose name was *John*. The same came for a witness, to bear witness of the Light, that all men through him might believe. He was not that Light, but was sent to bear witness of that Light. That was the true Light, which lighteth every man that cometh into the world. He was in the World, and the world was made by him, and the world knew him not.
>
> Gospel of St John 1:1-10 (King James Version)

Signs of Latinate Origins

Some words can quickly be eliminated from suspicion of a latinate origin; if a base word contains >k<, >w<, <th>, <sh> or <gh> it is unlikely to be Latinate. Those letters and digraphs are very characteristic of Old English words. On the other hand, any word which ends with the suffix <-ion>, or is *related* to a word which does, will almost certainly be of latinate origin. It follows, then, that such a word will not use any of the letters or digraphs referred to above.

The word ***decimate*** was the subject of an investigation which I recently suggested to a group of Year 6 children after one child had asked me what it meant. The first suggestion was that it might be related to ***decimal***, and therefore be something to do with numbers. Before they investigated exactly which number was concerned I asked for a little detective work on the word's origin. The related form ***decimation*** was a strong indication that the word is latinate, and reference was made to the dictionary for confirmation. The etymological entry was this:

[C17; from Latin *decimare*, from *decimus* tenth, from *decem* ten]

Maths lessons can be rich contexts for linguistic discussions and projects.

This first provoked a discussion as to why ***decimal*** numbers are so called, and the class teacher immediately promised a learning unit on number bases and revision of decimals in the maths lessons during the following weeks.

Next, someone asked what this had to do with ***December***, the twelfth not the tenth month. That child is now engaged on an investigative project on the history of the calendar which has led to the discovery that December *was* once the tenth month.

Finally we returned to the meaning of ***decimate***. The dictionary told us that it originally referred to the brutal practice of executing *every tenth man* in a mutinous section of a Roman army; it used to mean 'destroying a tenth part of something'. It is, therefore, a word with obvious connotations of savagery. But the last decade or two have seen the word being used in a different sense – to destroy or kill *a large proportion*. The children easily saw that this is quite a long way from the basic meaning of the word since one tenth is hardly *a large proportion*! Sadly, however, that earlier meaning of the word is now probably lost; even BBC newsreaders use it in this new, looser sense. It adds an unnecessary synonym to an existing stock of words which can be used to mean wholesale destruction. The last consequence of this investigation of ***decimate*** by this group of children was to make a collection of synonyms for annihilation.

Loan Words from Latin

Singular	Plural
cactus	cacti
gladiolus	gladioli
larva	larvae
formula	formulae
medium	media
stratum	strata
datum	data
candelabrum	candelabra

Latin loan words have provided English with a number of mainly technical or scientific terms. Often they end with <-us>, the plural of which is <-i> in Latin. Several end with <-a> whose plural is <-ae>; others end with <-um> with a plural <-a>. In the margin are examples of these Latin loan words; we usually keep the Latin plurals for these loan words, even in English. The last four of these are interesting because many people do not realize that the <-a> ending in these words is already plural. I often hear such nonsenses as, 'The mass media ***is*** ...' where it should be, 'The mass media ***are*** ...' I have also seen the word ****candelabras***, which can only be a plural of a plural!

A loan word is one which is imported from one language into another, often without alteration to its original spelling. For instance ***blitz*** is the German word for *lightning* and ***ski*** is a Norwegian word.

Latinate Words from French

Many words of French origin fused with Old English as a result of the Norman conquest; they are usually to do with government and administration. Another interesting group of words for investigation by children can be Norman equivalents for Old English animal names. Examples are given here.

Old English	Norman
cow, bull	beef
sheep	mutton
pig, swine	pork
fowl	poultry
deer, game	venison
calf	veal

The northern French of the conquerors differed in some respects from the French of further south. French had a number of words of Germanic origin which began with /w/; Northern French kept initial /w/ while the French of Paris changed it to /gw/, written <gu->. (This is why the Modern French equivalent of the name ***William*** is ***Guillaume***.) These variant spellings of the same Germanic word have given us interesting pairs of words, depending on which form of French they came from; some of these are shown in the margin.

From:

Norman	Parisian
ward	guard
wage	gage
warranty	guaranty
wise	guise

The spelling of ***guerrilla*** is interesting in this respect. Though it is actually a Spanish loan word, it entered Spanish in the first place from the Germanic *war* via the Parisian French ***guerre***. So the words *war* and ***guerrilla*** are closely related in form as well as in meaning.

More Recent French Imports

Many French words have come into English in more recent times, after Modern English had established itself. Clues in spelling can indicate that a word has come into English from or through French. Here are some of them.

- The digraph <ch> representing the sound /ʃ/. Words in this class include:

chevron	chalet	chassis	crochet	chauffeur
chef	brochure	chicanery	ricochet	chandelier

- The suffix <-eur>. Words in this class include:

chauffeur grandeur coiffeur masseur saboteur

- The string <eau> in words such as ***beauty*** and ***bureau*** and their relatives.
- The final string <-que>. Words in this class include:

unique boutique clique grotesque

Signs of Greek Origins

Almost all the words which have come into English from Greek have done so in relatively modern times and have supplied the need for technical and scientific terms. On the whole these words tend to be long. The orthographical clues which indicate a Greek origin include the following.

- The digraph <ch> representing the sound /k/.
- The letter >y< inside the word when it does not immediately follow a vowel.
- An initial <pn->, <ps-> or <pt->.
- The digraph <ph> representing /f /.
- Any of the following elements:

-ology	dia-	tele-	(r)rh	-gm	auto-	poly-	bio-
graph(y)	gram	scope	mania(c)		syn- / sym-		

Here are some words which were identified as being of Greek origin by primary children I work with. The indicators of Greek origin are printed in bold type.

e**ch**o	s**ch**ool	me**ch**anic	or**ch**id
diameter	**diagram**	**telegram**	h**y**pocrite
chorus	kilo**gram**	**telescope**	**microscope**
Christ(ian)	**ch**emistry	stoma**ch**	te**ch**nical
polyte**ch**nic	**poly**hedron	**poly**gon	**poly**thene
synagogue	**synch**ronize	**ch**ronometer	**ch**ron**ology**
rhinoceros	**rh**ombus	**rh**ododendron	**syn**copation
synod	**syn**thesizer	**sym**pathetic	**sym**bol
m**y**th	(a)**sym**metrical	**symph**ony	**sympt**om
pneumatic	**pn**eumonia	c**y**cle	**psychology**
pterodact**y**l	**ph**iloso**ph**y	**biology**	**phy**sical
Philip	klepto**mania**	cr**y**stal	m**y**stery
ara**ch**no**ph**obia	cata**rrh**	em**ph**asis	

... and many more – a **plethora** in fact!

You might also like to use a good dictionary to investigate the connection between the Greek word ***hemisphere*** and ***migraine***; this was a discovery made by a ten-year-old in one of my classes.

✎ **Neologism**: sometimes called 'nonce' words. A newly coined word usually, but not always, made up of elements of already existing words.

It is particularly in the area of Greek etymology that much entertainment is to be had with ***neologisms*** – the coining of new words. Here are some that have been generated from time to time by children I have been working with.

hypnophiliac	a child who found getting up difficult
elastochronological	a child who was never on time for anything
rhinorrhoea	a child who never had a handkerchief
megalorhinous	a child who never minded his own business
megalocephalous	a child who was rather bossy

Other Formations

Eponyms

Eponyms are words which are derived from the real names of people or places.

In a piece of writing I saw recently a child had written:

Last weekend I bought my mother a pot of ***fewshers***.

The spelling of that last word was the best that raw phonics could produce. The writer was given due credit but it could not be allowed to pass; it was an opportunity for a class diversion about the taxonomy of plants.

There has long been a convention of naming plants after the first person to describe them, usually adding the latinate suffix <-ia> to that person's name. The first person to describe the plant my writer wanted to spell was one Leonhard ***Fuchs*** (1501-66); his discovery is therefore called ***fuchsia***, and his name has since achieved immortality in the pots of a myriad front rooms! Instantly someone pointed out that there were several pots of ***tradescantia*** in the classroom; reference to the class dictionary confirmed that there was a botanist called ***Tradescant*** and a group project on Kew Gardens followed. Several children produced imaginative drawings of supposedly new plants of their own invention and we had a gallery of plants labelled, among other things, as ***jonesia***, ***thompsonia*** and ***wardia***.

☞ **It is an entertaining project for a class to collect eponyms; there is often an interesting story to be had from them which has repercussions for other areas of the curriculum .**

Lord ***Sandwich*** (1718-92) was such a compulsive gambler that the only way he would eat was to have his meal while he was still playing; the food was brought to him between two slices of bread and butter. The aristocratic name has given us a distinctly plebeian item of vocabulary!

Here are further eponyms to investigate. A class poster will show the class's growing collection.

cardigan maverick bloomer caesarean canter bedlam (in)clink bunkum

Portmanteau Words

These words, sometimes also called *blend words*, are formed by joining together or overlapping parts of two other words. The term *portmanteau words* was invented by Humpty Dumpty in Lewis Carroll's book *Alice Through the Looking Glass*. (A portmanteau is a large travelling case for carrying clothes.) Humpty Dumpty explains some of the words of the poem *Jabberwocky* to Alice:

brunch	breakfast + lunch
breathalyse	breath + analyse
guestimate	guess + estimate
motel	motor + hotel
smog	smoke + fog
paratroops	parachute + troop
workaholic	work + alcoholic
ginormous	gigantic + enormous
aerobatics	aeroplane + acrobatics
chortle	chuckle + snort
slimnastics	slimming + gymnastics
stagflation	stagnation + inflation
bit	binary + digit
maglev	magnetic + levitation

"Well, 'slithy' means 'lithe and slimy'. 'Lithe' is the same as 'active'. You see it's like a portmanteau – there are two meanings packed up into one word."

The accompanying table gives some examples of portmanteau words.

Children can be pretty inventive in generating their own. I was recently offered ***swurse*** (**swear + curse**). One of my individual pupils arrived triumphantly one day announcing that she was a ***dysprin*** – **dys**lexic but **pr**etty **in**telligent!

This last blend word has characteristics which make it very like the next category of word formation.

Acronyms

There are four categories of acronym.

✎ **Acronym**: An acronym is made up from the initial letters or initial segments of several words. The resulting sequence of letters is read as if it were an ordinary word.

Acronyms in upper case

NATO	**N**orth **A**tlantic **T**reaty **O**rganization
AIDS	**A**cquired **I**mmune **D**eficiency **S**yndrome
BASIC	**B**eginners' **A**ll-purpose **S**ymbolic **I**nstruction **C**ode
RADA	**R**oyal **A**cademy of **D**ramatic **A**rt

Acronyms which are proper nouns

Aslef	**A**ssociated **S**ociety of **L**ocomotive **E**ngineers and **F**iremen
Naafi	**N**avy, **A**rmy **a**nd **A**ir **F**orce **I**nstitute

Acronyms often unrecognized

radar	**ra**dio **d**etecting **a**nd **r**anging
laser	**l**ight **a**mplification by **s**timulated **e**mission of **r**adiation
posh	**p**ort **o**utward **s**tarboard **h**omeward (but this is disputed)
quasar	**quas**i-stellar **r**adio source
quango	**qu**asi-**a**utonomous **n**on-**g**overnmental **o**rganization
sonar	**so**und **n**avigation **a**nd **r**anging
zip [code]	**z**one **i**mprovement **p**lan

The expanded acronym

This class of acronym, currently much in vogue, is represented by the word

yuppie young urban / upwardly mobile professional + <-ie>

Here the expanded acronym generates a new base element **<yup–>** to which is added the diminutive or characterizing suffix <-ie>. The new acronym can itself form new complex words such as ***yuppiedom, yuppify*** and ***yuppification.***

Onomatopoeia

These words are formed from sounds which seem to suggest and reinforce their meanings. Examples include:

murmur	hiss	twitter	blip	buzz	bang
pizazz	cuckoo	tweet	peewit	gobbledegook	

☞ **Organize a timetable spot in which children share with the rest of the class any interesting etymologies they have encountered during the past week.**

Researching Etymologies

The interest to be had from investigating etymologies should be shared with children. It is an essential part of knowledge about the language and adds to a sense of excitement in its use. To conclude this chapter I include lists of words for investigation, by both yourself and your class. **Make sure that proper dictionaries are available – those with etymological entries for each word.**

Identifying a Source Language

The following words come from miscellaneous languages, often originally as loan words. The fact that they are not of English origin will often mean that they do not conform to the conventions and patterns of English spelling.

I have found it useful to 'map' these words on to a large copy of a map of the world; investigations can then be made to see what proportion of these words originated in countries that were once part of the British Empire.

bungalow	pyjamas	algebra	mach[ism]o	amen
yoghurt	trek	slogan	scoff (= 'eat')	gazette
boomerang	amok	bonanza	filibuster	alcohol
whiskey	clan	smithereens	kerfuffle	galore
brandy	yacht	budgerigar	pencil	crony
twig (= 'understand')		commandeer	mammoth	pal

Curious and Amusing Etymologies

Unexpected amusement, often wry, is to be had from many words. You will, for instance, discover that a ***Tory*** was originally an Irish bandit, that your ***nostril*** is a nose-hole, that ***school*** comes from the Greek for leisure, and that to be ***astounded*** you may have to be struck by lightning!

nostril	daisy	junk	bloke	gossip
silly	window	atonement	school	tawdry
Tory	mobcap	disaster	bugbear	checkmate
currant	influenza	caterpillar	gormless	gerrymander
escape	astonish	liquorice	haversack	werewolf
aftermath	Lent	barmy	jazz	poppycock
desk	mush! (the command to dogs pulling a sleigh)			

A small group of words results from what is called 'mistaken division' of a word. We have all encountered the mistaken division of ***another*** as **a nuther*. Perhaps the only reason that this division has not become standard is because of the continued and frequent currency of the base word *other*. Not so with the following:

an ewt (OE ewte) → a ***newt***

a numpire (ME from Old French noumpere) → an ***umpire***

The words ***adder, orange, nickname, lone*** and ***apron*** are also mistakenly divided words. Others can be collected by the class and added to a suitable poster.

CHAPTER 9: REFERENCING AND WORD ATTACK

Standard Dictionaries and Their Limitations

☞ **Dictionaries are about definitions, etymologies and usage. Their function is not primarily to be manuals of spelling.**

Dictionaries are important, crucial even. Every classroom should have one in pride of place, it should constantly be used and be seen to be used. But in terms of spelling there is an important fact which must be understood: you can only check spellings in a dictionary with any consistent efficiency when you already know how to spell since every correct detail about a target word needs to be known in order to locate it. This elementary fact escaped me when I was a young teacher.

'See if you can find it in the dictionary.' I am embarrassed when I think of the number of times I used to parry a child's request for help with that instruction. As one disgruntled child said to me in my first year of teaching, 'How do you expect me to find the word when I can't spell it!' The principal reason why dictionaries are of little use for the basic business of spelling is that ***spelling is only an incidental concern of dictionaries.***

☞ **A dictionary is a tool of use only to a mature speller, or to someone who *already knows* how to spell the target word; for the early learner it is of little help for spelling. Don't ask children to find a word in a full dictionary unless they already have the correct spelling to hand.**

The convention of strict alphabetical order of entries of *whole* words is another limitation of the usefulness of dictionaries for the seeker after a target word. Using a dictionary assumes facility in a complex process which relies on starting with knowledge of every constituent detail of the whole target word. Since a dictionary lists each entry in strict alphabetical order of each of its constituent letters in the proper sequence of all of them, a search is likely to fail unless you get every single letter in its correct order. Investigating all the possible alternatives for every letter place may well mean an impossibly long and tedious process.

Strict alphabetical ordering will only accidentally result in the bringing together of words which are morphologically related. For instance, ***receive*** is likely to be listed separately from ***reception*** and ***receptacle*** with, perhaps, the totally unrelated word ***recent*** intervening. And, of course, such morphologically related words as ***deception, intercept, inception, precept, conceptualize*** and ***accept*** are unspottable from the entry on ***receive***.

Every class *should* have a dictionary; it will need to be consulted on matters of meaning and usage. When a spelling of a word is known a good dictionary will also be a source of etymological information relevant to the spelling of the known word. Such a class dictionary must be a proper one, not a simplistic and truncated affair. It should have pride of place and teachers should give it status by being seen constantly to be consulting it and making a 'ceremony' of it every time they do so. I know of one teacher who bought an old wooden lectern at a junk shop and installed a large dictionary on it in a special central place in the classroom. Above all teachers should alert children to the function of a dictionary as a tool for checking unknown or imprecise *definitions* of words and for investigating *etymologies*. ***No standard dictionary should be used as the classroom reference tool unless it contains etymological entries.***

☞ **Whatever reference book children need to consult, it is important to remember that they always need lots of practice in both listing and finding words in alphabetical order.**

Dictionaries Intended for Spelling

Clearly there is a need for a form of dictionary whose prime concern is orthography rather than definition and usage. Several versions have been developed.

Limited Entry Dictionaries

One response has been to produce truncated dictionaries with a severe limit on entries – what I call 'kiddi-dictionaries'. Such dictionaries have a problem of identity: they don't know whether they are for spelling or for definitions.

☞ **Check children's knowledge of the alphabet itself. In my experience it is often the case that teachers assume that someone else has taught their children the order of the letters. And if they do know their alphabet, children often do not know how to rank words according to letters other than the initial.**

☞ **One or two kiddi-dictionaries could usefully be kept in the classroom for practice in locating words in the alphabetical ordering system *but only when the child has the correct spelling to start with and you have ensured that the target word is actually in that dictionary.***

Because they severely limit entries the words listed are known to children, so they are unlikely to use them for investigating *meanings* of words. If they are for spelling they don't need to include definitions for simple known words. But even if they are supposed to be a spelling aid they are not necessarily of much real help.

Let's assume that children fail to find a target word in such a book; they cannot know whether

- they have made a mistake in their alphabetical ordering skills, **OR**
- they have the wrong spelling to start with (and a single misplaced letter may cause failure), **OR**
- the target word just isn't listed in the kiddi-dictionary because the entries are severely limited.

Truncated kiddi-dictionaries, with their restricted range and lack of etymological content, are of little use for anything except for elementary referencing practice in the use of alphabetical order.

The consequences, then, are clear: kiddi-dictionaries – produced with the kindest of motives and beautifully presented as they occasionally may be – are of limited usefulness and may even be counterproductive to developing confidence in spelling. If you have a class set of them then the best thing to do is to keep just a few of them for practice in locating words in alphabetical order and offer the rest to the next School Car Boot Sale and use the proceeds to buy a real dictionary.

Since a conventional dictionary is inappropriate for establishing the *spelling* of a target word publishers have recently been producing ***spelling dictionaries*** which do not concern themselves with definitions and meanings. The elimination of entries about meanings and usage results in a welcome reduction in bulk and makes the book appear less intimidating to a young learner.

These new 'spelling dictionaries' list misspelled words with the correct spelling afterwards. The drawbacks of this presentation are:

1. The number of possible misspellings of a single word are often legion. In an entertaining paragraph Bullock (11.41) points out that there are theoretically 596,580 possible different ways of spelling ***scissors*** if you use only phonic criteria, and a test of 1000 children produced 209 different wrong spellings of ***saucer***! So children still have a problem if their own misspelling is not listed; where do they go then? You still have to rely on the book listing your own particular misspelling.

2. ***The appearance of a misspelling in print can only reinforce that incorrect form, consolidating it in the visual memory of the writer. It is seriously misleading and damaging to do so.***

Such spelling dictionaries, then, are not likely to be of much practical use and can actually be harmful, particularly to the very children who will be using them because their spelling is weak in the first place.

Computer Spelling Checks

Most word processing packages now offer spelling checks. It is a common assumption that these are an effortless and foolproof means of correcting any text. But their usefulness – particularly to those who have conceptual and perceptual difficulties in the first place – is actually limited. They can cause unwarranted confidence and misleading complacency.

The paradox is that, as with dictionaries, computer spelling checks tend to be of full use only to those who can already spell. Spell-checkers will not identify a *wrong* word which is *spelled correctly*. For instance, they will not call attention to anything wrong in the following examples from children's work:

The shop is open ***form ate*** o'clock. The owl tried to ***sees*** the mouse.

Put the picture ***hire*** up the wall. His illness ***weekend*** him a lot.

Simple spell-checkers will highlight a word which they do not recognize; fine – but you still have to find the correct spelling. Many spell-checkers now offer a list of alternatives for a word unrecognized by the system. Here are some of the suggested corrections made by the spell-checker on my PageMaker system. The first is a simple misspelling – ***terget***; here are the alternatives offered:

target	turgid	treated	turret	egret	greeted	iterate
tragic	targeted	treaty	targets	tricot	turreted	derogate

I can read and spell, so I had no trouble in identifying the correct spelling I needed, so the correction of ****terget*** in my manuscript was quite straightforward.

PageMaker also highlighted ***unspottable*** for me. In fact, of course, that word is spelled correctly, but the programme doesn't 'know' it and offers me: *inspectable, unspeakable, inhospitable, unsupportable.* If I am lacking in orthographical confidence what am I to make of all that? After all, my original spelling was correct.

Surprisingly my generally very sophisticated system doesn't recognize ***kindest*** and offers an entertaining set of alternatives:

kinkiest kindliest chunkiest kindles kinetics kinghoods kinds shindies

I have to be a confident speller to know that my original spelling of ***kindest*** was right and that none of the suggested alternatives was appropriate.

The conclusion is obvious: computer spelling checks are for the orthographically mature to identify their typing errors and occasional oversights; I wouldn't be without mine and it is a godsend. But the benefits of computer spelling checks for the learner can be overrated and may even increase perplexity.

Reference Strategies

Clearly, then, overreliance on existing printed reference materials is misplaced. So too is an obstinate ideology which, relegating spelling to an irrelevance to thinking, asserts that all can be sorted out for a final draft by microtechnology.

Learners need proper reference strategies of their own. By these they can make informed judgements about the structure of words and achieve a sound construction of a target word.

Strategies for the correct representation of a target word are of two dimensions. The first strategy attacks the word by means of contextual clues or through different words which have similar meanings but unrelated forms. This will assume a knowledge of synonyms. The second dimension – the more powerful – attacks the word through internal and analytical clues connected with the meanings of words which are of similar form.

Synonym: A word that means the same or nearly the same as another, different, word.

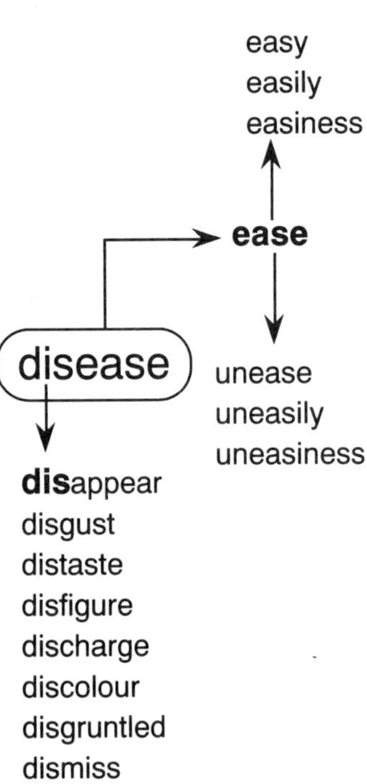

Children should know what synonyms are, and use simple words as a route to referencing the spelling of more complex synonyms.

The External Strategy of Word Attack

With this strategy the learner uses a known and simple *synonym* of the target word as a means of word attack.

A young learner working with me needed to write the word ***disease***. She produced ***dezese**, had inevitably failed to find it in a dictionary, and came to me for help. I suggested that she thought of a synonym whose spelling she was certain of and introduced her to the Longman Dictionary of Synonyms. The class had done some work on collecting synonyms and they knew that synonyms are different words which have similar though not exactly the same meanings as each other. She quickly suggested ***illness***, saying that she was certain that she could spell it. She looked up ***illness*** and quickly recognized ***disease*** from the list of entries. Because she was in a class where the teacher supported a climate of excitement about words she then noticed that the structure of the word was actually <dis-> + <**ease**> and produced the word web given here for her personal collection.

Another learner in the same group, perplexed that he could not locate the word in the dictionary that he had confidently spelled as ***nurishment**, used the synonym method on his own initiative: he looked up *food* and recognized his target word with ease. Someone else who needed ***necessity***, knowing it was 'awkward', found it via the entry for ***need.*** Yet another found ***automobile*** very quickly by looking up the entry for *car*.

Knowledge of this process will consolidate into an effective word attack skill. Here is another example in which the learner brought together a number of aspects of knowledge about real orthography.

The child I was observing wanted to check the spelling of a word he had recorded in his first draft as /**sachrated**/ (the slash brackets signalled that he knew that his phonetic representation needed further attention). His first line of attack was to try to isolate the base element to make a word web. He removed the instantly recognizable suffix <-ed> and wrote ***sachrate**; but when he wanted to add <-ion> he realized that there was an extra segment he had not previously accounted for and wrote ***sacheration.** He now went to the dictionary; when S-A-C-H- proved fruitless he tried S-A-T-C-H- with similar lack of success. At this point I considered intervening. My offer of help was declined and I was told, 'It's all right; I do know how to spell *wet* so I'll try the dictionary of synonyms.' He enjoyed his success when he found his target word and his parting comment to me was, 'I wasn't expecting the <tu> – do you think it's got anything to do with the planet ***Saturn***?' Such hypothesizing showed that he was a confident orthographer. (I later discovered that, admittedly remotely, there actually is an etymological connection between ***saturate*** and ***Saturn***!)

I noted what a good climate the class teacher had generated. She allowed the time and space for children to engage in such investigations by eliminating all pressure on children to produce writing in quantity just for the sake of it.

The Analytical Strategy of Word Attack

This strategy does not look to synonyms as a route to the target word, but concentrates on the structure of the word itself. It relies on the child's understanding of the standard word structure of **base word + affixes**. The writer first prunes the target word of any recognizable prefixes in order to isolate the base element. Here is an example of this in operation.

A child I was watching had prepared a report on a football match and was dealing with the word /**intasepted**/. He rewrote his tentative phonetic version of this word and divided off prefixes and suffixes that he recognized:

in–**tasept**–ed

He played with **tasept** for a short time and soon decided that he knew of no other word with that base element. 'Is it <inter-> like in ***Intercity*** and ***international***?' he asked me. I confirmed that he was right. He now tried:

inter–**sept**–ed

He consulted the dictionary but could not find ***intersept**. He then wrote ***sept***, and told me that it probably wasn't right because his target word had nothing to do with the number seven. He knew this, he told me, because the class had done a spelling project on the months of the year and he knew that *Sept**ember*** had once been the *seventh* month. He then crossed off the letter >s< and substituted the letter >c<, making the spelling of the base element <**cept**> instead. This now brought success as he looked up ***intercept*** in the dictionary.

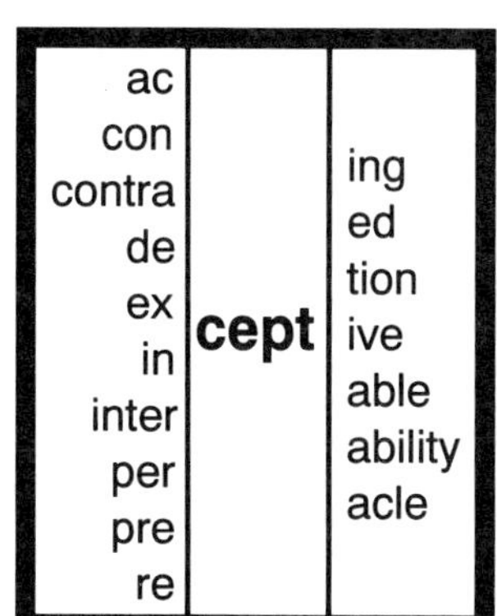

That learner was already a mature speller. I suggested to him that he might like to make a matrix on the base element <**cept**>. He did so at home and now thanks to him and his family I have the accompanying copy of his matrix in my collection.

This analytical approach to word attack is the one which most closely corresponds with the real structure words and should, therefore, constantly be reinforced with learners.

In a class where spelling activity follows the sort of pattern shown in this book there will be a climate of curiosity about words. Children lucky enough to work in such a climate will be encouraged to give in to the temptation to linger with a reference entry such as this one. It is a powerful means of vocabulary extension to allow learners this lateral curiosity; it is a case of spelling activity generating an expansion of experience of words rather than being confined to those words already in the spoken vocabulary of the child. It is a wise teacher who removes pressure on children to produce writing in quantity, and so allows them time to be 'side-tracked' by these reference entries and thus increase the range and power of their vocabulary.

In order, then, to be able to engage in referencing through word attack it is clear that a writer will need to be familiar with:

1. Segmenting and the analytical identification of affixes and base elements.
2. Alphabetical ordering of header word entries in reference books.

These basic word-building skills are well within the capabilities and range of activities of primary children.

In general it will also be clear that the principle that **spelling is a thinking process** is reinforced each time the representation of a target word is sought. This is in strong contrast with conventional mark/correct procedures which apply only to single and isolated words, corrected and copied individually when the only word attack strategy is rote memorization.

CHAPTER 10: ORGANIZING THE TEACHING OF SPELLING

Spelling Needs Teaching

Writing is a medium of learning in much of the curriculum. Word building and the representation of meaning in writing will inform teaching in various subject areas, reinforcing work across the curriculum. Incidents of teaching spelling, then, will occur in all teaching contexts. Since spelling occurs throughout the curriculum there is often a temptation to leave the specific teaching of orthography to opportunities which might happen to arise in the course of other activities.

☞ **Link the teaching of word building principles to relevant topics and themes in all areas of the curriculum.**

This laissez-faire attitude discourages attention to spelling in its own right. In the last few decades attitudes to orthography and the way children should encounter it have tended to play down attention to specific teaching of spelling. Influential ideas of Schonell and developmental ideologies associated with Piaget have been taken to encourage the view that specific teaching of spelling is unnecessary.

The Influence of Schonell

The name of F.J. Schonell is associated with word lists intended for spelling activities. His work has been influential and even though his word recognition test is (rightly, I believe) waning in popularity, his views about spelling linger on. In particular it is not usual to challenge his dictum that

> the child should be taught the word when he wants to write it.

☞ **Raising the profile of orthography in teaching and directing quite specific attention to it in the allocation of teaching time will empower and increase the range and fluency of written expression.**

This statement has a superficial ring of common sense but its consequences are debilitating. It relegates the teaching of spelling to mere reaction. But ***spelling is not a passive process confined to one word at a time.*** Teaching of spelling needs to be proactive because engagement with orthography in its own right is an enrichment of linguistic activity. Knowing about the internal structures of individual words brings awareness of others of similar form or meaning, broadening the vocabulary.

Teaching according to Schonell's edict tends to limit writers to words they already know. By waiting until learners try to use a word before giving them its spelling or correcting their attempt we reduce their work to a succession of separate and individual word-problems. It disempowers learners by encouraging cliché and 'safe', simplistic words which stand a good chance of avoiding 'corrections'.

Even worse, this attitude can constrict writers by denying them ownership of the very processes of word building they need. Ability to work with word structures is an *enabling* process. It gives deeper insights into the meaning of words and alerts learners to connections between words that they might otherwise not have noticed. This in turn can influence the quality of larger-scale writing. If you go along with Schonell's dictum that children should only learn to spell words they use then they are likely only to use the words they can spell and the inward spiral of repetition and banality is intensified and reinforced.

☞ **Children are liberated by their increasing ownership of the orthographic processes in writing. They find the urge to play with their increasing word power in their own texts to be irresistible.**

There has been another, related, teaching attitude which has tended to denigrate attention to spelling: the notion that ability to spell and effective writing are somehow almost incompatible. Self-expressionism has been particularly vocal in the dismissal of spelling as an enabling skill. But it is vital to rescue spelling from the refusal to see that self-expression needs the skills to be able to generate it. Form and structure are needed to mediate the content. Understanding spelling gives access to ranges and subtleties of meaning which are the stuff of the generation of written images and the tools of expression in writing.

Leaving Spelling to Be Absorbed

It is also a beguiling ideology which would have us believe that there is no need specifically to teach spelling in time slots of its own as it will be picked up from other encounters with language. This notion probably owes something to the insistence that children 'discover' everything they learn for themselves.

It is also possible that this unwillingness to teach may be a result of now discredited models which suggest that learning takes place in distinct and strictly sequential stages, where the learner moves step by step through a hierarchy of skills in an established and linear order. The idea is appealingly simple.

There is a related notion that children's minds, too, go through distinct stages characterized by an ability to think only in a specific way. This gives rise to an idea of 'readiness'. Domination by this ideology has resulted in teachers assuming that children must have reached a particular stage of conceptual development before they are even *able* to engage with a certain activity. Few teachers these days would still approve of this retardation of learning opportunities in reading, but the idea lingers on in attitudes to spelling. It is assumed that children's 'intuitive etymologies' will automatically bring understanding of all they need to know of spelling when the time is right.

Being in the thrall of such a developmental model can result in effective abdication of the teaching process. If you assume that children move *naturally and automatically* through specific and definable stages at roughly predictable ages then the temptation is to 'let it happen'. The sort of language used in texts by people regarded as experts can also subtly reinforce this assumption. Here is an example from an influential educationist's comments on what she calls the Transitional Stage:

> Children begin to recognize acceptable letter patterns, put vowels in every syllable ...
>
> (Bentley, page 2)

This implies that we should wait for children to discover themselves the principles of a system that has taken centuries to evolve. It would be better to rephrase the quoted comment into something like this:

> In order to help learners to achieve the Transitional Stage they **should be shown how** to generate and recognize acceptable letter patterns and **be informed that** a vowel needs to be present in every syllable ...

This would not be to interfere with children's learning; it would be constructively to *intervene* in it.

A strictly linear model of learning has particularly failed to take into account the value of constantly *revisiting* a specific concept, not merely as revision but for re-sorting and reclassifying its elements on the basis of experience of other concepts.

Jerome Bruner has given us a more helpful model in his hypothesis of **the spiral curriculum.** In this model teaching is seen as the regular revisiting of the same basic concepts, encountered in progressively complex forms. Each time a concept is revisited greater sense is constructed from it; interrelated connections and correspondences with other basic concepts are progressively perceived.

In order properly to approach teaching any subject in a 'spiral' manner its real content must be fully understood. The conventions and patterns of spelling intertwine and interact; when any spelling theme is being dealt with it will have to be linked with related orthographical conventions each time it is visited.

We should be offering children a series of *themes* in English orthography. Professional judgement will control the appropriateness and, above all, the *pace* at which they operate the choice of theme. Any theme will from time to time be revisited by learners at any stage of competence, even the highest. In my own teaching I operate with the whole range of these themes at all stages from Reception onwards, with children in schools, with teachers on Inservice courses, and with those with specific learning needs whether of difficulty or needs associated with giftedness.

The sound teacher of spelling has to be aware of the real structures of orthography and will not merely be an adept at finding tricks for remembering individual and isolated words, however virtuosic and entertaining.

A Note on Mnemonics

✎ **Mnemonic**: a device for assisting the memorization of a single fact when that device has either no or a false connection with the fact to be learned.

A common strategy for teaching 'difficult' spellings is to associate the particular difficulty with an artificial device for memorizing it. For instance, the colours of the rainbow can be remembered in the right order from the initial letters of **R**ichard **O**f York **G**ave **B**attle **I**n **V**ain (**R**ed, **O**range, **Y**ellow, **G**reen, **B**lue, **I**ndigo, **V**iolet).

As a memory prompter a mnemonic is intrinsically unconnected with the fact needing memorization. Therein lies its danger when applied to spelling – it only applies to an isolated word and has no relevance to broader orthographical processes. And, of course, over-use of mnemonics for spelling will give negative messages to learners about the English orthographical system, suggesting inexplicability and illogicality.

A further danger in some mnemonics is that they can even confuse understanding of the real orthographical structures of words. Examples are the use of the word te**ache**r to remember *ache* and the sentence 'It's gr**eat** to eat' to remember the vowels in *great*. Neither pair of words has a connection morphologically, etymologically or even phonologically – only a coincidence of letters.

☞ **Beware of expending energy on devising ruses which apply to single, isolated words; concentrate instead on teaching skills which put the real structures of orthography into children's ownership.**

Teachers should, then, exercise great caution in using mnemonics for spelling. They should be a last, rather than an early, resort. I will confess to the occasional use of 'Fry the end of your friend' as a mnemonic for the initial string of ***friend***. On the other hand, when I associate ***answer*** with ***swear*** (in the sense 'to make a declaration') I am making a *real* etymological association.

Organizing Time

Once the need to allocate a time slot to spelling is accepted we need to look at how that relates to time given to reading and to the interrelated functions of handwriting and spelling.

Link Spelling with Reading

We have already noted that good readers will not automatically be good spellers. We cannot claim to be attending effectively to spelling by leaving it to be a by-product of reading.

☞ **Progress in spelling and writing can radically improve reading skills; poor readers *especially* should be targeted for intensive work in spelling and writing.**

Yet the uneven relationship between reading and spelling produces the apparent paradox that although reading ability will not automatically generate an ability to spell, nevertheless *ability to construct and spell words will increase ability to read*! Normally the context helps the understanding of a word in reading, but when the context fails to help then knowledge of individual word structure will come to the rescue. Individual word-attack processes are more prominent in spelling than in reading; a learner who can *construct* words efficiently through a personal repertoire of letter-strings which correspond to units of meaning and sound will *know what to look for* when reading a word for which the context provides no clues.

It is increasingly being understood that *children progress with their early reading at least as much through writing as they do through actually reading!*

We might conclude that time actively spent on orthography could be subsumed under a general heading of learning to read. A practical result of this could be that the considerable allocation of time made to hearing individual reading might be cut down somewhat and the time freed used for word building, which will in turn nourish the ability to read.

Link Handwriting with Spelling

☞ **Handwriting affects spelling because it is the means of its implementation and the medium of its learning, so don't teach them separately.**

The importance of linking handwriting directly with the learning of spelling has been dealt with in Chapter Four. When children learn to *write* the integrated movement patterns which correspond to the letter-strings from which words are built these patterns of movement are imprinted in the motor memory. We learn and remember spellings through writing, the tactile dimension which underlines the regularity of these patterns and therefore their predictability. Clearly it will be a priority to use a form of handwriting which is free from inefficiencies, incongruities and any obstacles to its fluency. Link the teaching of the writing of letter-strings with morphemes and base elements and the beneficial results of these periods of combined handwriting and spelling will be felt even in reading progress.

Use Time for Teaching rather than Testing

The justification for testing is the notion that making children learn a specific list of words each week for a test will efficiently increase the number of words a child can spell correctly. Yet it has been understood for some time that this system of spelling tests can guarantee no *long-term* retention of the spelling so 'learned'.

All that testing usually does is to indicate which words a child can *not* spell and increase the general level of anxiety about spellings.

I am sure that teachers know that spelling tests are not all they are cracked up to be; I certainly did, though I used to be unable to say exactly why. Elements of this lack of effectiveness in what, commonsense might suggest, looks to be a systematic method of instruction include:

- The isolated nature of each word learned for the test – isolated, that is, from words which are related to it in form and meaning – mean that the learning effort is confined to a single word.
- The climate of threat and danger generated by tests often leads to an avoidance of risk-taking. Children will be encouraged to avoid writing words whose spelling they are unsure of and go for the safe option.

The reason for the continuing presence in classroom life of spelling tests is probably to be accounted for by the need felt by many teachers to be seen to be doing *something* about spelling. If, however, you free the time usually taken in the preparation for and administration of traditional spelling tests you could have an hour or two a week at your disposal in order to teach real orthography.

Choosing Spelling Themes

☞ **Time spent by teachers on attention to word structure was seen to determine actual progression in spelling, but children receiving no teaching, and children blindly following a printed word list with no instructions about how to learn the words, deteriorated in their ability to write words that conformed to precedent in English.**

(Peters, page 21)

Add the time taken in the organization and administration of spelling tests to the further hour or so sometimes allocated to handwriting and devote it all instead to orthography and you have a significant chunk of the timetable to reallocate to properly constructive word building. This time can be used to introduce and sustain specific **word building themes**. Some initial suggestions could include the patterns of suffixing, recognizing prefixes, ways of representing the 'long' vowels, the related letter-strings <tion>, <ture> and <tive>, or any of the other conventions and patterns of orthography.

Whole class experiences of a spelling theme are possible since individual learners will engage at a level of complexity appropriate to themselves. Each element of the structures of orthography is a suitable context for simultaneous activity by learners at varying levels of sophistication. Orthographical themes are open-ended rather than restricted so there is room for the cautious and the ambitious, the tentative and the confident, the inexperienced and the expert.

Decisions about which theme to choose for a class's attention depend on:

- what they need appropriately to cope with, given their past experience and present understanding of orthography.
- links that can be made with current themes in other areas of the curriculum.
- 'gaps' in knowledge which reveal themselves through marking individual scripts in the class and through occasionally hearing reading.

Above all make sure that specific and regular time-allocations for orthography are made and maintained. **Whole-class lessons on spelling are wholly appropriate!**

Weekly Experiences

There should be regular and recognized slots in the weekly timetable for:

- the introduction, exploration, or development of a recognizable and coherent orthographical theme or sub-theme.
- a word game which involves some preparation and research. **Call My Bluff**, with children taking it in turns to be on the presenting panel, is a favourite.
- an opportunity for any child to share new discoveries about words. Personal news time is a feature of primary classes; orthographical discoveries of a similar nature can often be of more general interest and value.

Organizing Response

Helping children towards maturity in orthography operates in two dimensions. The one will be input of information – the direct teaching element, usually in the context of a whole class lesson. We take a *proactive* stance towards spelling by taking steps to ensure that word building is given regular time in a class's learning programme.

We should also work out positive means of *reacting* to the orthographical needs of every child as seen in a current piece of individual writing. These responses must avoid meaningless mechanistic reactions which will not engage learners in word construction skills. The question arises about what practical responses should be made to spelling mistakes in children's written work.

☞ Don't expect children to correct and learn every single spelling mistake in a script; select for attention only the word(s) which have priority for the writer.

Marking Personal Scripts

Traditional responses to marking scripts are of two sorts. In a modification of the testing idea the weekly test is replaced with a list of a child's misspellings at the end of each piece of work. Apparent advantages of this are first that words to be copied out again and learned arise from the child's own work; secondly anyone inspecting the exercise book will see that spelling is being attended to.

I did this myself for several years but was never happy with it. This entirely mechanistic process embedded in no meaningful context and of no relevance to words other than the one being corrected was unlikely to motivate learners and, significantly, did not help in general word construction skills. Of more importance, children's knowledge that each misspelled word would need to be copied out correctly several times did nothing to encourage risk-taking.

The second response to marking has been to correct all the spelling mistakes in a script and make the writer re-write the entire passage correctly in the expectation that the correct spellings will just 'sink in'. This response is about as efficacious as the expectation that correct spelling will be picked up from reading.

Teachers know that the lack of effectiveness of these two mark/correct responses is only too evident in the constant recurrence of the same spelling mistakes.

Word Webs and Matrices

Word webs are a different matter from blanket marking or scribbling a single wanted word in a small book. Making word chains demands a thinking process which has to identify and organize the morphemes of the target word; it operates in a context of meaning and consolidates knowledge of word construction.

This is the result of a collaborative venture between a six-year-old and the people at home.

come → comes
coming
income
outcome
become → becomes
becoming
newcomer
comedown
comeback

Here is an illustration of how making a word web was a useful response to a six-year-old's need to consolidate the spelling of the common word *come*. Phonics is of little use here, in fact her spelling of it as ***cume** showed that phonics was actually hindering her. I judged that it was perhaps too early to talk about the historical reasons for the letter >o< in the word.

This spelling needs to be internalized principally through the motor memory. Merely copying out the word several times might lead slowly to this but would involve tedium and consequent alienation. Instead I set the child the task of including the base word <**come**> in as many different combinations as she could think of. Children in this class were encouraged to consult their peers and the people at home as they collected these combinations. The result is given here.

By the time this simple word web had been generated and written the orthography of <**come**> was fully established. The non-phonetic >o< had been written in the base element eleven times, each in a different final word but in every case as a result of conscious word building. Not only was the presence of this non-phonic >o< consolidated by generating this word chain, but the presence of the final silent >e< was also emphasized by the need to replace it with <-ing> when that suffix was added, thus giving experience of an interrelated spelling pattern at the same time.

It was not the meaningless replication procedure which mere copying out of the same word would have been.

An approach such as this will, of course, mean that you do not call attention to every single one of the spelling errors in a script. Plainly it is overloading a learner to expect all miscues to be corrected and 'learned' simultaneously. The teacher will make a judgement as to which spelling has the priority for attention.

In the script mentioned above the six-year-old writer had also produced the following misspellings:

*Jagyer *stering weel *moterway *sumtimes

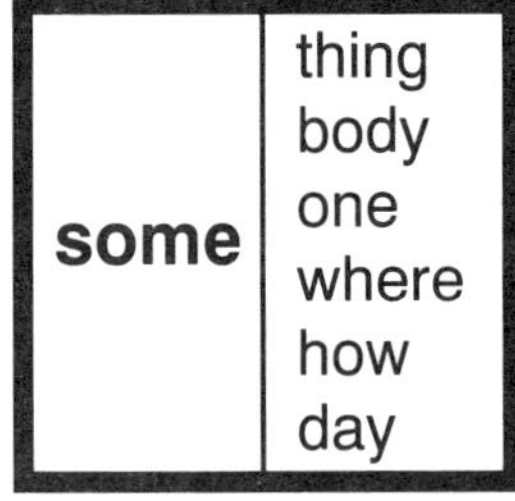

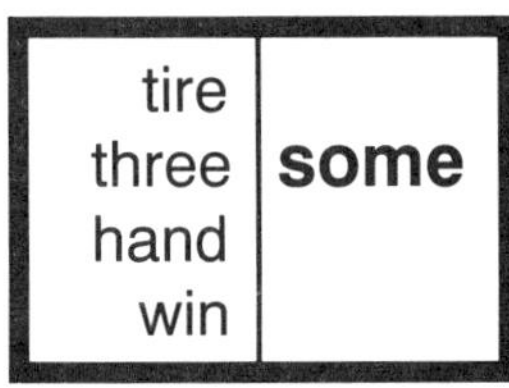

Besides the attention I gave to *come* (she had, you will remember, written ***cume**) I decided also to attend to ***sumtimes**. This was because (i) the element <**some**> is very common and (ii) it bears a strong orthographical relationship to *come*. Since she had correctly written the ***times*** element I concentrated her attention on the *some* element by giving her the matrices from which she would be able to construct several words. Interestingly she also produced ***toothsome*** – a favourite word, she explained, of her mother's.

The other misspellings were put right only for the final public form of the document when all the redrafting was complete. What I had done was to establish priorities for attention and to avoid a counterproductive overload.

Making word matrices like this to respond to a child's specific needs in word building is an entertaining process and makes 'marking' a much more satisfying and challenging activity for teachers. You will find that you quickly become adept at producing suitable matrices and will soon build up a collection of your own which will form a useful resource.

☞ **Don't make children copy out corrections several times: instead give them a word matrix based on the target word whose spelling needs to be attended to.**

Such word webs and matrices made *by the child* in response to their own spelling needs can build up into a collection of personally produced resource materials. These are of greater use than the traditional notebooks of isolated words.

Wider Responses from a Script

An older child I was working with produced these mistakes in a short script.

*imeadiately *earlyst *equiped *familer *misalanious *headake

He was a ten-year-old of average-to-good general abilities. I did not want to daunt his evident confidence in trying words out by overloading him with 'corrections'. I made the following decisions on how to respond to the script which was fairly typical of what the class was producing.

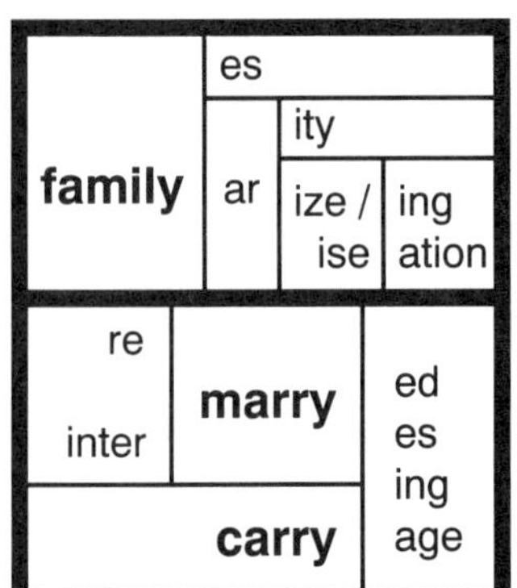

1. Devote class spelling time to revisiting the theme of what happens to final consonants when a vocalic suffix is added. That would remind the class of the need to double the letter >p< in<**equip**> + <-ed> ➔ **equipped**.
2. Give a one-off class session on what happens to the three base words *family, carry* and *marry* when suffixes are added. It would involve revisiting the pattern which governs how the vowel letters >i< and >y< interchange. The session would also include the revision of the comparative and superlative suffixes <-er> and <-est>. This would enable the writer to make the correct construction of <**early**> + <-est> ➔ **earliest.**

   You will note that <-est> is usually pronounced /ist/, but it is spelled with an >e< because of its link with <-er>. The different suffix <-ist>, though sounding the same as <-est>, has the different meaning of 'a person who engages with what the base word is about' – e.g. typ**ist**, social**ist**, perfection**ist**.

3. Start a class poster on which we would collect words built from the base element <**medi-**> ("middle"). This will lead towards the structure of <im-> + <**medi**> + <-ate> + <-ly>.

toothache	
headache	*aches*
faceache	*ached*
brainache	*aching*
earache	
backache	

The only 'correction' I specified for the writer himself was the proper spelling of *ache*. He was orthographically mature enough to ask whether the representation of /k/ in the word as <ch> was because the word was Greek. I told him that it was the only case I knew in which /k/ is represented by <ch> in a word which is not Greek; there is, however, a reason why this Old English word is spelled in this way and I promised to tell him that reason some time later. I set him the task of producing at least five compound words of which <**ache**> was an element. What he produced is given here.

As for ***misalanious** I decided only to respond to that by saying that I would attend specially to that later, but I congratulated him on knowing that the final segment which sounds /-ŭs/ is always written <-ous> in an English word.

Word Webs

These powerful learning tools are constructed by writing a starter word at the centre of a working space; words which are related to its constituent morphemes are then developed from it. The simplest webs are confined to words which contain only the base element of the central starter word.

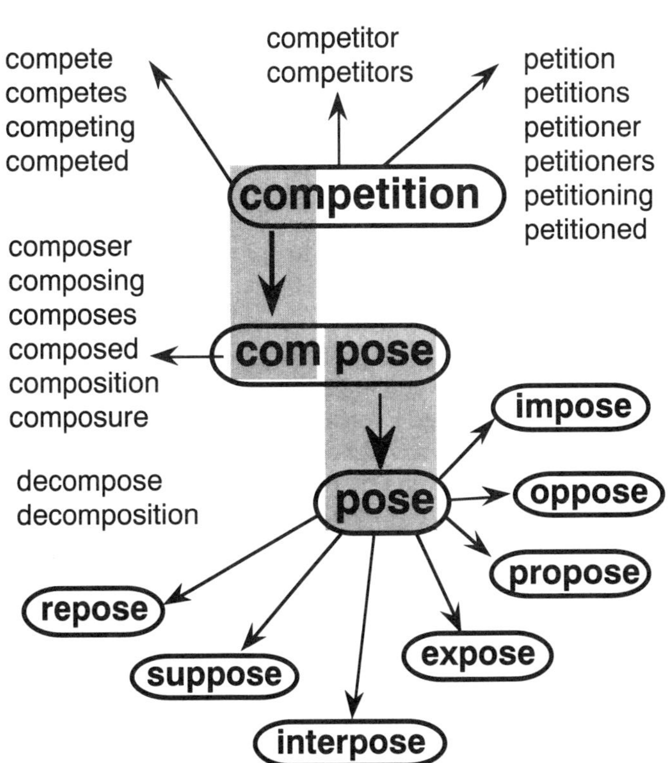

The obvious advantages of representing a word as part of a web are:

- The spelling of the starter word is constantly represented in relationship with other words of connected meaning, even when the sound of the base element changes in different combinations. Spelling's morphological nature is constantly reinforced.
- Word webs can be supplied ready-made to illustrate and consolidate a particular point of word construction or they can be set as small-scale projects in word investigation.
- They are suitable for individual or for group work and are very collectable.

In a development of the word web a large sheet of paper is pinned to a wall – a passageway is good – and a pen is kept nearby, perhaps attached to it on a piece of string. Every time someone passes by they have to add a further word to the web.

This web is a record of one such that had been going for a short while. It shows just how open-ended this activity is; there is never a time when a further word cannot be added to a word web.

Resources for Individuals

I now move on to consider what personal records or resources individual children may need to assemble for their own use.

Children's Own Spelling Books

There is a traditional organizational response to children's spelling needs in their everyday writing – personal spelling notebooks, usually arranged in some sort of alphabetical sections. Every time children ask for a spelling either they or the teacher write the word under the appropriate initial letter in this book. The arrangement may appear to be sensible but it can be overrated as a tool of progress. In practice it usually proves to be of little use for several reasons:

- Children rarely use it for reference when they are seeking a target word. Like published kiddi-dictionaries its limited scope makes it a limited resource.
- When it acquires a number of entries they are only collected under the *initial* letters of each word; there is no alphabetical system or order *within* a letter entry and it becomes increasingly difficult to locate a particular word even if you are sure that you have written it somewhere. It needs constant revision and rewriting.
- Words are given whole with no analytical element and therefore no pathway to learning the word; isolated entries are not connected with the words to which they are related in form and meaning.
- Children use these books as a means of transfer of a needed word from teacher to page for the current piece of writing only. The word is then ignored since it only had relevance to the moment. Children frequently ask for words which are already in their spelling books.

The presence of such spelling books results from an expectation of a faultless first draft of writing. Since children know that all incorrect spellings will be marked, even in a first draft, there is no climate in which experimentation with word building can take place. Instead, when young writers come across a word about which there is even a slight doubt many will abandon the flow of their writing to stalk the teacher in order to 'get a spelling', probably joining a trailing queue to do so. It is a golden opportunity for the task avoider too! Others will merely abandon the effort to attempt an appropriate or interesting word if it presents any doubts at all and go for the simple uninteresting synonym or fall back on to cliché.

These spelling books fail as instruments of learning and as facilitators of fluency.

A Personal Resource Collection

I have suggested that blanket marking of spellings, imposition of corrections, or little spelling books for children to wave at you are either of no real help or even counterproductive. I have also recommended a constructive response to personal scripts in the form of word matrices and webs. It is precisely these that children should be collecting for their own use and reference.

Here is an outline of what each child should have.

1. **A note book** which is devoted specifically to word building, the combination of handwriting and spelling. It would contain the target words investigated during class lessons as well as personal notes.
2. **A file or folder** in which to store the collection of word webs and matrices – both those given by the teacher in response to personal scripts and those generated by the learner.

3. A growing **collection** of words which are of etymological interest discovered during routine class work.

Editorial Partnerships

☞ **Organizing a class into regular editorial partnerships for first checking of word building considerably reduces queues for word checking directly from the teacher.**

It is a useful managerial structure to organize children into editorial partnerships. These function as collaborative pairings for the discussion and checking of target words as well as for the editing of early drafts of scripts whose destination is to be 'public documents' but which have not yet reached that stage.

The progress of constructing a target word is as follows: the writer follows the segmenting strategy given earlier (page 50) and generates as much of the word as possible, leaving gaps or empty boxes for segments which are uncertain. These are then shared with the editorial partner for checking, comment and possible completion. Only if the editorial partnership cannot resolve something about the word will the teacher be consulted for the confirmation or resolution of problems.

Organizing Space

The recognition of the importance of orthography in learning not only implies time being made available, it also suggests that space be allocated to it.

A Scriptorium

Every class should have easy access to a reference area of its own. Because of the essential link between writing and spelling, this area should have facilities for careful writing and calligraphy too – proper writing pads with a selection of writing implements, papers and guidelines. Because of this link with writing I have tended to use the term *scriptorium* for such an area (a scriptorium was the reference and writing area of the monastery, the seat of learning in the mediaeval and renaissance world).

Pride of place should be given to a proper and full dictionary. If possible this should be on a sturdy bookstand on which it can rest securely while being consulted. Those who do consult this tome should be encouraged to leave it open at the page they use; the visual message of a reference tool which is encountered already open is powerful – much better than approaching a 'closed book'!

Also available for use in this scriptorium, perhaps on a table-top book rest, should be such other reference tools as a Dictionary of Synonyms and a Thesaurus. Other specialist reference books (Quotations, Word Origins, Phrase and Fable, Historical Slang, etc.) will appropriately be present in older classes of primary schools.

Reference Posters

A prominent and accessible place on the classroom walls should be reserved for reference posters. These should show essential elements of word building which are of general and constant use. The most powerful of these will be a reference poster of prefixes. Other possible posters include those which show the class's collection of suffixes, and perhaps interesting or productive base elements.

These posters should not be static and unchanged but reflect the growing awareness and discoveries of the class. When, for instance, a new prefix is identified or introduced it should be added to the poster with some sort of status-giving ceremony.

Specific Learning Needs

Teaching methodologies may vary widely in consistency and form but most children seem to cope with learning in school in spite of what we do to them. This intuitive ability to learn carries the majority reasonably smoothly through their school days whatever the predominating ideology or atmosphere may be, and whatever variety of teaching methods they encounter. They might not go as far with unsound teaching as they might have done with more sound approaches, but they will cope.

But there is a significant minority of children in all our classes who fail as a result of one learning difficulty or another. For these learners the teacher's first duty is to make the climate of the classroom setting supportive and not threatening or debilitating. But just being kind will not necessarily help learners to unravel their learning difficulties. It is imperative that children with specific learning needs encounter only conceptually sound and coherent frameworks for their learning.

We know that the movement memory is important in learning spelling, so fluent and consistent handwriting is a powerful route into spelling. An early priority, then, is to rescue them from printing and pencils as a matter of urgency.

If the obstacle of inappropriate handwriting is compounded by exposure to the perplexity of plainly wrong spelling strategies then not only have the special needs of these children not been attended to, but they will also have been subjected to hindrance and confusion. The over-prioritization of phonics is the widest single hindrance to the rescue of children with specific learning needs in language. Confining children to simplistic phonics, irrelevant mnemonics (page 92), unhelpful and inconsistent 'rules', and a printed script may actually be *causing* the problems of significant numbers of children.

Children with specific learning difficulties in language are particularly fortunate if their teacher ensures that everyone in the class is given an efficient, economical, and fluent hand, integrally linking handwriting with reading and spelling. Above all they will be helped into word attack skills through the morphological structures which are the real basis of word building.

Children with no particular learning difficulties may cope with whatever incoherent teaching of writing and spelling we encumber them with, but even they will not achieve their full potential without our recognizing their early entitlement to fluency in word building. A conclusion that should be drawn, then, is that **if the whole class is given a properly fluent handwriting style and conceptually sound teaching of orthography, not only will the majority of children be enabled to go that much further than they might otherwise have done, but many of the children liable to failure under the usual piecemeal attitude to word building will not fail either.**

Summary of the Structures for Teaching

The diagram below summarizes structures of organization of time and space for teaching. Remember particularly that:

- Word building, the combination of handwriting and spelling, is a suitable open-ended subject for whole class teaching.
- Spelling themes should regularly be revisited.

- 'Corrections' copied out several times should be eliminated; instead misspelled base words should become the basis of chains, matrices and webs.
- Classroom routines should include setting up an easily accessible scriptorium, producing and maintaining reference posters, opportunities for individual presentations which share orthographical discoveries, and the establishment of editorial partnerships.

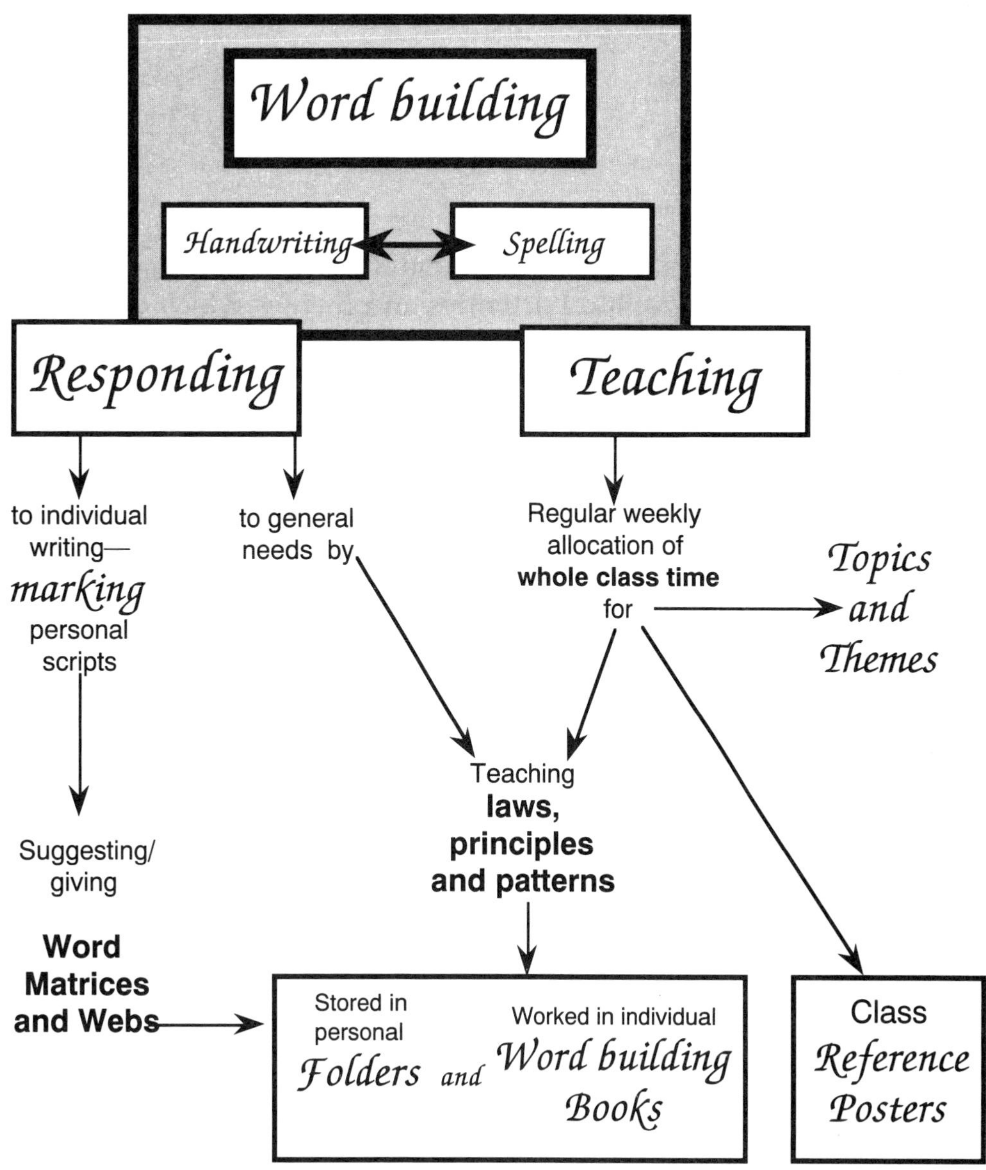

PART THREE

SELECTED ACTIVITIES AND THEMES

This part of the book offers you resources for teaching orthographical activities and themes which can be implemented following the structures and processes given in Parts One and Two.

Only a small representative sample of such activities can be given if the book is to avoid becoming impossibly bulky. Further detailed resources may become available as separate publications in due course.

Four orthographical 'themes' are explained:

1. Orthography for early learners.
2. The letter-string <igh>.
3. The vocalic suffixes.
4. Working with the plural suffix.

Photocopiable resource sheets are provided for developing and consolidating work in these themes.

Three further resource sheets are provided for general work; they should be self-explanatory.

1. Orthography for Early Learners

Learning the Alphabet

The version of the alphabet song given here is suitable for work with even quite young children. It is set to a traditional well-known tune and simple guitar chords are given for it. Remember to use letter *names* when singing the song.

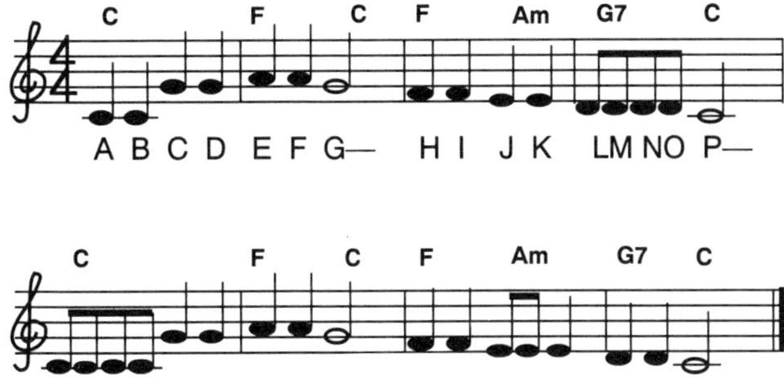

Learning the alphabet with this song has the advantage that you learn the letters in groups rather than as a single, very long sequence. It is a combination of smaller, more manageable sequences: **ABCDEFG**, **HIJK**, **LMNOP**; **LMNOPQ**, **RST**, **UVW**, **XYZ**. Learning to group letters in a way such as this means that children will soon be able to start a sequence of letters at various points through the alphabet so that they will not necessarily have to start at A in order to reach a given letter. This will bring its most obvious benefits when they are learning the processes of referencing.

Learning to Segment

☞ Children should learn to segment any words they use by chanting them, tapping out the rhythm of the segments on their own or on a partner's hand. They should then count the segments in the word they are segmenting.

Introduce the two terms **monosyllable** and **polysyllable** even to very young children. They love the terminology and relish the use of longer words. Sources of words to segment include:

- Children's own names, and those of the people they live with.
- Streets where they live.
- Towns and countries they have heard of.
- Characters and places from stories they know or are told.

Several teachers I know incorporate these segmenting activities with aspects of music-making. As soon as possible children should practise identifying the first segment of a word, the last segment, the second segment, and so on.

Real Sounding Out

☞ Be very careful not to undermine sounding out by using the phonetic alphabet – that will generate the unhelpful habit of hiccoughing fragmentation of words.

Teach the proper process of sounding out as soon as possible.

- Demonstrate how to draw out the word as a *continuous* sound by saying it out loud very slowly.
- Constantly concentrate on what the word feels like in the mouth.

Early practice should only be with monosyllables which do not contain consonant blends. Here are some to try.

bad	bed	lid	hop	up	mad	hen	dig	fog	but
jam	met	bin	got	mum	fan	jet	fit	box	sun
leg	is	on	hug	sat	yes	pin	nod	us	at

Note that <th>, <sh> and <ch> use two letters but each is only one phoneme; children should know from the beginning that sometimes a single sound needs a pair of letters to represent it. Include such words as the following in your early sounding out.

that	then	this	thing	both	thin	shall	shell	fish	wish
ship	push	chat	check	chin	chop	chug	each		

- When you start identifying the sounds don't confine yourself to initial sounds; practise identifying the *last* sounds too.
- As soon as children know the vowels (which should be very soon) practise identifying the vowel in each of the words.
- Professional judgement will indicate when to show children the letters / graphemes which represent the sounds they identify, but it should be sooner rather than later that you combine sounding out with writing the words for all the children to see.
- Write out the word as you sound it out; the sound and the movement should be continuous and synchronized.

These are the two-consonant blends which occur at the beginning of words; share them with the children and ask them to supply words which begin with the blends.

sp-	st-	sc-	sk-	sm-	sn-	sl-	sw-	tw-	dw-	bl-	cl-
gl-	fl-	pl-	pr-	br-	tr-	dr-	cr-	gr-	fr-	thr-	shr-

Here are the three-consonant blends which can occur at the beginning of words. Again, share them and ask for words which begin with them.

spr- spl- str- scr- squ- (= /skw/)

Here are monosyllables which contain initial and final consonant blends:

trip	stun	grab	melt	milk	crest	grim	flap	from
fact	brush	stop	chest	film	loft	frost	prod	self
next	act	and	sand	bend	fond	wind	grunt	camp
sent	spent	bench	print	hunt	romp	jump	lunch	

Combine segmenting with sounding out. First segment words, then sound out each segment to identify its constituent sounds and their order. Write out the final word, making sure you do so segment by segment, spelling it out as you do so.

expect	himself	itself	myself	adopt	upset
magnet	depend	expand	defend	talcum	ambush
upon	intend	begin	belong	beyond	Batman

Vowel Spotting

☞ Teach recognition and writing of the vowels as soon as possible. Use the photocopiable sheet (page 73) to show the arrangement in which they should be written.

Teach the rule that every word must contain at least one vowel and confirm this by instituting vowel spotting in any text which comes to hand. This could be books, posters, notices, packages, your own writing, or even newspapers and magazines.

Some children will be ready very soon to begin searching for and spotting common vowel digraphs. They should learn to write and know the sounds that these digraphs represent. Point out the variants< ai> /<ay> and <oi> /<oy> since this will be a suitable point at which to introduce the rule about a final >i<. At first

ai/ay /ā/
ee/ea /ē/
oi/oy /oɪ/
ou /ow/

introduce it in its simplest form: **you can't have a letter >i< at the end of a word – use >y< instead**. Share the knowledge that if you are building words you choose <ay> and <oy> if the sound is at the end of the word because to use <ai> and <oi> would make the word end with an >i<. Here are some words to build with these digraphs; let the children decide which form they must use.

pain	rain	day	fail	nail	say	repay	play
train	stain	wait	aim	stay	stray	explain	oil
boil	soil	spoil	boy	foil	dismay	joy	enjoy
coin	join	joint	point	avoid	destroy		

The First Suffixes

Just as segmenting should be among the earliest encounters of learners with word building, so should awareness of affixes. Basic matrices are for the suffixes <-ly> and <-ful>. A matrix for the suffixes <-ness> and <-less> can be introduced very soon afterwards.

☞ **When you are using <-ing> as a suffix only build it on to base words which are not affected by vocalic suffixes. If you are unsure of these principles look at the section in this chapter on The Vocalic Suffixes (page 109).**

The letter string <-ing> serves as one of our most common suffixes; it can also be used as a phonetic building block.

It is appropriate at an early stage to introduce children to the simple suffixing pattern that **when a base word ends with a single silent >e<, it is removed when you add the suffix <-ing>**. Children will need to know the following terminology:

single: only one, not double;
silent: not representing a sound on its own.

The test for whether a final >e< is silent is to sound out the word and identify the last sound. If that sound isn't /ee/ then the final >e< is silent. For instance when you sound out the word *have* you get /hăv/, so the final >e< is silent:

have + -ing → having

Sound out the word *be* and you get /bee/, so the final >e< is not silent:

be + -ing → being with the >e< retained

Here are some base words which end in >e<. Children can be asked to add <-ing> to all of them, deciding whether to remove the >e< first or not. The process can be written like a sum, as has been done with ***have*** and ***be*** above.

have	love	be	live	like	see	use
save	take	chase	agree	hate	care	dive
behave	hate	glue	referee			

Early Experiences of Compounds

Some important and common words are compounds. Some matrices appear on the resource sheet to give experience of them. They also give practice in writing such words as *some* and *any* which are not simplistically phonic.

Resource Sheet 1: Basic Word Building

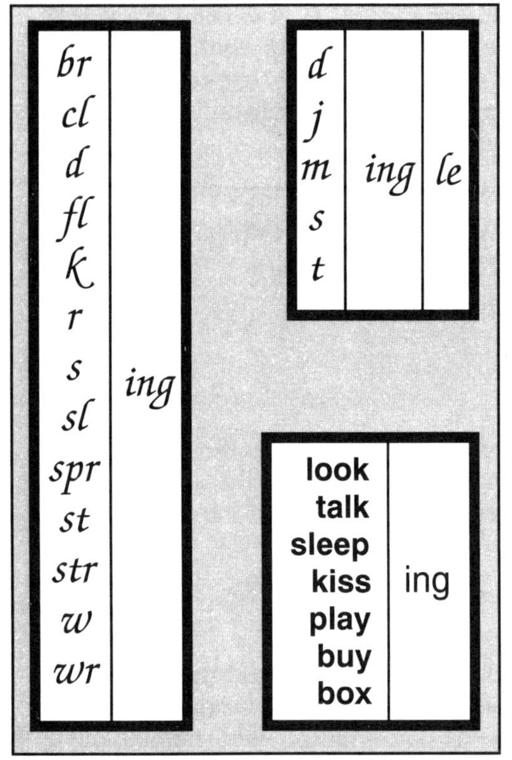

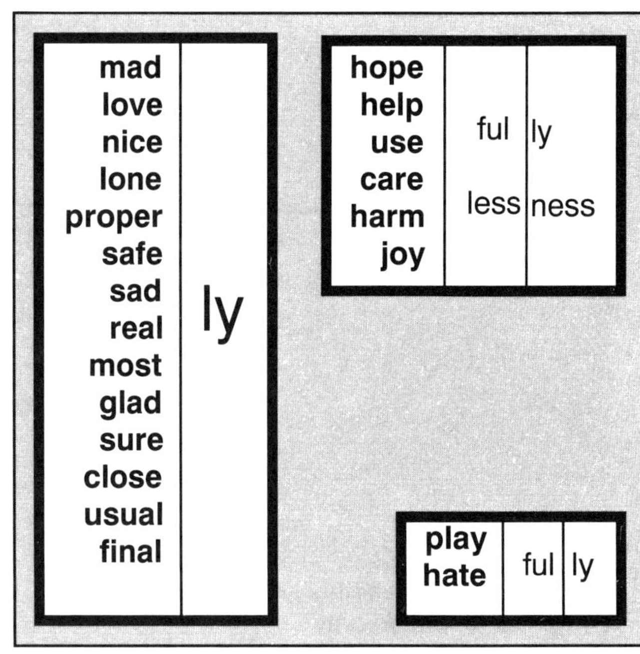

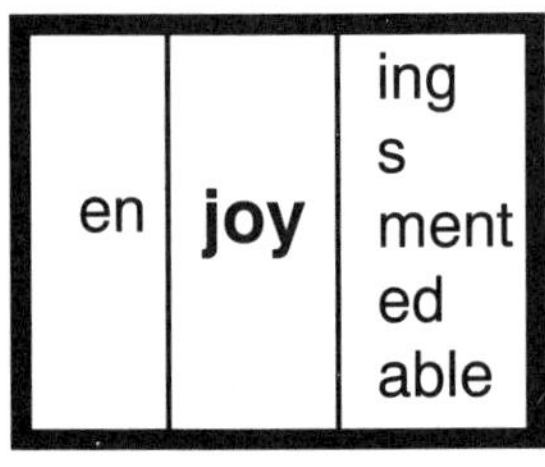

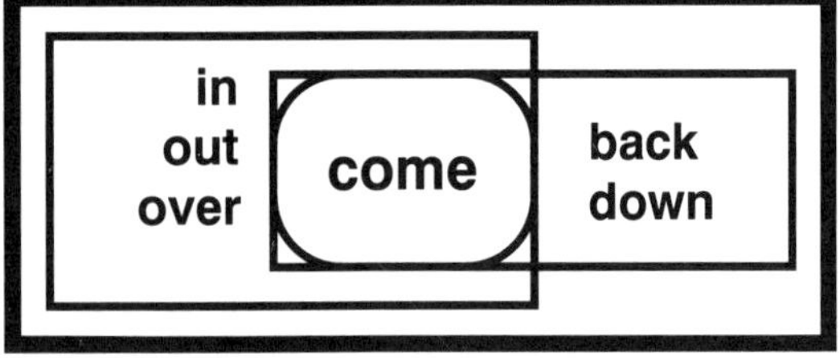

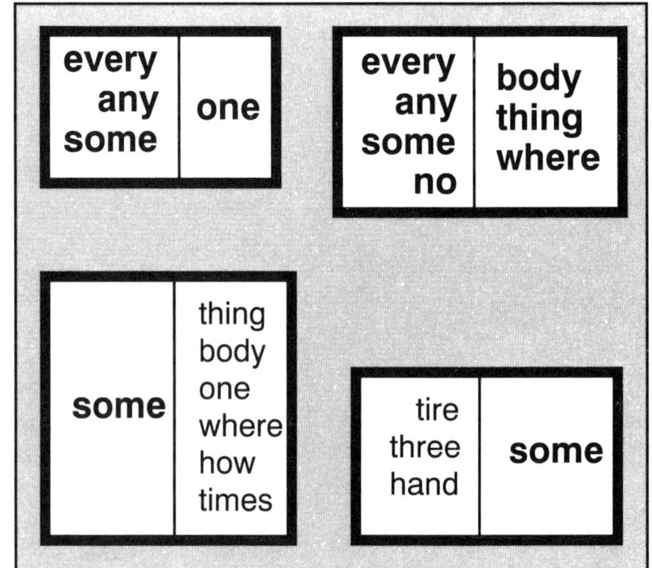

2. The Letter-string <igh>

☞ Teach <igh> as a single written unit, emphasizing its unity by dotting the >i< only after the >h< has been written. Early learners should say the /ī/ sound as they dot the >i<. Early learners should also say this letter-string in one breath when they are spelling out; thus *highly* will be H-IGH (pause) L-Y.

Chapter 6 introduced <igh> and gave some introductory materials; page 61 should be referred to with these notes. Like anything containing the digraph <gh> this letter-string is assumed to be difficult. It is not. It follows consistent patterns, is a very productive starter for a word building project, and is suitable even for early learners.

The Basic Pattern

Two facts about this string should be known by children:

1. **When preceded by a consonant <igh> always represents the 'long' >i<.**
2. **A word which contains <igh> is of Old English origin.**

Use the matrix to generate base words which contain the string <igh> representing 'long' >i<. Check the etymology of each after it has been written.

These Old English words attract basic affixes – the prefix <-un> and suffixes <-ly>, <-ful>, <-ness>, <-less>, <-s>, <-y>, <-er>, <-est> and <-ed>. Experiment with each of the base words, developing them by adding basic affixes. This activity can generate a large number of words. Here are a few:

blighted	higher	flighty	almighty	midnight
sighed	brightness	sprightliness	unsightly	frightfully

Vowel + <igh>

When the string <igh> is preceded by a consonant it will represent 'long' /ī/. When a vowel precedes it the sound it normally represents is 'long' /ā/.

Consonant + <igh> → /ī/ **Vowel** + <igh> → /ā/

In practice only >a< and >e< can precede <igh>. A matrix given on the resource sheet will generate most words which result from vowel + <igh>.

Homophones

The words which use <igh> to represent /ī/ and /ā/ are a fruitful source of homophones which can help children consolidate their understanding of the principle that variant spellings represent various meanings. Here is a starter list of pairs of homophones for sharing and discussing with the children. It is a good subject for a class collection.

higher hire	sighed side	sighs size	might mite	right write rite
sight site	knight night	sleigh slay	eight ate	weigh way
weight wait	neigh nay			

☞ Don't refer to *<ght> as a string; it is not a constituent string of the system and referring to it as if it were can only hinder children's understanding of the presence of the <gh> digraph in our orthography.

The String <ugh>

The patterns associated with the related string <ugh> are not as straightforward as those for <igh> – though they are still nowhere near as awkward and complicated as many would have us believe. They are best dealt with as a separate topic.

Keep the string <ugh> separate from <igh>, but refer to each in exactly that sequence since they are actual letter strings of the orthographical system.

Resource Sheet 2: The Letter-string <igh>

far-
long-
short-
clear-
fore
hind
un
sight
ly
ed
ness
less
s
ing
see
ing
er

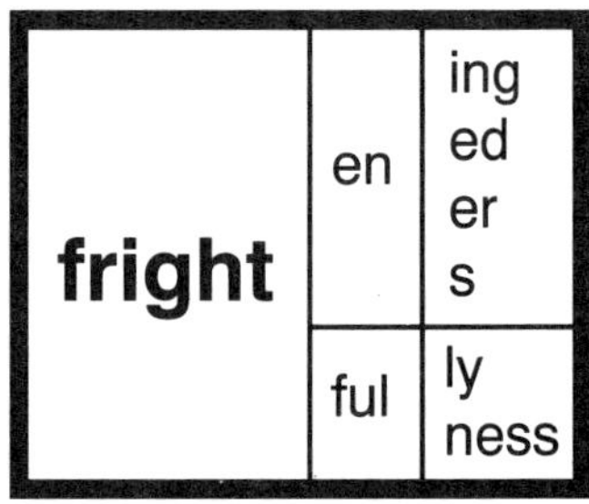

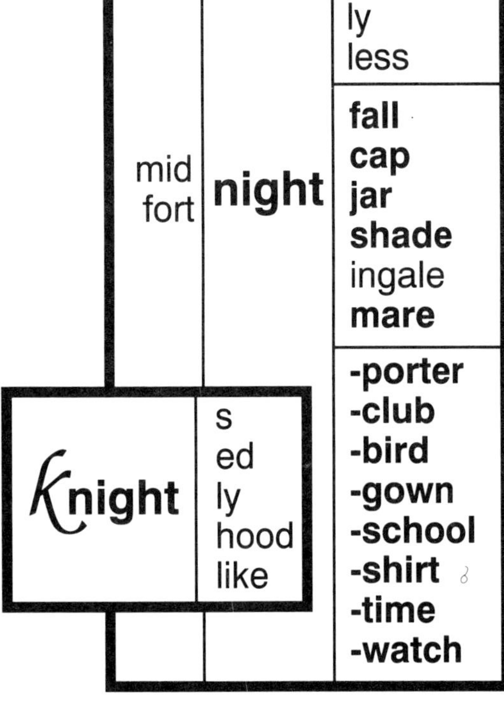

bright
fright
light
tight
en
ing
ed
er
s

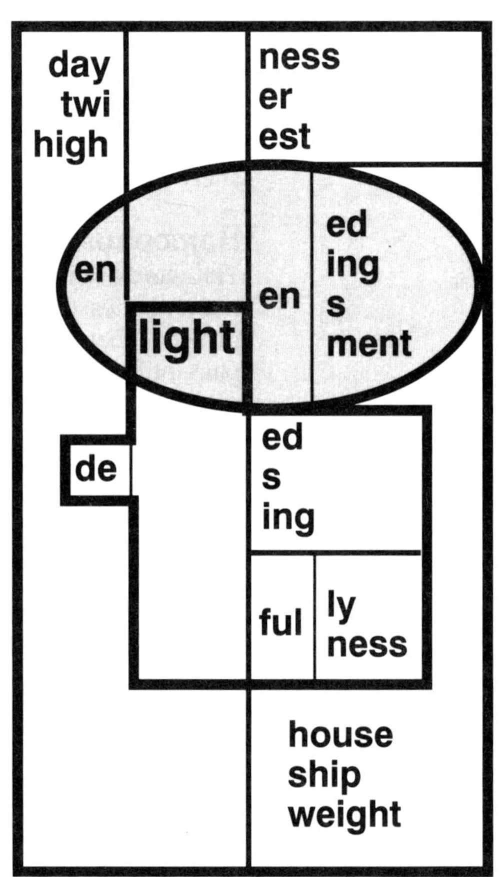

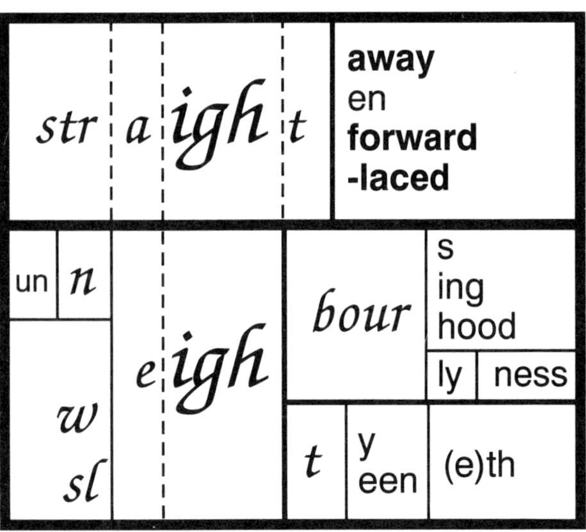

The vocalic suffixes can affect the last letter of base words. This project expands the patterns introduced on pages 65-68 which should now be re-read.

3. The Vocalic Suffixes

If the base word ends with a vowel, you usually just add the vocalic suffix without making any changes. So

do + ing → ***doing*** boo + ing → ***booing*** woo + ed → ***wooed***

Final Single, Silent >e<

If, however, the base word ends with a **single, silent >e<**, then *replace* that >e< with the vocalic suffix.

come + ing → *com[e]ing → ***coming*** brave + er → *brav[e]er → ***braver***

BUT agree + ing → ***agreeing*** be + ing → ***being***

Remember that the >e< must be *single* (not double as in *flee*) and it must be *silent*, which means that it is not directly representing part of the sounds of the word (as it does in *be*).

Try adding appropriate suffixes to the following:

wire go [un]do boo love place write
[be]have [mis]take become income [re]move be

If the final >e< of the base word is in the combination <oe> or <ye> then in order to avoid ambiguities that combination is regarded as indivisible:

shoe + ing → ***shoeing*** hoe + ing → ***hoeing***
eye + ing → ***eyeing*** dye + ing → ***dyeing***

Avoid Writing >i< Twice

If the base word ends with >y<, then the pattern you know from elsewhere applies – >y< does not occur inside a word unless you know of a reason for it:

pretty + er → ***prettier*** happy + est → ***happiest***

Remember the law that in an English word you do not write >i< twice in succession; use <yi> instead.

bully + ed → ***bullied*** **BUT** bully + ing → ***bullying*** (not *bulliing)

Try adding the suffixes <-ed> <-es> <-ing> to the following base words:

spy fly try imply reply copy cry carry

Avoiding Triple >e<

Remember the law that you don't write three successive letters the same:

agree + ing → ***agreeing*** **BUT** agree + ed → ***agreed*** (not *agreeed)

Add appropriate vocalic suffixes to the following base words:

[be]love [en]twine [re]late complete flee argue [dis]agree
boo see glue rescue busy write tune [re]place referee

Base Words Ending with a Consonant

Base words which end with a consonant sometimes double that last letter when a vocalic suffix is added, depending on the structure of the base word.

Monosyllabic Base Words

In the early stages of teaching this pattern confine your work to **words which have only one segment**. On the next page is a reminder of the two questions which have to be asked. If the answer to *both* questions is YES, then YES, you do double the last consonant of the base word when you add a vocalic consonant.

1. **Does the base word end with a *single* consonant?**
2. **Is there a *single* vowel before that last consonant?**

If the answer to either question is NO, there is no doubling. You must have yes twice if doubling is to happen.

Reminders:

- >w< will not double; its name tells you that a final >w< is not 'single' and it is not even a consonant.
- >x< represents a combination of two consonantal sounds packed inside one letter: >x< represents /k/+/s/ (as in ***expect***) or /g/+/z/ (as in ***exact***).

Polysyllabic Base Words

It is a natural consequence of segmenting to recognize the difference between *monosyllables* and *polysyllables* (words which have more than one segment). Here is an activity which will help establish that difference.

The Monosyllable Game

I have had some entertaining (and demanding) times with groups of children establishing this concept by playing **The Monosyllable Game**. Specify a period of time during which only monosyllabic words are allowed for all conversation, or even writing. It is not that there is any necessary virtue in the exclusive use of monosyllables; the point is that in order to select them you have to recognize polysyllables and avoid them by finding monosyllabic alternatives.

When children are at home with distinguishing between mono- and polysyllables, introduce what vocalic suffixes do to the final consonants of polysyllables.

Accounting for 'Stress'

Various systems have been used over the years for indicating the stress in words; modern dictionaries are more or less united in a convention that is only appropriate in combination with the International Phonetic Alphabet and does not fit easily into ordinary alphabetical writing.

Not all the segments in a polysyllable are equally stressed. For instance, in the word ***party*** it is the first segment that is stressed – **par**-ty – and in the word ***refer*** it is the second segment that is stressed – re-**fer**.

We do not usually indicate stress in ordinary writing. I recommend a fairly old convention which makes use of the acute accent (´) by placing it over a vowel in the stressed segment when you need to show in ordinary writing where the stress is. So, the two words mentioned above would be written as **párty** and **refér**. One way of highlighting the concept is to make a collection of words in which you change the meaning when you change the stress. Here are some of them:

content	invalid	refuse	conjure	desert (cf. also dessert)	
convert	minute	perfect	object	project	record
present	upset	forearm	entrance	extract	console

You will find many more; they make an interesting investigative project. In the individual intensive work that I do with dyslexic children, I never need more than one half-hour session to establish the concept. A class of mainstream children should master it in a session or two.

The Third Question

When you are sure that the children can easily identify the segment where the stress is and mark it as such they will be prepared for this next stage. It is the time to reveal to them that there is actually a third question which needs to be asked. Here are the two questions you already know with the third question added.

1. Does the base word end with a single consonant?
2. Is there a single vowel before that?
3. Is the stress in the last segment of the word?

All *three* questions must be answered YES if the last consonant is to double. Here are examples of the **third question** in operation.

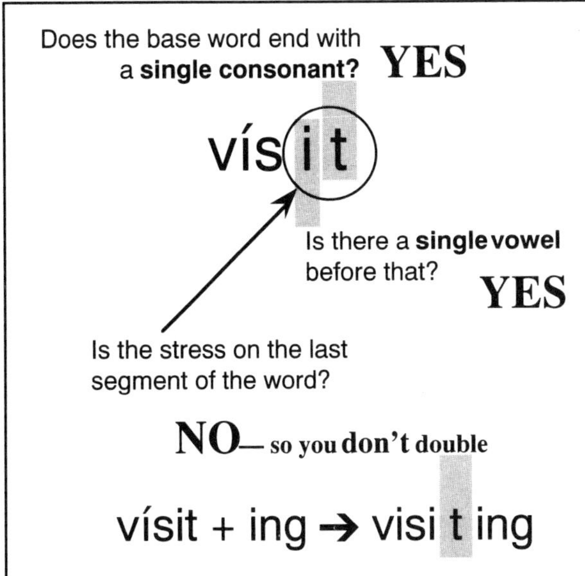

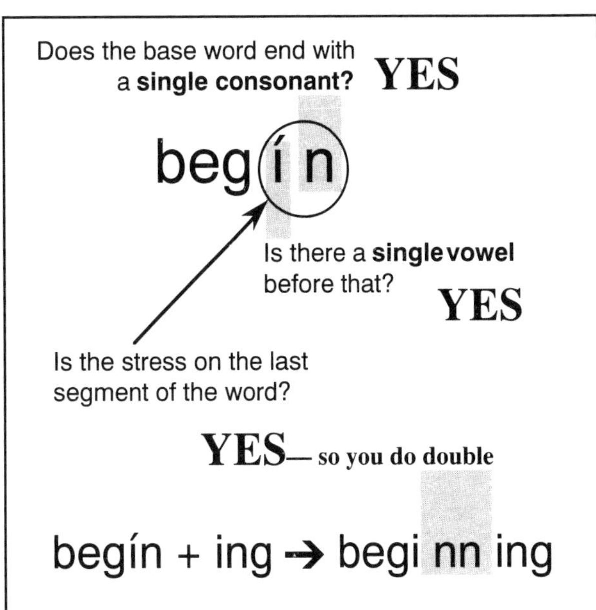

There is no inconsistency between *benefited* with one >t< and *fitted* with two since both forms result from the same pattern. To compare the two forms is to make what is called a 'false analogy': there is no morphological or etymological connection between *fit* and *benefit*.

We are now in a position to decide which is the correct form – ***benefitted*** or ***benefited***? The word without the suffix is **bénefit** with the stress in the *first* segment, so the stress is not on the last segment of the word. Doubling, then, does not take place, so the correct spelling has to be ***benefited*** with only one >t<.

When the Base Word Ends with <l>

If the final consonant of the base word is a single >l< then the stress pattern of the word is ignored. In British English the >l< is usually doubled. So:

sígnal+ed → ***signalled*** márvel+ous → ***marvellous*** contról+er → ***controller***.

The pattern does not operate with the three suffixes <-ish>, <-ist>, and <-ism>.

dévil+ish → ***devilish*** feúdal+ism → ***feudalism*** indivídual+ist → ***individualist***.

Now try adding appropriate vocalic suffixes to these base words.

pílot háppen forbíd gárden ópen límit abándon devélop prefér óffer prófit compél tárget trável equíp bánquet invént díal

Compound Words

For the purposes of suffixes, compound words are treated as if they were split back into their component elements. For example, before adding suffixes to *leapfrog*, separate it into its elements and deal with the last element only. When the suffix is added, then the elements are recombined: leapfrog + ed = leap-<**frog**> + <-ed> <**frog**> + ed → frogged leapfrog + ed → ***leapfrogged.***

Practise on these compound words; add vocalic suffixes where appropriate:

outfit horsewhip zigzag hobnob sleepwalk

☞ Constantly remind learners of the principle that where possible homophones reflect the differing meanings in different spellings.

Resolving Ambiguities

You would expect that when you add the suffix <-ing> to the base word ***singe***, you remove the final single, silent >e< and replace it with the suffix, resulting in ***singing**, which clearly causes ambiguity. This can be resolved by re-inserting an >e<: thus **singe + ing ➔ singeing**. Try adding <-ing> to the following pairs of words: *swing* / *swinge*; *rout* / *route*.

This principle of using spelling to resolve ambiguity is also seen with the homophones ***die*** and ***dye*** when vocalic suffixes are added to them. See what happens to each word when the suffix <-ing> is added.

1. die

Apply the pattern that replaces a single, silent >e< with a vocalic suffix, and you get ***diing**. This form goes against the law that you do not write >i< twice in succession; you use <yi> instead. So the spelling becomes **dying**. Compare **tie + ed ➔ tied**, but **tie + ing ➔ tying**; try it with ***lie*** and ***vie*** as well.

2. dye

Apply the pattern that replaces a single, silent >e< with a vocalic suffix, and you get ***dying**. But this form is identical to die + ing. In order to resolve the ambiguity, another pattern, referred to on page 109, comes into effect: the combination <ye> remains unalterable. The correct form, therefore, is **dye + ing ➔ dyeing**.

'Hard' and 'Soft' >c<

The letter >c< represents at least two sounds. When >c< represents /k/ it is said to be 'hard', and when it represents /s/ it is 'soft'. The pattern is straightforward: when >c< is immediately followed by >e<, >i< or >y< then >c< always represents the 'soft' sound; otherwise it represents the hard sound. In ***cot*** (/kot/) and ***panic*** (/panik/) it is 'hard', while in ***cellar*** (/seler/) and ***pencil*** (/pensl/) it is 'soft'.

Add the suffix <-able> to **<<u>notice</u>>**; applying the basic pattern which replaces the final single, silent >e< with the vocalic suffix gives the form ***noticable**, in which the >c< has to be 'hard'; the word can only represent /*notikabl/. The other pattern now comes to the rescue and you insert an >e< after the >c< in order to 'soften' it. You now have the correct form ***noticeable***. Here are further examples:

un + en + **force** + able; un + pro + **nounce** + able; out + **rage** + ous; inter + **change** + able

Flow Charts

These can form a rich topic or project, and it could easily last for half a term or more. The subjects of charts need to involve:

1. Suffixing to a base word that ends with a vowel.
2. Interchanging of >y< and >i< when suffixing takes place.
3. Monosyllabic base words (using just two questions).
4. Polysyllabic base words (using the three questions).
5. Suffixing to compound words.

Groups can have the task of producing a flow chart which deals with just one of these subjects. Drafts can be offered to other groups for checking and editing, which will also help the sharing of strategies. When each of these subjects is accounted for with its own separate flow chart, it may be possible to amalgamate all into one comprehensive flow chart. Reserve a large area of display space for the result! Alternatively, ready-made flow charts can be given to each learner to include in their file of spelling resources. Some such are given here.

Resource Sheet 3

START

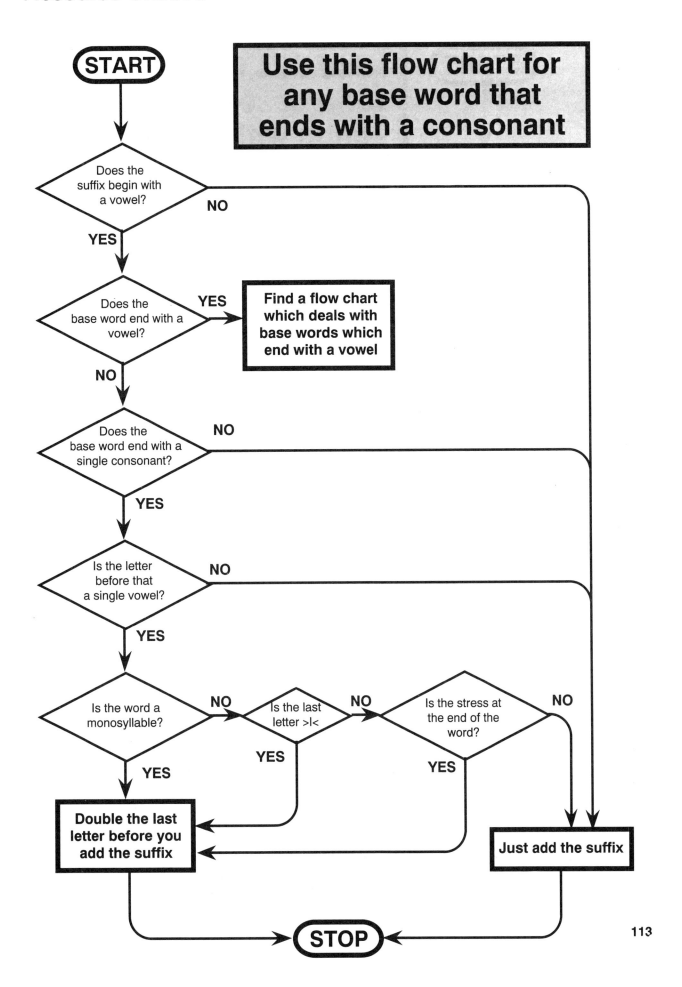

Use this flow chart for any base word that ends with a consonant

Does the suffix begin with a vowel?
- NO → Just add the suffix
- YES ↓

Does the base word end with a vowel?
- YES → **Find a flow chart which deals with base words which end with a vowel**
- NO ↓

Does the base word end with a single consonant?
- NO → Just add the suffix
- YES ↓

Is the letter before that a single vowel?
- NO → Just add the suffix
- YES ↓

Is the word a monosyllable?
- YES → Double the last letter before you add the suffix
- NO → Is the last letter >l<
  - YES → Double the last letter before you add the suffix
  - NO → Is the stress at the end of the word?
    - YES → Double the last letter before you add the suffix
    - NO → Just add the suffix

Double the last letter before you add the suffix → STOP

Just add the suffix → STOP

Resource Sheet 4

START

Use this flow chart for a base word that ends with a vowel

Does the suffix begin with a vowel?
- NO → Just add the suffix
- YES ↓

Does the base word end with a vowel?
- NO → **Find a flow chart which deals with base words which end with a consonant**
- YES ↓

Is that vowel a single, silent >e<?
- YES → **Remove the >e< and replace it with the suffix** → STOP
- NO ↓

Does the base word end with a >y<?
- NO → Just add the suffix
- YES ↓

Is the letter before that a vowel?
- YES → Just add the suffix
- NO ↓

Does the suffix begin with an >i<?
- NO → **Change the >y< to >i< before adding the suffix** → STOP
- YES → **Just add the suffix** → STOP

STOP

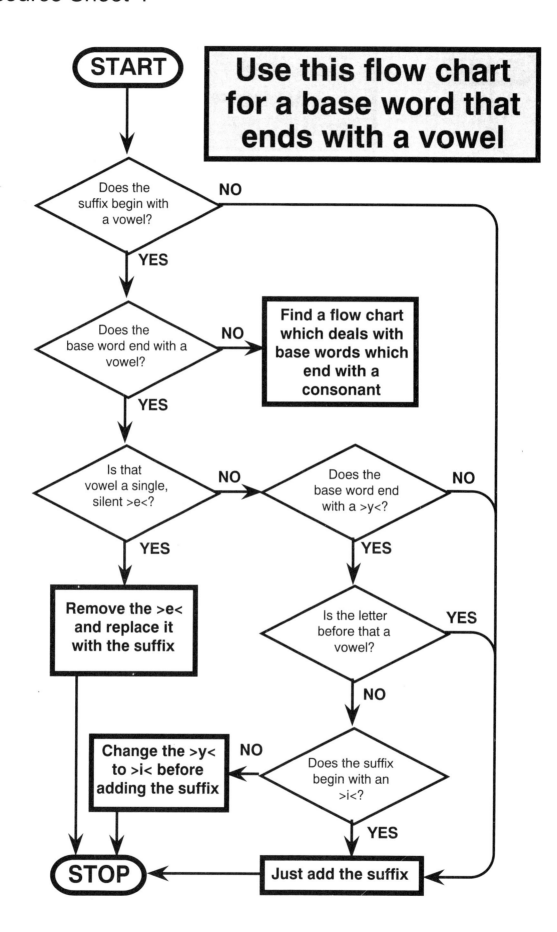

☞ Make a class catch-phrase of the slogan, 'Don't use an apostrophe to make a word into the plural.'

4. Working with the Plural Suffix <-(e)s>

The vast majority of English words represent their plural by adding a suffix whose form is either <-es> or just <-s>. This plural suffix behaves like any other suffix – IT DOES NOT NEED AN APOSTROPHE!

☞ It is an early priority that learners should know what the plural is, and be able to use the proper term.

Learners need, therefore, also to know the term **singular**. Tell them that the **singular** is what we call a **single one**, while the plural is what we call several. A simple test for the singular and the plural forms of a word is to say out loud, 'A single *** but several ***.' For instance, with the word ***hat*** you say, 'A single ***hat*** but several ***hats***.' So the singular is ***hat*** and the plural is ***hats***.

☞ The plural suffix is <-(e)s> and never spelled with >z< however it is pronounced.

When the plural has the same number of segments as its corresponding singular then just add <-s>.

shell	walnut	plan	chicken	bar	book
camera	computer	number	word	carrot	dog

Use <-es> with an extra segment

If the plural has one more segment than the singular then <-es> is needed. This is a result of the basic law that **every segment of an English word must have a vowel in it**. Here are some words to practise on. Say the plural form out loud; if the word forms its plural with an extra segment then you need to use <-es>.

fox	witch	crash	dish	wash	class
church	bus	wish	box	hutch	brush
coach	dress	ash	peach	match	gas
stitch	glass	branch	express	success	scratch

When the base word already ends with >e< then only >s< will be needed for the plural of most of them since such words don't increase their segments in the plural. Some words which end with >e< *will* increase their segments for the plural; in this case the pattern known from the vocalic suffixes will apply:

<**base**> + (-es) → bas[e] + (-es) ➔ ***bases***

apple	rule	table	plate	stone	nose
pole	tale	referee	glove	telephone	

Use <-es> after any change in spelling

If the orthography or the phonology of the base word changes when it forms the plural then use the full suffix <-es>, even if an extra segment isn't needed. There are two cases where this happens.

1. When the base word ends with >y<

Because children already know the patterns connected with the letter >y< and the way it is replaced with >i< when it is no longer at the end of the word they will automatically know what to do with the plural of a word ending with >y<.

Here are two examples.

☞ There is no such suffix as *<-ies>; when a plural ends with <ies> the >i< is actually part of the base word.

city + <-(e)**s**> ➔ **cities** because:

- in the plural the >y<, no longer at the end of the word, has to change to >i<.
- this has changed the form of the base word so you use the full plural suffix <-es>. You always use this full form if the base word changes in any way to form the plural.

day + <-(e)s> ➔ days because:

- the letter before the final >y< is another vowel; this is one of the patterns which remains unalterable whatever you do to the word.
- the form of the base word hasn't changed for the plural and there isn't another segment so you only need to use <-s>.

Here are some words to practise on.

party copy family puppy story boy pony cry
valley spy lady canary diary hobby supply key
monkey army fly lily tray daisy guy chimney

2. When the base word ends with /f/
Words which end with /f/ will end with the spellings >f<, <ff> or <fe>. These words often (but not always) change the /f/ into /v/ in their plurals. If they do, then the spelling is changed to >v<, and since that base word has now changed it take the full suffix <-es>. E.g. **half ➔ halves.** Speech backed up by reference will be the best guide as to whether to change /f/ of the singular into /v/ in the plural.

thief §proof ¶calf §oaf sheaf wolf loaf
shelf ¶dwarf ¶scarf thief ¶hoof knife wife
self ¶wharf §belief §roof §waif leaf ¶handkerchief

¶ – These words can either retain /f/ in the plural and take just <-s> or change the /f/ to /v/ and form the plural <ves>

§ – These words never change /f/ to /v/

Note that ***staff*** has two plurals; ***staves*** is a musical term, otherwise use ***staffs***.

Words Which End with >o<

A word which ends with >o< is not of English origin, except basic monosyllables like ***do*** and ***go*** . On the whole a word which ends with >o< will represent its plural just with <-s>. But when the word has become very common or absorbed almost entirely into English it represents its plural with the full suffix <-es>: potato ➔ potato**es;** domino ➔ domino**es.** Others include:

tornado hero volcano echo cargo torpedo tomato go

This subject is an opportunity for another class poster headed PLURALS OF WORDS ENDING IN >o<. The subheading would be Form the plural as <os>, except the following: words such as those listed above should be added to the poster with some sort of ceremony each time a member of the class discovers and reports one.

Never use <oes>:

- when final >o< is preceded by a vowel: cuckoos radios videos embryos
- with abbreviations: hippos kilos
- with names: Figaros Romeos

Avoiding Ambiguity with an Apostrophe

The apostrophe should never be used to form a plural unless the circumstances are exceptional and nothing else will do. Use the apostrophe only when there is a risk of confusion, for instance: Dot your i's (Dot your ***is*** would be confusing). By contrast the apostrophe is not really needed in the following because there is no risk of confusion: And cross your ts.

Resource Sheet 5: The Plural Suffix –(e)s

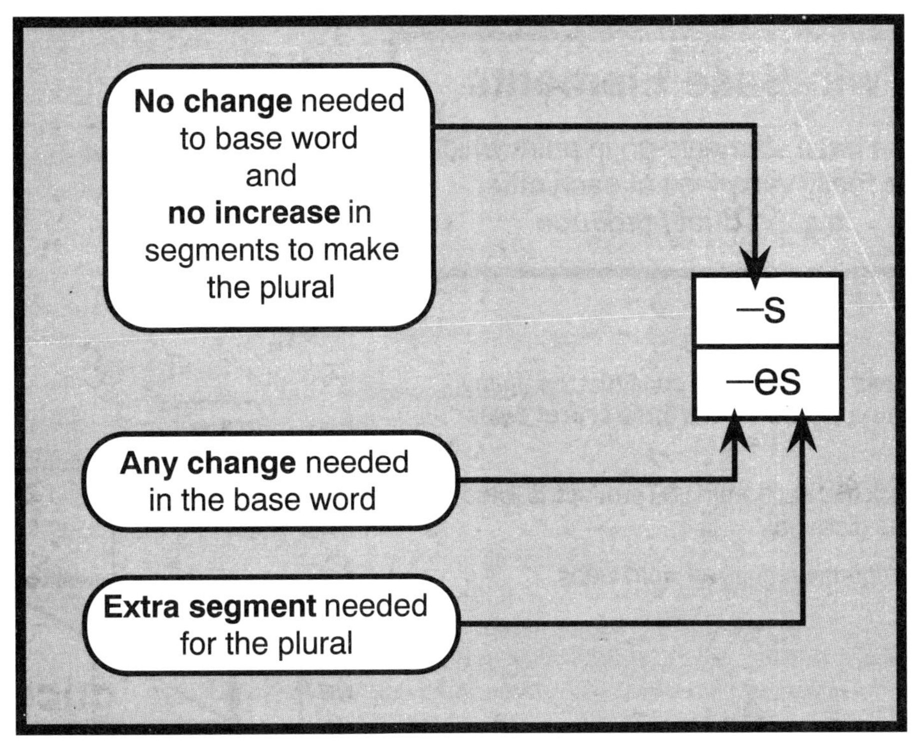

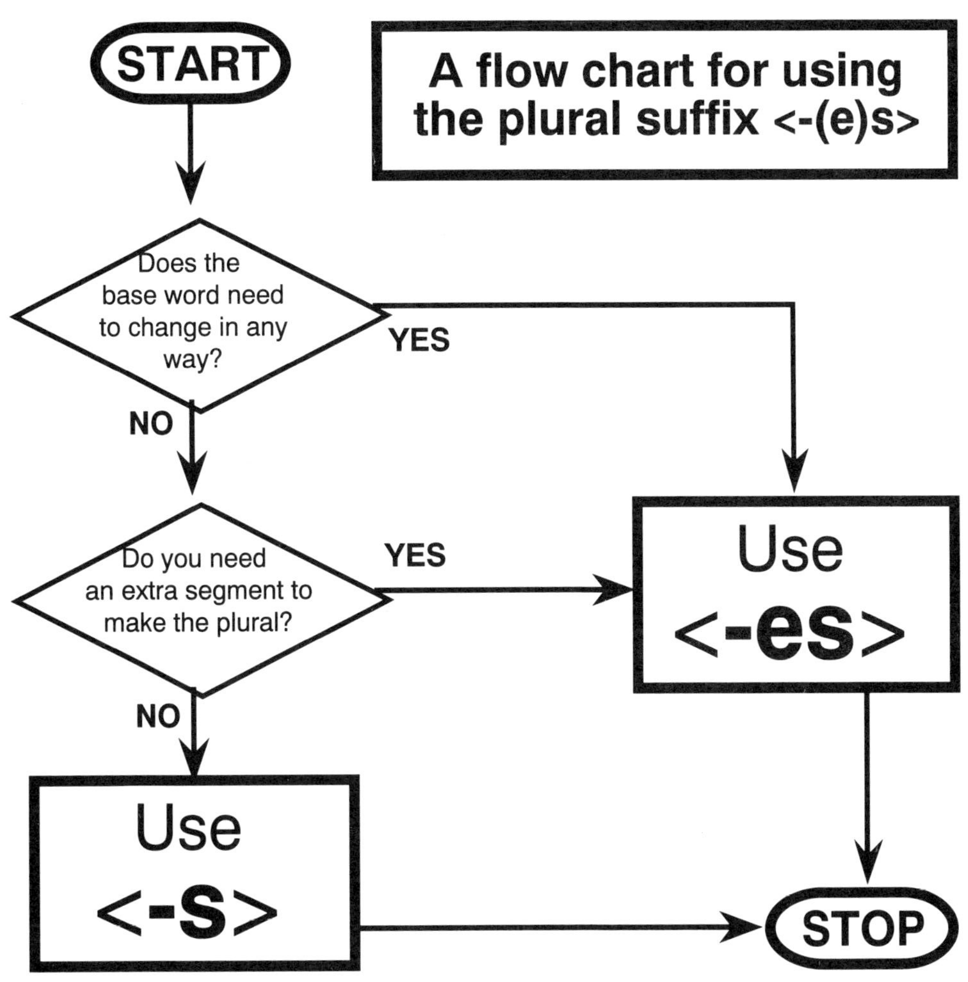

Resource Sheet 6

Twin Base Elements

Some base elements go in pairs which are really variations of each other – e.g. pro**duct** / pro**duce**

Use these diagrams to construct as many words as you can from the three sets of 'twins' given.

1. Check that each word you produce is listed in the dictionary.
2. Arrange the results as word webs.

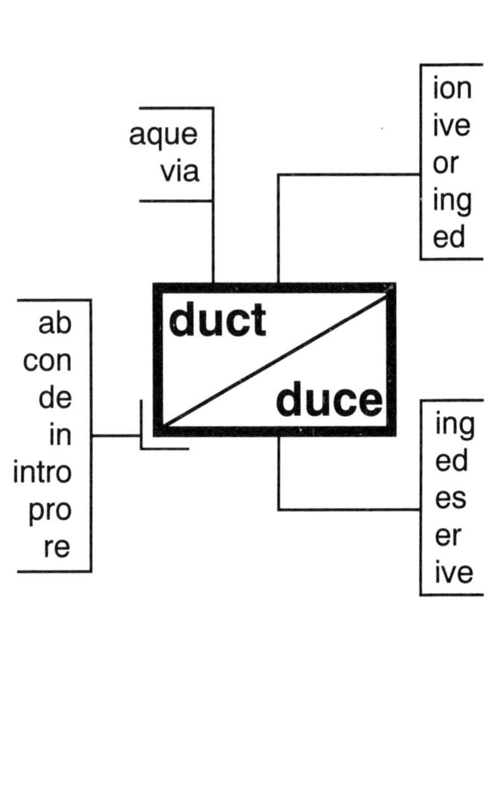

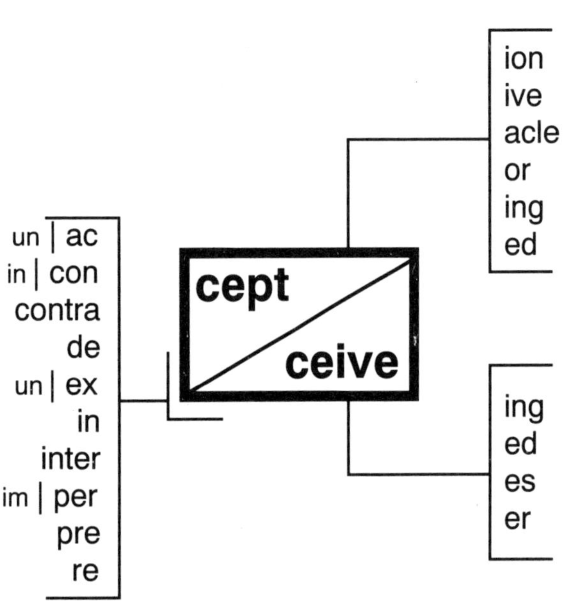

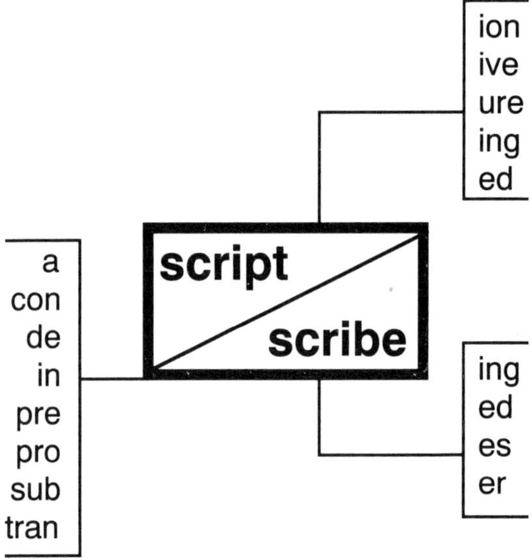

Resource Sheet 7: Some More Ambitious Matrices

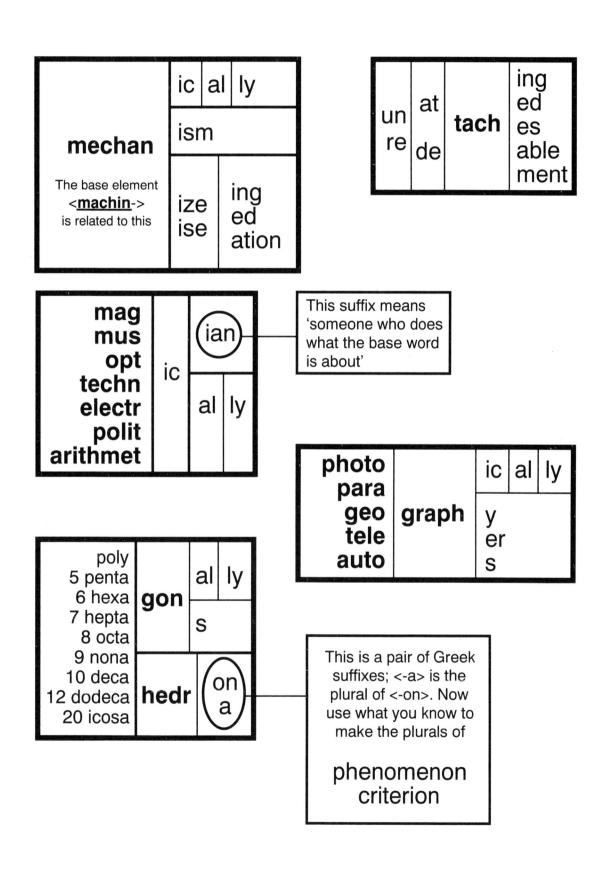

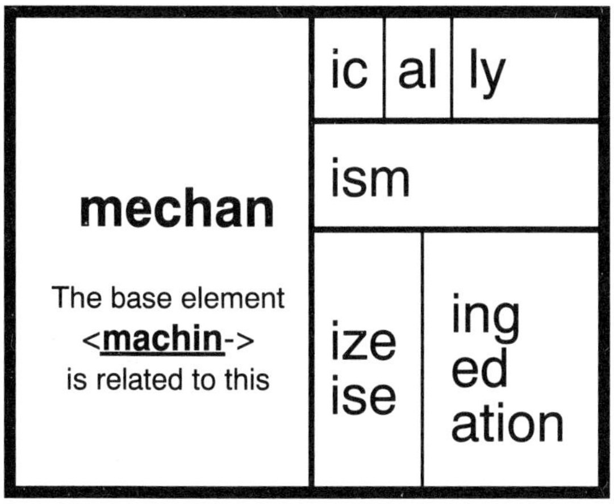

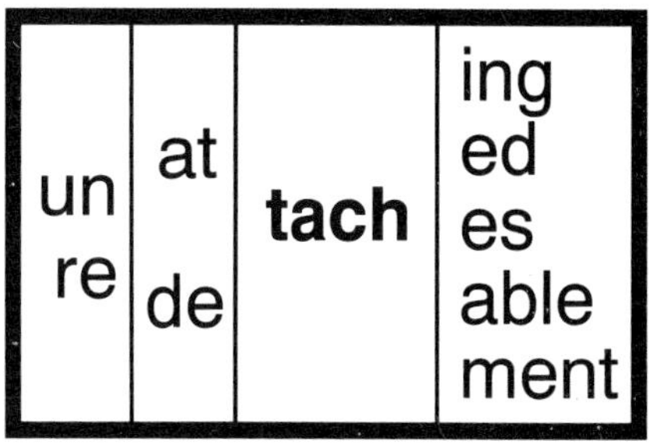

mechan The base element <**machin**-> is related to this	ic | al | ly ism ize, ise | ing, ed, ation

un re	at de	**tach**	ing ed es able ment

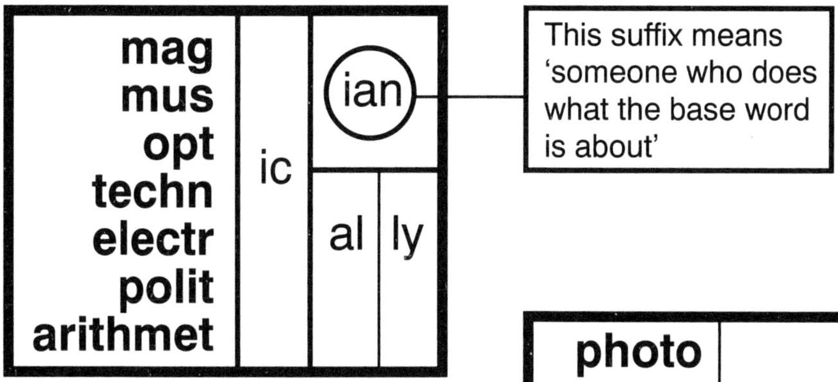

mag **mus** **opt** **techn** **electr** **polit** **arithmet**	ic	(ian) al | ly

This suffix means 'someone who does what the base word is about'

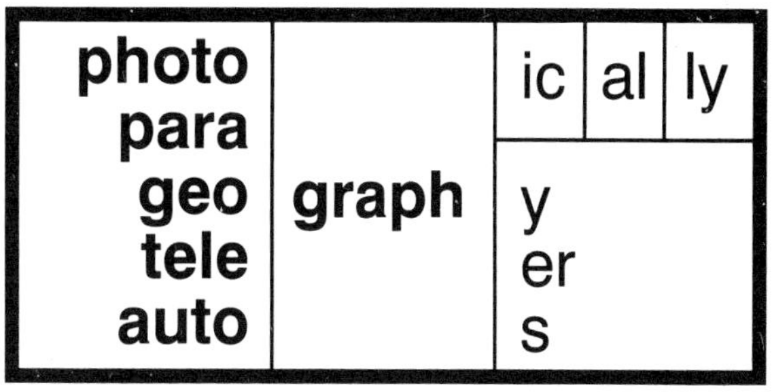

photo **para** **geo** **tele** **auto**	**graph**	ic | al | ly y er s

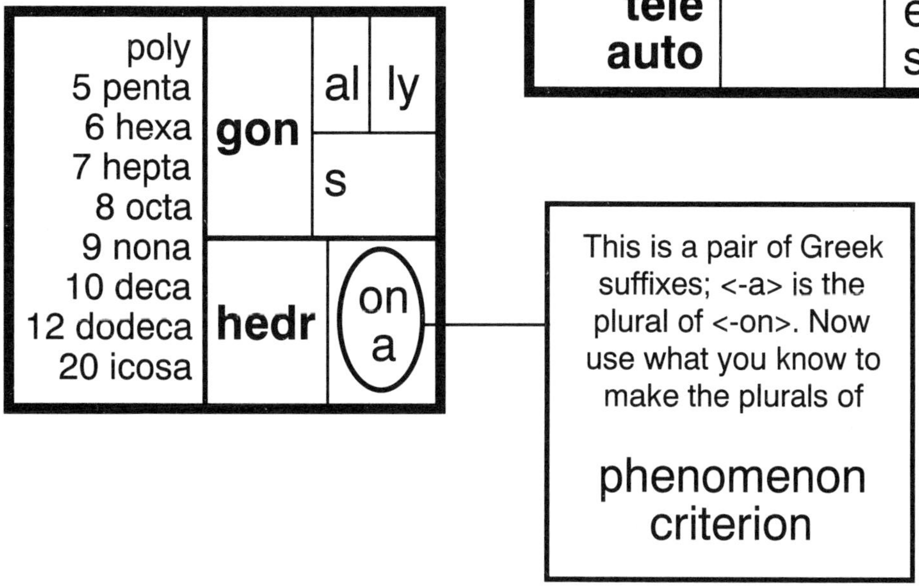

poly 5 penta 6 hexa 7 hepta 8 octa 9 nona 10 deca 12 dodeca 20 icosa	**gon**	al | ly s
	hedr	(on a)

This is a pair of Greek suffixes; <-a> is the plural of <-on>. Now use what you know to make the plurals of

phenomenon
criterion

Resource Sheet 8: A Project with the Base Element <**cess**> and its homophone <**sess**>

Check all your resulting words in the dictionary.

Arrange what you discover as word webs.

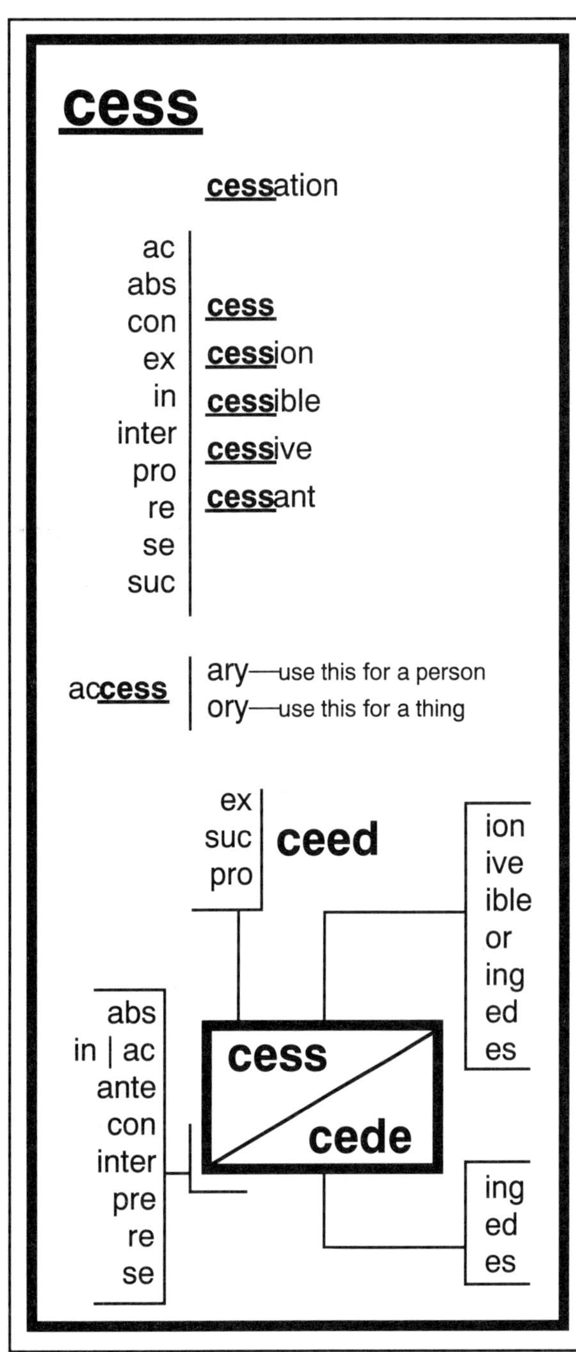

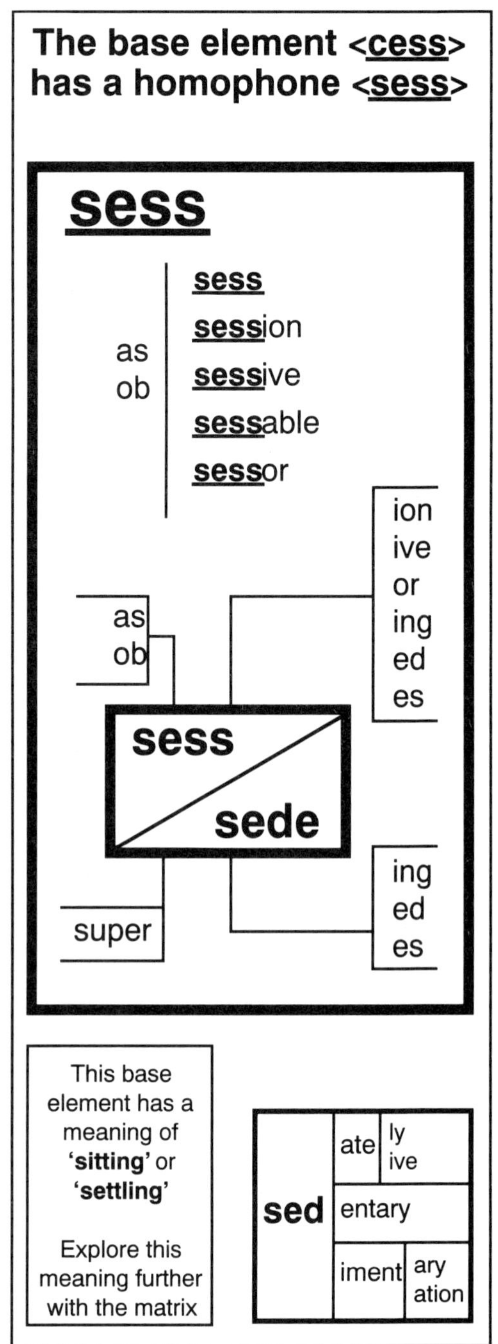

Bibliography

Bentley, D.	*Teaching Spelling*	University of Reading, 1990
Bruner, J	*Towards a Theory of Instruction*	Harvard, 1966
Bullock, A. (Chairman)	*A Language for Life*	HMSO, 1975
Burchfield, R.	*The English Language*	OUP, 1985
Claiborne, R.	*The Life and Times of the English Language*	Bloomsbury, 1990
Cox, C. B.	*English for Ages 5 to 11*	HMSO, 1988
DES	*English in the National Curriculum*	HMSO, 1990
Frith, U.	*'Unexpected Spelling Problems' in Cognitive Processes in Spelling*	Academic Press, 1980
Greene, J.	*Psycholinguistics*	Penguin, 1972
Hank, P. (Editor)	*Collins Dictionary of the English Language (2nd Edition)*	Collins, 1986
O'Kill, B.	*Dictionary of Word Origins*	Longman, 1983
Peters, M.	*Spelling Caught or Taught?*	Routledge, 1985
Pratley, R.	*Spelling it Out*	BBC, 1988
Ramsden, M.	*Putting Pen to Paper*	Southgate, 1992
Schonell, F.	*The Essential Spelling List*	Macmillan, 1932
Smith, F.	*Writing and the Writer*	Heinemann, 1982

Index